graphis annual 85|86

85|86

graphis annual

The International Annual of Advertising and
Editorial Graphics

Das internationale Jahrbuch der Werbe-
graphik und der redaktionellen Graphik

Le répertoire international de l'art graphique
publicitaire et rédactionnel

Edited by / Herausgegeben von / Réalisé par:

Walter Herdeg

graphis annual

Graphis Press Corp., Zurich (Switzerland)

GRAPHIS PUBLICATIONS

GRAPHIS, International bi-monthly journal of graphic art and applied art
PHOTOGRAPHIS, The international annual of advertising and editorial photography
GRAPHIS POSTERS, The international annual of poster art
GRAPHIS PACKAGING VOL. 4, An international survey of package design
CHILDREN'S BOOK ILLUSTRATION VOL. 3, VOL. 4, An international survey of children's book illustration
GRAPHIS DIAGRAMS, The graphic visualization of abstract data
FILM + TV GRAPHICS 2, An international survey of the art of film animation
ARCHIGRAPHIA, Architectural and environmental graphics
GRAPHIS EPHEMERA, Artists' Self-Promotion

GRAPHIS-PUBLIKATIONEN

GRAPHIS, Die internationale Zweimonatsschrift für Graphik und angewandte Kunst
PHOTOGRAPHIS, Das internationale Jahrbuch der Werbephotographie und der redaktionellen Photographie
GRAPHIS POSTERS, Das internationale Jahrbuch der Plakatkunst
GRAPHIS PACKUNGEN BAND 4, Internationales Handbuch der Packungsgestaltung
KINDERBUCH-ILLUSTRATION BAND 3, BAND 4, Eine internationale Übersicht über die Kinderbuch-Illustration
GRAPHIS DIAGRAMS, Die graphische Visualisierung abstrakter Gegebenheiten
FILM + TV GRAPHICS 2, Ein internationaler Überblick über die Kunst des Animationsfilms
ARCHIGRAPHIA, Architektur- und Umweltgraphik
GRAPHIS EPHEMERA, Künstler-Eigenwerbung

PUBLICATIONS GRAPHIS

GRAPHIS, La revue bimestrielle internationale d'arts graphiques et d'arts appliqués
PHOTOGRAPHIS, Le répertoire international de la photographie publicitaire et rédactionnelle
GRAPHIS POSTERS, Le répertoire international de l'art de l'affiche
GRAPHIS EMBALLAGES VOL. 4, Répertoire international des formes de l'emballage
ILLUSTRATIONS DE LIVRES D'ENFANTS VOL. 3, VOL. 4, Un aperçu international des illustrations de livres d'enfants
GRAPHIS DIAGRAMS, La visualisation graphique de données abstraites
FILM + TV GRAPHICS 2, Un panorama international de l'art du film d'animation
ARCHIGRAPHIA, La création graphique appliquée à l'architecture et à l'environnement
GRAPHIS EPHEMERA, Autopromotion des artistes

Distributors / Auslieferung / Distribution:

USA: WATSON-GUPTILL PUBLICATIONS, INC., 1515 Broadway, New York, N.Y. 10036 – **(ISBN: 0-8230-2137-8)**
CANADA: HURTIG PUBLISHERS, 10560-105 Street, Edmonton, Alberta T5H 2W7, tel. (403) 426-2469
FRANCE: GRAPHIS DISTRIBUTION, Milon-la-Chapelle, F-78470 St-Rémy-lès-Chevreuse, tél. 052-13-26
ITALIA: INTER-ORBIS, Via Lorenteggio, 31/1, I-20146 Milano, tel. 422 57 46
SPAIN: COMERCIAL ATHENEUM, S.A., Consejo de Ciento, 130-136, Barcelona 15, tel. 223 1451-3
AMERICA LATINA, AUSTRALIA, JAPAN AND OTHER ASIAN COUNTRIES, AFRICA:
FLEETBOOKS S.A., c/o Feffer & Simons, Inc., 100 Park Avenue, New York, N.Y. 10017, tel. (212) 686-0888

All other countries / Alle anderen Länder / Tout autres pays:

GRAPHIS PRESS CORP., 107 Dufourstrasse, CH-8008 Zurich (Switzerland)

PUBLICATION No. 180 (ISBN 3-85709-185-1)

Contents   Inhalt   Sommaire

Abbreviations

Abkürzungen

Abréviations

Argentina	ARG	Argentinien	ARG	Afrique du Sud	SAF
Australia	AUS	Australien	AUS	Allemagne occidentale	GER
Austria	AUT	Belgien	BEL	Argentine	ARG
Belgium	BEL	Brasilien	BRA	Australie	AUS
Brazil	BRA	Bulgarien	BUL	Autriche	AUT
Bulgaria	BUL	Dänemark	DEN	Belgique	BEL
Canada	CAN	Deutschland (BRD)	GER	Brésil	BRA
Czechoslovakia	CSR	Finnland	FIN	Bulgarie	BUL
Denmark	DEN	Frankreich	FRA	Canada	CAN
Finland	FIN	Grossbritannien	GBR	Danemark	DEN
France	FRA	Hongkong	HKG	Espagne	SPA
Germany (West)	GER	Iran	IRN	Etats-Unis	USA
Great Britain	GBR	Irland	IRL	Finlande	FIN
Hong Kong	HKG	Israel	ISR	France	FRA
Iran	IRN	Italien	ITA	Grande-Bretagne	GBR
Ireland	IRL	Japan	JPN	Hongkong	HKG
Israel	ISR	Kanada	CAN	Iran	IRN
Italy	ITA	Mexiko	MEX	Irlande	IRL
Japan	JPN	Niederlande	NLD	Israël	ISR
Mexico	MEX	Norwegen	NOR	Italie	ITA
Netherlands	NLD	Österreich	AUT	Japon	JPN
Norway	NOR	Polen	POL	Mexique	MEX
Poland	POL	Schweden	SWE	Norvège	NOR
South Africa	SAF	Schweiz	SWI	Pays-Bas	NLD
Spain	SPA	Spanien	SPA	Pologne	POL
Sweden	SWE	Südafrika	SAF	Suède	SWE
Switzerland	SWI	Tschechoslowakei	CSR	Suisse	SWI
Turkey	TUR	Türkei	TUR	Tchécoslovaquie	CSR
USA	USA	USA	USA	Turquie	TUR

Cover/Umschlag/Couverture: Ikko Tanaka

We extend our hearty thanks to the many contributors from all over the world who, by their work, made it possible for us to compile this international overview of graphic design. We trust we may continue to count on their interest and cooperation in the future.

Unser herzlicher Dank gilt allen Einsendern aus zahlreichen Ländern, die es uns mit ihren Arbeiten ermöglichten, diese internationale Übersicht auf dem Gebiet der graphischen Darstellung zusammenzustellen. Wir hoffen, auch weiterhin auf ihr Interesse und ihre beständige Mitarbeit zählen zu können.

Que soient ici remerciés tous les collaborateurs du monde entier qui, en nous envoyant leurs travaux, nous ont permis de réaliser ce panorama de la création graphique internationale. Nous espérons qu'ils continueront à nous témoigner leur intérêt et à nous assurer de leur appui.

IKKO TANAKA, the designer of our cover, was born in Nara, Japan, in 1930. On graduating from the Kyoto City College of Fine Arts, he worked as art director at the Nippon Design Center before establishing his own design studio in Tokyo in 1963. His posters, on show worldwide, have won him acclaim. He is the recipient of the silver award at the International Poster Biennale in Warsaw, and he has also received many awards for his outstanding exhibition displays. Three books have been published on his work so far, and in 1983 he received the "Yamana Award" from the Japan Advertising Club.

IKKO TANAKA, der Gestalter unseres Umschlags, wurde 1930 in Nara, Japan, geboren. Nach Abschluss seines Kunststudiums am Kyoto City College of Fine Arts arbeitete er als Art Director im Nippon Design Center, bis er 1963 sein eigenes Design-Studio in Tokio eröffnete. Durch seine Plakate, die weltweit ausgestellt wurden, fand er schnell Anerkennung – er erhielt die Silbermedaille der Internationalen Plakat-Biennale in Warschau –, und er wurde mehrfach auch für seine hervorragenden Ausstellungs-Gestaltungen ausgezeichnet. Drei Bücher sind bisher über seine Arbeiten erschienen; 1983 erhielt er den «Yamana Award» des Japan Advertising Club.

IKKO TANAKA, l'auteur de notre couverture, est né à Nara (Japon) en 1930. Ce diplômé du Kyoto City College of Fine Arts a été directeur artistique au Nippon Design Center avant de s'établir à son compte à Tokyo en 1963. Ses affiches lui ont valu la renommée – il est l'auréat de la médaille d'argent de la Biennale internationale de l'affiche de Varsovie. De nombreux prix ont en outre récompensé ses remarquables créations au service d'expositions. Trois ouvrages ont été consacrés à cet artiste; et en 1983 il a reçu le «Yamana Award» du Japan Advertising Club.

Steven Heller

Cult of the New

STEVEN HELLER is the art director of *The New York Times Book Review* and he also frequently writes on graphic design and illustration—past and present. His books include: *Man Bites Man: Two Decades of Satiric Art; Art Against War* and *The Art of New York*. He has edited *Seymour Chwast: The Left-Handed Designer* and also the forthcoming *Innovators of American Illustration*. He is co-director of Push Pin Editions and teaches in the Master of Fine Arts Programme at the School of Visual Arts, New York.

In 1940 Thomas Maitland Cleland, a formidable American graphic artist und designer, addressed an assembly of his peers, and offered some very harsh words about modern currents in graphic design. He zealously decried "the restless craving for something new", aiming his arrow-sharp barbs at the young exhibitionists who were flagrantly breaking the rules of type and page design. "The embarassing ineptitude of the current efforts towards a new typography are even more distressing than similar contortions in other fields," he harangued. "Typography is a servant of thought and language to which it gives visible existence. When there are new ways of thinking and a new language, it will be time enough for a new typography. I suggest that those who cannot abide the conventions of typography are mostly those who have never tried them."

Though the verity of Cleland's statement was shrouded by an all too severe and dogmatic disdain for all "isms" (especially Modernism)—and all who practised them, regardless of their inventiveness—it also hit a responsive chord, then as now. Indeed, if the speech were given today, many in the field would applaud in agreement the critique that too much contemporary graphic endeavour derives, not from an understanding of precedents, but from (as Cleland put it) "alluring shortcuts and seductive philosophies—a disturbing babel of undigested ideas and indigestible objectives." Throughout the past forty-five years so much has changed for the better in the design field; technologically, philosophically and even politically, yet graphic endeavour appears to have finally come full circle in the eighties, like an Escher beast who eats its own tail.

Happily, graphic design is being taken more seriously by scholars, and so the collective design milestones from the Gilded Age to the present are now ubiquitous in books and exhibitions. The designer's universe of knowledge has never been wider, but the resulting design practice is dangerously derivative of the past. In fact, the eighties are typified by *déjà vu* conceits and mimicked stylizations. Therefore it is merely the surface of the remarkable ground-breaking innovations of the seminal European and American twentieth-century art and design movements that have been capriciously rehashed and reapplied by adherents of the "new wave"—a wave, it might be added, that has already washed up on shore many times before. For any historical material to be nourishing it must be slowly absorbed and understood. Today though, it is voraciously consumed and quickly regurgitated whole; the results of which reveal ignorance of the original function and rationale. The fact that Constructivism, for example, simply looks modern, is not a good enough reason to reprise it out of context.

In 1955 the American designer and teacher, Bradbury Thompson, astutely wrote: "Although the designer works with conviction based upon fact, he must create in the spirit of his own time, showing in the designs an essential understanding, rather than a laboured copying of the masters." Despite these wise words it should come as no surprise that many practitioners not only attempt to reinvent the proverbial wheel, but try at the same time to rediscover fire as well. Every generation hopes to pioneer better means of communication, but communication easily falls prey to design for design's sake in the service of personal commitment to a compelling social, political or personal cause (such as the revolutionary fervour experienced during the early part of the century). Perhaps the argotic term, "Post-Modern", which refers to the marriage in architecture and design of classical and modern vernaculars, is the most honest of the contemporary "styles" since its usage is an admission that there is nowhere *new* to go. Hence, suggesting a return to tradition, if only for the moment.

György Kepes, the designer, critic and author, succinctly underscores the perennial crisis of achieving *newness* with a commentary made in the early 1950's: "Today's obsession for speed and quantity has profoundly influenced the ways in which we think and feel. Mass production and mass communication, with their characteristic standardized thoughts and vision, have over-worked ideas, making them exhausted stereotypes." This thought is congruent with today's debates about contemporary design education and practice, and addresses the sorest of points. For who is responsible for propagating "exhausted stereotypes" but lazy teachers and compliant students?

Perhaps it is a cliché simply to discuss this issue; after all, the criticisms are similar decade after decade. No doubt, an overview forged by time is the only legitimate way to answer the question of whether or not the current generation has contributed significantly to the legacy or the lexicon of graphic design. However, the immediate and forthright discussion of the merits and demerits of current trends, fashions and specific works will establish ground rules for how to judge contemporary endeavour in the future. Hence, generating critical commentary, of which there is now a paucity, is of utmost importance. Further, historical grounding is also necessary, as Kepes stated in 1957: "To give direction and order to this formlessness we have to go back to our roots. We need to regain the health of our creative faculties, especially our visual sensibilities." And to add to that, we have to recognize the rules, if only to intelligently rebel against them.

The GRAPHIS ANNUALS, which span the last twenty-three years, provide a primary resource for design and illustration criticism. They chart the rise and fall of varied trends and conceits, and expose the viewer to international cross-currents that cannot be viewed anywhere else. Indeed, the collected annuals are a visual timeline of graphic communication from which history can be written. However, even more important than the above, the annuals focus on individual practitioners and their achievements—not as part of groups, schools or movements, but rather as reflecting their times and their own needs as applied artists.

Discussing in positive terms his quest for the new in 1956, Robert Osborn, the acerbic graphic commentator, said: "What we require are new means to make our sensations visible and, more importantly, felt." Ultimately it is on the shoulders of the visionary designer or illustrator to create something legitimately new, and thus lasting. And perhaps the means of measurement, be it for this or any generation, is rooted in Osborn's observation. While visual gymnastics may grab the eye and entertain for the moment, they will eventually fall flat. Lasting design achievement is born of understanding, passion—and, of course, the will.

Steven Heller

Kult des Neuen

STEVEN HELLER ist Art Director für den *New York Times Book Review*, eine regelmässig erscheinende Literaturbeilage der Zeitung. Er selbst schreibt über Graphik-Design und Illustration der Gegenwart und der Vergangenheit. Zu seinen Büchern gehören: *Man Bites Man: Two Decades of Satiric Art; Art Against War* und *The Art of New York*. Er ist Herausgeber des Buches *Seymour Chwast: The Left-Handed Designer* und auch des demnächst erscheinenden *Innovations of American Illustration*. Er ist Mitherausgeber der Push-Pin-Editionen und unterrichtet an der School of Visual Arts, New York, innerhalb des Kunstprogramms (Master of Fine Arts Programme).

Thomas Maitland Cleland, ein hervorragender amerikanischer Graphiker, hielt 1940 vor Berufskollegen eine Ansprache, die einige sehr harte Worte über moderne Strömungen im Graphik-Design enthielt. Mit leidenschaftlichen Worten verurteilte er das «rastlose Verlangen nach etwas Neuem», wobei er pfeilscharfe Spitzen gegen die jungen Exhibitionisten richtete, die unverhohlen mit allen Regeln der Typographie und des Layouts gebrochen hatten. «Die beschämende Unbeholfenheit der gegenwärtigen Bemühungen um eine neue Typographie ist sogar noch jämmerlicher als ähnliche Verirrungen auf anderen Gebieten», führte er vorwurfsvoll an. «Typographie steht im Dienst des Gedankens und der Sprache, sie macht diese sichtbar. Wenn es neue Wege des Denkens und eine neue Sprache gibt, bleibt noch immer Zeit genug für eine neue Typographie. Ich bin der Meinung, dass die meisten, die sich nicht an die Gesetze der Typographie halten, es noch nie probiert haben.»

Obgleich die überstrenge und dogmatische Verachtung aller «ismen» (besonders des Modernismus) – und aller ihrer Befolger, ungeachtet ihrer erfinderischen Qualitäten – Clelands an sich wahre Behauptung fragwürdig erscheinen liess, so fand sie damals doch auch Anklang, und das wäre auch heute der Fall. Viele Fachleute würden sich uneingeschränkt der Kritik anschliessen, dass ein grosser Teil des zeitgenössischen Graphik-Designs nicht auf dem Verständnis des Vergangenen aufbaut, sondern (wie Cleland es formulierte) «auf verführerischen Patentlösungen und Philosophien – ein verwirrendes Babel unverdauter Ideen und unverdaulicher Ziele». Während der vergangenen fünfundvierzig Jahre hat sich auf diesem Gebiet, technisch, philosophisch und sogar politisch gesehen, sehr vieles positiv verändert, und doch scheint das Graphik-Design in den achtziger Jahren einen Kreis geschlossen zu haben, ähnlich wie eine von Eschers Kreaturen, die sich in den eigenen Schwanz beisst.

Der Wissenshorizont des Graphik-Designers war nie grösser als heute, und doch imitiert er in seiner Arbeit auf bedenkliche Weise die Vergangenheit. Tatsächlich sind *déjà-vu*-Manierismen und nachgeahmte Stilisierungen typisch für die achtziger Jahre. Von den wichtigen, wegweisenden Neuerungen der schöpferischen Kunst- und Design-Bewegungen des 20. Jahrhunderts in Europa und Amerika wurde nur die Oberfläche von den Anhängern der «New Wave» willkürlich verwendet und aufgewärmt – einer Welle, so sei hinzugefügt, die schon manches Mal ans Ufer geschwappt ist. Jedes historische Material, soll es von Nutzen sein, muss langsam aufgenommen und verstanden werden. Heute wird es jedoch gierig verschlungen und schnell als Ganzes wieder ausgestossen, wobei die Ergebnisse Unkenntnis der ursprünglichen Funktion und logischen Grundlage erkennen lassen. Die Tatsache zum Beispiel, dass Konstruktivismus einfach modern aussieht, ist nicht Grund genug, ihn völlig zusammenhangslos wieder aufzunehmen.

1955 schrieb der amerikanische Designer und Lehrer Bradbury Thompson sehr treffend: «Obgleich der Designer sich bei seiner Arbeit auf Tatsachen stützt, muss er sie in Einklang mit dem herrschenden Zeitgeist bringen; statt eines mühsam erzwungenen Kopierens der Meister muss seine Arbeit Verständnis des Wesentlichen erkennen lassen.» Trotz dieser weisen Worte wird es nicht überraschen, dass in der Praxis viele so vorgehen, als gelte es, das Rad neu zu erfinden und gleichzeitig auch noch das Feuer zu entdecken. Jede Generation hofft, bessere Kommunikationsmittel zu finden, aber Kommunikation wird leicht zum Opfer des Designs um des Designs willen, im Dienste eines persönlichen Engagements für eine zwingende soziale, politische oder persönliche Angelegenheit (so wie die revolutionäre Leidenschaft, die man anfangs dieses Jahrhunderts erlebte). Vielleicht ist die Bezeichnung «Post-Modern», welche sich auf die Verbindung von klassischer und moderner Sprache in Architektur und Design bezieht, die ehrlichste der modernen «Stilrichtungen», weil ihre Anwendung ein Zugeständnis ist, dass es kein Neuland gibt, das man betreten könnte. Somit wird eine Rückkehr zur Tradition vorgeschlagen, sei es auch nur für den Augenblick.

In einem Kommentar in den frühen fünfziger Jahren umreisst György Kepes, der Designer, Kritiker und Autor, die immer wiederkehrende krisenhafte Sucht nach dem Neuen: «Die heutige Besessenheit von Tempo und Quantität hat einen tiefen Einfluss auf unser Denken und Fühlen. Massenproduktion und Massenkommunikation, mit ihren charakteristischen standardisierten Gedanken und Visionen, haben Ideen über-strapaziert und sie zu erschöpften Klischees gemacht.» Dieser Gedanke deckt sich völlig mit den heutigen Debatten über Design-Unterricht und -Praxis und trifft den wundesten Punkt. Denn wer sonst als bequeme Lehrer und allzu folgsame Schüler ist verantwortlich für die Propagierung «erschöpfter Klischees»?

Vielleicht ist schon die Diskussion dieses Themas ein Klischee; schliesslich ähneln sich die Kritiken von Jahrzehnt zu Jahrzehnt. Zweifellos ist ein durch die Zeit gereifter Rückblick das einzig legitime Mittel um zu entscheiden, ob die heutige Genera-tion bedeutend zum Vermächtnis oder Lexikon des Graphik-Designs beigetragen hat. Andererseits kann die spontane und unverblümte Diskussion der Verdienste und Mängel der gegenwärtigen Trends, Moden und spezifischer Arbeiten Grundregeln für die spätere Beurteilung dieser Bemühungen aufstellen. Somit ist kritischer Kom-mentar, den man heute häufig vermisst, von äusserster Wichtigkeit. Ausserdem ist eine historische Grundlage notwendig, denn, wie Kepes 1957 sagte: «Um der Form-losigkeit Richtung und Ordnung zu geben, müssen wir auf unsere Wurzeln zurück-greifen. Wie müssen unsere kreativen Fähigkeiten gesunden lassen, insbesondere unser visuelles Feingefühl.» Dem sei hinzugefügt, dass wir die Regeln erkennen müssen, und sei es nur, um auf intelligente Weise gegen sie zu rebellieren.

Die GRAPHIS-ANNUAL-Jahrbücher, welche die letzten 23 Jahre umfassen, bieten eine wichtige Informationsquelle für die Design- und Illustrationskritik. Sie zeigen u. a. Aufstieg und Fall verschiedener Trends und manierierter Spielereien auf, und der Betrachter wird mit internationalen Gegenströmungen konfrontiert, die er in dieser Form sonst nirgends zu sehen bekommt. Die gesammelten Jahrbücher bieten einen chronologischen Überblick der Entwicklung der graphischen Kommunikation, nach dem sich die Design-Geschichte schreiben liesse. Wichtiger als dies ist jedoch die Tatsache, dass die Jahrbücher sich auf individuelle Künstler und ihre Arbeit konzen-trieren – nicht auf Teile von Gruppen, Schulen oder Bewegungen, sondern auf den Graphik-Designer als Spiegelbild seiner Zeit und seiner eigenen Anliegen.

Robert Osborn, ein strenger Kritiker des Graphik-Designs, umschrieb 1956 in einer Diskussion sein Streben nach dem Neuen in folgenden Worten: «Was wir brauchen sind neue Wege, um unsere Gefühle zu visualisieren, und, was noch wichtiger ist, um sie spürbar zu machen.» Letztlich liegt es also beim Designer und Illustrator, etwas wahrhaft Neues von Bestand zu schaffen. Vielleicht sind die Massstäbe für die Beur-teilung dieser oder einer anderen Generation in Osborns Bemerkung zu suchen. Wenn visuelle Verrenkungen auch für einen Augenblick die Aufmerksamkeit auf sich ziehen und unterhalten mögen, so werden sie sich schliesslich als oberflächlich erweisen. Design-Leistungen, die Bestand haben, werden aus Verstehen, Leiden-schaft – und natürlich auch aus dem Willen heraus geboren.

Steven Heller

Culte de la nouveauté

STEVEN HELLER est le directeur du *New York Times Book Review*, un supplément littéraire du journal qui paraît régulièrement, en même temps qu'un auteur prolifique spécialisé dans les aspects dia- et synchroniques de l'art publicitaire et de l'illustration. Citons parmi ses ouvrages: *Man Bites Man: Two Decades of Satiric Art; Art Against War; The Art of New York*. Il a dirigé l'édition de *Seymour Chwast: The Left-Handed Designer* et de l'ouvrage à paraître sur les *Innovators of American Illustration*. Codirecteur des Editions Push Pin, Steven Heller enseigne à la School of Visual Arts de New York dans les classes du Master of Fine Arts Programme.

En 1940, Thomas Maitland Cleland, ce formidable graphiste et designer américain, se lançait devant ses pairs dans une violente diatribe contre les tendances modernes qui se faisaient jour dans l'art publicitaire, réservant ses pointes les plus acérées aux jeunes exhibitionnistes «éperdus de nouveauté à tout prix» et qui transgressaient allègrement les règles de la typographie et de la mise en pages. «Les inepties choquantes des efforts en cours pour réaliser une nouvelle typographie», s'exclamait-il, «sont encore plus affligeantes que les contorsions similaires auxquelles on se livre dans d'autres domaines. «La typographie est au service de la pensée et de la langue, auxquelles elle confère une existence visible. Lorsque de nouveaux modes de pensée et de langage auront vu le jour, il sera bien assez tôt pour mettre au point une nouvelle typographie. J'estime que ceux qui ne peuvent observer les conventions de la typographie sont essentiellement ceux qui ne s'y sont jamais essayés.»

La vérité de ce constat, toute voilée qu'elle fût par le mépris trop sévère et trop dogmatique que Cleland affichait pour les «ismes» (en particulier pour le modernisme) nonobstant l'ingéniosité des novateurs, est incontestable, à l'époque comme aujourd'hui. Le même discours repris à 45 ans de distance susciterait l'approbation de tous ceux, et ils sont nombreux, qui estiment comme Cleland que trop de travaux graphiques contemporains procèdent de «raccourcis séduisants et de philosophies alléchantes – une Babel insensée d'idées mal digérées et d'objectifs indigestes.» Pourtant, en près d'un demi-siècle, tant de choses ont changé en bien, technologiquement, philosophiquement et même politiquement; mais la création graphique semble avoir bouclé la boucle au cours des années 80, à la manière d'un monstre d'Escher qui se mord la queue.

L'univers des connaissances accessibles au designer n'a jamais été aussi vaste, et pourtant la pratique du design s'inspire dangereusement du passé. De fait, ce qui caractérise les années 1980, ce sont des concepts et des stylisations mimétiques qui relèvent du déjà-vu. Ce n'est par conséquent que la surface des remarquables et radicales innovations des mouvements séminaux dans l'art et le design d'Europe et d'Amérique qui s'est vu grattée, broyée et accomodée à la sauce des tenants de la «nouvelle vague» – une vague qu'on a vu déferler sur le rivage bien des fois dans le passé. Pour qu'un matériau historique puisse affirmer ses vertus nourricières, il faut l'absorber lentement et le comprendre, alors que, de nos jours, il est dévoré tout cru et régurgité entier à une vitesse éclair. Le résultat témoigne d'une totale incompréhension de la fonction originale et du pourquoi des assimilats. Le simple fait – pour ne prendre qu'un exemple – que le constructivisme a l'air moderne ne justifie aucunement son emploi hors d'un contexte significatif.

En 1955, l'Américain Bradbury Thompson, professeur et designer, était pleinement conscient du problème quand il écrivait que «bien que le designer travaille avec conviction en s'appuyant sur des faits, il doit créer dans l'esprit de son propre temps et faire preuve dans ses compositions d'une compréhension essentielle des maîtres qui l'ont précédé, et non pas s'attacher à les copier servilement.» Ces sages paroles n'empêchent pas de nombreux professionnels non seulement de redécouvrir la roue proverbiale, mais aussi en même temps de redécouvrir le feu. Chaque génération cherche à inventer de meilleurs moyens de communication, mais la communication court toujours le risque de devenir un prétexte à de l'art (du design) pour l'art au service d'un engagement personnel en faveur d'une cause sociale, politique ou personnelle obsessionnelle, telle que la ferveur révolutionnaire au début du siècle. Peut-être le terme argotique de «post-moderne» appliqué à l'alliance du classique et du moderne en architecture et en design représente-t-il le plus honnête des «styles» contemporains, puisque son usage même implique qu'il n'y a nulle part où aller si l'on recherche la *nouveauté*. De la sorte, il suggère un retour au moins momentané à des valeurs traditionnelles.

György Kepes, le designer, critique et auteur bien connu, souligne d'un commentaire succinct, au début des années 50, la crise éternelle où la recherche de la *nouveauté* plonge le monde professionnel: «L'obsession de la vitesse et du quantitatif qui prévaut aujourd'hui a profondément influencé la manière dont nous pensons et ressentons les choses. La production de masse et la communication de masse, avec leurs trains standardisés de pensée et de vision, ont épuisé les idées, les transformant en stéréotypes usés.» Ce constat est tout à fait adéquat au débat qui se déroule un peu partout de nos jours au sujet de l'éducation du designer et de la pratique du design; il en vise même le point le plus affligeant — car qui est responsable de la propagation de «stéréotypes usés», si ce ne sont des enseignants paresseux et des étudiants complaisants et conformistes?

Peut-être aussi est-ce un simple cliché que de soulever ce problème, qui est repris décennie après décennie. Il est évident qu'un certain recul est nécessaire si l'on veut juger en toute légitimité la valeur de la contribution que la génération actuelle apporte au patrimoine de l'art publicitaire. Toutefois, la discussion immédiate et franche des mérites et des tares des tendances, modes et œuvres contemporaines sert à jeter les bases de l'évaluation future des réalisations de notre temps. C'est pourquoi il paraît indispensable de stimuler les commentaires critiques, encore fort rares. La perspective historique est également nécessaire. Comme le rappelait Kepes en 1957: «Pour donner une orientation et un ordre déterminé à cette absence de forme, il nous faut revenir à nos racines. Nous devons récupérer la pleine santé de nos facultés créatrices, tout particulièrement notre sensibilité visuelle.» Et qui plus est, il nous faut retrouver les règles, quitte ensuite à les mettre en question de manière intelligente.

Les GRAPHIS ANNUALS, qui couvrent maintenant une période de 23 ans, nous livrent une source primordiale de critique en matière de design et d'illustration. On y trouve le va-et-vient des tendances et concepts au sein d'un réseau créatif international qui n'est visualisé nulle part ailleurs. L'ensemble de ces annuels représente un guide à travers le temps, qui permet d'écrire l'histoire de la communication graphique. Et puis, l'important, c'est que ces annuels mettent en vedette des praticiens individuels et leurs réalisations, non pas en tant que membres de tel groupe, école ou mouvement, mais en tant que témoins de leur époque et des besoins qu'ils éprouvent en leur qualité de professionnels des arts appliqués.

Discutant en termes positifs sa recherche de la nouveauté en 1956, Robert Osborn, commentateur incisif de la scène graphique, déclarait: «Ce qu'il nous faut, c'est des moyens nouveaux pour rendre nos sensations plus visibles et — ce qui me paraît encore plus important — mieux ressenties.» En dernier ressort, c'est au designer ou illustrateur visionnaire de créer quelque chose de légitimement nouveau destiné à perdurer. Et peut-être l'étalon pour juger cet effort, dans cette génération et dans celles qui la suivront, est-il implicite dans l'observation d'Osborn. La gymnastique visuelle pourra retenir l'œil et le distraire l'espace d'un moment, pas plus. Toute réalisation durable dans le domaine du design naît de la compréhension, de la passion — et, bien entendu, de la volonté.

Index to Artists
Verzeichnis der Künstler
Index des Artistes

Index to Designers
Verzeichnis der Gestalter
Index des Maquettistes

Index to Art Directors
Verzeichnis der künstlerischen Leiter
Index des Directeurs Artistiques

Index to Publishers
Verzeichnis der Verleger
Index des Editeurs

Index to Agencies and Studios
Verzeichnis der Agenturen und Studios
Index des Agences et Studios

Index to Advertisers
Verzeichnis der Auftraggeber
Index des Clients

■ Entry instructions may be requested by anyone interested in submitting samples of exceptional graphics or photography for possible inclusion in our annuals. No fees involved. Closing dates for entries:
GRAPHIS ANNUAL (advertising and editorial art and design): 31 January
PHOTOGRAPHIS (advertising and editorial photography): 30 June
GRAPHIS POSTERS (an annual of.poster art): 30 June
Write to: Graphis Press Corp., Dufourstrasse 107, 8008 Zurich, Switzerland

■ Einsendebedingungen können von jedermann angefordert werden, der uns Beispiele hervorragender Photographie oder Graphik zur Auswahl für unsere Jahrbücher unterbreiten möchte. Es werden keine Gebühren erhoben.
Einsendetermine:
GRAPHIS ANNUAL (Werbe- und redaktionelle Graphik): 31. Januar
PHOTOGRAPHIS (Werbe- und redaktionelle Photographie): 30. Juni
GRAPHIS POSTERS (ein Jahrbuch der Plakatkunst): 30. Juni
Adresse: Graphis Verlag AG, Dufourstrasse 107, 8008 Zürich, Schweiz

■ Tout intéressé à la soumission de travaux photographiques et graphiques recevra les informations nécessaires sur demande. Sans charge de participation.
Dates limites:
GRAPHIS ANNUAL (art graphique publicitaire et rédactionnel): 31 janvier
PHOTOGRAPHIS (photographie publicitaire et rédactionnelle): 30 juin
GRAPHIS POSTERS (annuaire sur l'art de l'affiche): 30 juin
S'adresser à: Editions Graphis SA, Dufourstrasse 107, 8008 Zurich, Suisse

Editor and Art Director: Walter Herdeg
Assistant Editor: Joan Lüssi
Project Managers: Romy Herzog, Heinke Jenssen
Designers: Marino Bianchera, Martin Byland, Ulrich Kemmner
Art Assistants: Peter Wittwer, Walter Zuber

1

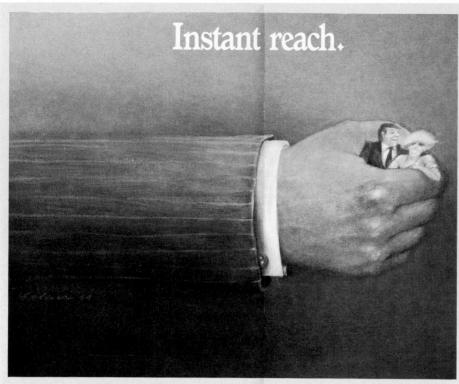

ARTIST / KÜNSTLER / ARTISTE:

1, 4, 6 Jerzy Kolacz
2 Miro Malish
3 Marvin Mattelson
5 Eduardo A. Cánovas

ART DIRECTOR

1, 2 Paul Grissom
3 Steve Ohman
4, 6 James Ronson
5 Eduardo A. Cánovas

AGENCY / AGENTUR / AGENCE:

1, 2 Reactor Art & Design
3 Marschalk
4, 6 Young & Rubicam
5 Estudio Cánovas

26

5

1, 2 Double-spread advertisements for two television magazines to attract advertisers. Based on readership analyses, they claim that the magazines capture the country's largest share of magazine readers. Fig. 1 is in tones of grey; Fig. 2 in tones of green, orange and brown. (CAN)
3 Full-page advertisement for W. R. Grace & Co. in brown tones, claiming that much of American business expects profits to be served up like fast-food burgers. (USA)
4, 6 Examples from an advertising campaign for the magazine *Time* bearing the same slogan and stating that the magazine is highly competitive in the Canadian marketing media. (CAN)
5 Black-and-white magazine ad for a medicine for prenatal and neonatal patients. (ARG)

1, 2 Doppelseitige Inserate für zwei Fernsehzeitschriften, die auf der Basis einer Leserschaftsanalyse um Inserenten werben. Abb. 1, vorwiegend in Grautönen, bezieht sich auf die sofortige Erreichung des Publikums, Abb. 2, in Grün-, Orange- und Brauntönen, auf die Lesezeit. (CAN)
3 Langfristige Planung – statt einer auf kurzfristige Erfolge (hier der Hamburger) ausgerichteten Geschäftspolitik – ist Gegenstand dieses ganzseitigen Inserats für W. R. Grace & Co. (USA)
4, 6 Beispiele aus einer Inseratenkampagne für die Zeitschrift *Time* unter dem Slogan: «Wenn *Time* berichtet, verstehen die Leute.» (CAN)
5 Für ein Medikament, das für das ungeborene und das neugeborene Kind bestimmt ist. (ARG)

1, 2 Annonces double page pour deux revues de programmes TV qui, se basant sur une enquête auprès des lecteurs, recrutent des annonceurs. Fig. 1: allusion à l'impact immédiat sur le public, camaïeu de gris; fig. 2: au temps de lecture, tons verts, oranges, bruns. (CAN)
3 Cette annonce pleine page pour W. R. Grace & Co. préconise une planification à long terme – au lieu d'une politique commerciale aux effets à court terme (comme le hamburger). (USA)
4, 6 Exemples tirés d'une campagne d'annonces pour le magazine *Time* sous le slogan: «Quand *Time* raconte, tout le monde comprend.» (CAN)
5 Pour un médicament destiné au fœtus et au nouveau-né. (ARG)

6

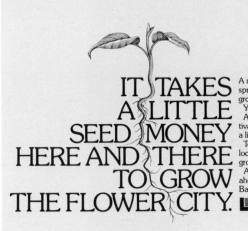

IT TAKES A LITTLE SEED MONEY HERE AND THERE TO GROW THE FLOWER CITY.

A new business takes root. Rows of shops sprout up. A major manufacturer breaks ground for another factory.
Year in, year out, Rochester prospers. At Lincoln First we've helped others cultivate that success over the years. Planting a little here. A little there. And then some.
Today, as then, we continue to support local business and industry, laying the groundwork for tomorrow.
And as the city grows through the years ahead, so can you. With Lincoln First Bank. We've got what you need to succeed.

Lincoln First Bank, N.A.

7

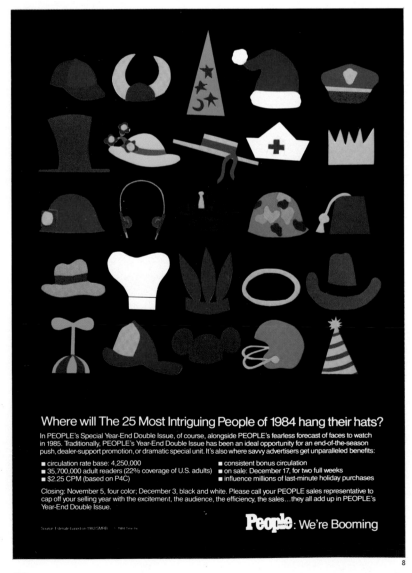

Where will The 25 Most Intriguing People of 1984 hang their hats?

In PEOPLE's Special Year-End Double Issue, of course, alongside PEOPLE's fearless forecast of faces to watch in 1985. Traditionally, PEOPLE's Year-End Double Issue has been an ideal opportunity for an end-of-the-season push, dealer-support promotion, or dramatic special unit. It's also where savvy advertisers get unparalleled benefits:

- circulation rate base: 4,250,000
- 35,700,000 adult readers (22% coverage of U.S. adults)
- $2.25 CPM (based on P4C)
- consistent bonus circulation
- on sale: December 17, for two full weeks
- influence millions of last-minute holiday purchases

Closing: November 5, four color; December 3, black and white. Please call your PEOPLE sales representative to cap off your selling year with the excitement, the audience, the efficiency, the sales...they all add up in PEOPLE's Year-End Double Issue.

People: We're Booming

8

THE REPORTER WHO WOULDN'T REPORT

INSIDE STORY: WITH HODDING CARTER ON PBS. FRIDAY, MARCH 23, AT 9 P.M.*

Should journalists make every detail public when their private lives are involved in the news?

Reporter Rita Jensen thought not. Even when she discovered her roommate was underground revolutionary Kathy Boudin.

Rita never lost her convictions. But somehow she did lose her job. Discover "The Curious Predicament of Reporter Rita Jensen." On public television's Inside Story. Funded by General Electric.

Let Hodding Carter introduce you to a journalist who put her private life ahead of public curiosity.

*National PBS airdate. Check your local listings for date and time.

GE IS A TRADEMARK OF GENERAL ELECTRIC CO

9

Comme on fait son nid on se couche, ça tombe sous le sens.

10

Rester sur place quand on peut avancer, ça n'a pas de sens.

11

7 Doppelseitiges Inserat in Schwarzweiss mit grüner Pflanze für eine Bank: «Für die Saat braucht man hier und dort ein wenig Geld, damit eine blühende Stadt entstehen kann.» (USA)
8 Inserentenwerbung für eine Doppelnummer der Zeitschrift *People* zum Jahresende. (USA)
9 Ganzseitiges Schwarzweiss-Inserat, in dem ein Fernseh-Interview mit einer Reporterin angekündigt wird, die über einen Fall, der ihr Privatleben berührte, nicht berichtete. (USA)
10–12 Aus einer Kampagne mit doppelseitigen Inseraten für die Bank Crédit Agricole. Die mehrfarbigen Illustrationen beziehen sich auf verschiedene Bereiche, in denen die Bank helfen kann: im Privatleben («Wie man sich bettet, so liegt man»), im Geschäftsleben (damit man vorwärtskommt) und in Fällen, wo Werbemittel notwendig sind, um der Anonymität zu entgehen. (FRA)

7 Annonce double page pour une banque, en noir et blanc, avec plante verte. «On n'a pas besoin de beaucoup d'argent pour la graine qui fera fleurir la ville.» (USA)
8 Publicité pour un numéro spécial de fin d'année du magazine *People*. (USA)
9 Annonce pleine page en noir et blanc de l'interview télévisée d'une journaliste qui omit de parler d'un sujet, car il touchait sa vie privée. (USA)
10–12 Exemples d'annonces double page d'une campagne du Crédit Agricole. Les illustrations polychromes se rapportent aux divers domaines dans lesquels la banque offre son soutien: vie privée, affaires, et chaque fois que des moyens publicitaires sont nécessaires à la promotion: «Accepter d'être anonyme, ça n'a pas de sens.» (FRA)

12

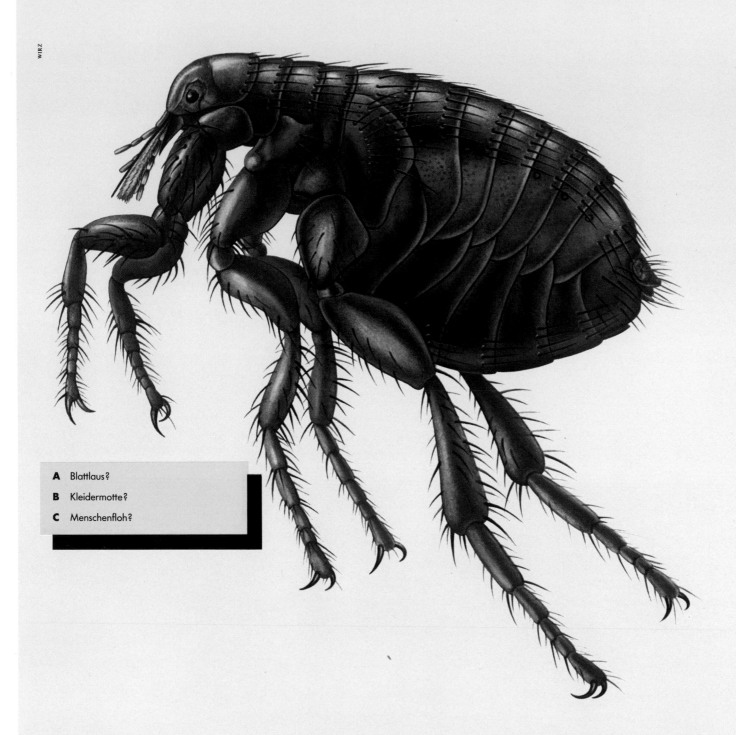

Advertisements/Inserate/Annonces

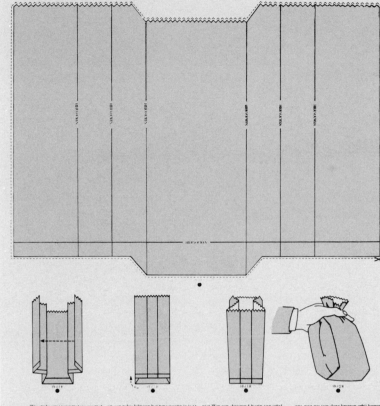

13 Is it an aphid, a moth or a flea? It's a flea, and if you want to know more about other small matters that crop up in everyday life, you need the *Neue Zürcher Zeitung*, says this full-page advertisement in its plea for new subscribers. (SWI)
14 "Free from the Nutsspaarbank, a harmless bang for New Year's Eve." For a bank. (NLD)
15, 16 Full-page advertisements with colour illustrations for PSDI, developers of software systems for project management, which help to put the manager ahead of his competitors. (USA)

13 Fundiertes Wissen, auch in nicht alltäglichen Bereichen (gezeigt ist der Menschenfloh), ist das Thema dieses ganzseitigen Inserats für die *Neue Zürcher Zeitung*. (SWI)
14 «Gratis von der Nutsspaarbank, ein harmloser Knall für Silvester.» Für eine Bank. (NLD)
15, 16 Inserate mit mehrfarbigen Illustrationen für PSDI, einen Software-Hersteller. Hier soll veranschaulicht werden, wie der Kunde sich dank des Programms von der Konkurrenz unterscheiden wird. (USA)

13 Acquérir des connaissances précises, même dans des domaines inhabituels (reconnaître une puce), tel est l'objet de cette annonce pleine page de la *Neue Zürcher Zeitung*. (SWI)
14 «La Nutsspaarbank vous offre un pétard inoffensif pour la St-Sylvestre.» (NLD)
15, 16 Annonces avec illustrations en couleurs pour PSDI, producteur de logiciel. Il s'agit de démontrer comment le client, grâce à son programme informatique, se différenciera de ses concurrents. (USA)

14

15

16

31

17

The No Curves Auto Loan

Our same day auto loan takes the curves out of buying a new car.
We understand how it feels to buy a new car. It's a big decision! And once you decide, you'll want the most direct route to financing, at a rate you can afford.

First Wisconsin's No Curves Auto Loan means that your loan can be approved in just five hours or less. With our straight-forward approach, you can be on the road the same day.

Whether you currently bank with First Wisconsin or would simply like a new car loan. We can help you figure out what you can afford and how much your monthly payments will be—before you go shopping. This gives you a better idea of how to plan your purchase.

So don't spin your wheels waiting for a new car loan. Come to First Wisconsin and get behind the wheel. You'll get a competitive rate and fast service.

III FIRST WISCONSIN

18

L'Espresso. Per saperne di più.

19

17 Double-spread advertisement for *Italtel*, a company in the field of telecommunications. The illustration relates to the specific research this company undertakes in its products. (ITA)
18 Newspaper ad for the First Wisconsin Bank, which promises assistance with car loans. (USA)
19 "*L'Espresso*. In order to know more." Full-page advertisement in black and white from a press campaign for this weekly magazine reporting on politics, economy and culture. (ITA)
20 Advertisement for the Bamerindus Bank in *Grafica*, a trade magazine for graphics. (BRA)
21–24 Examples from IBM's promotional campaign for their typewriters. (USA)

17 Doppelseitiges Inserat mit mehrfarbiger Illustration für *Italtel*, ein Computer-Unternehmen, das hier auf seine gezielte Forschungstätigkeit aufmerksam macht. (ITA)
18 Zeitungsinserat für die First Wisconsin Bank, die auf problemlose Autokredite hinweist. (USA)
19 «*L'Espresso*. Um mehr zu wissen.» Ganzseitiges Inserat in Schwarzweiss aus einer Pressekampagne für *L'Espresso*, ein Wochenmagazin für Politik, Wirtschaft und Kultur. (ITA)
20 Inserat für die Bamerindus Bank in *Grafica*, einer Fachzeitschrift für Graphik. (BRA)
21–24 Beispiele aus einer Anzeigenkampagne für IBM-Schreibmaschinen. (USA)

17 Annonce double page avec illustration polychrome pour *Italtel*, une entreprise d'informatique, qui attire ici l'attention sur ses activités dans la recherche. (ITA)
18 Annonce de journal signalant l'avantage du crédit auto de la First Wisconsin Bank. (USA)
19 «*L'Espresso*. Pour en savoir plus.» Annonce pleine page noir et blanc tirée d'une campagne pour *L'Espresso*, hebdomadaire consacré à la politique, l'économie et la culture. (ITA)
20 Annonce pour la Bamerindus Bank parue dans *Grafica*, magazine de graphisme. (BRA)
21–24 Exemples tirés d'une campagne d'annonces pour les machines à écrire IBM. (USA)

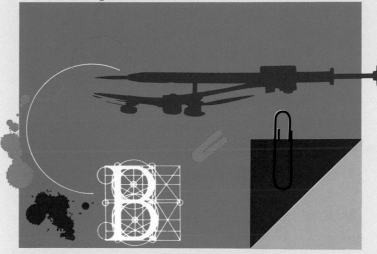

20

21

22

23

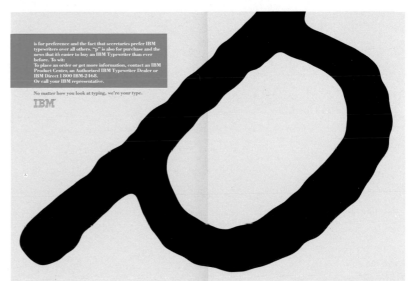

24

We're a part of and yet apart from the automobile business.
They do things their way.
We do things our way.
In 1949, their way was a garish, gas-guzzling hulk of sheet metal and chrome. The car.
Our way was a small, homely, humble attempt at good basic transportation. The Beetle.
It embodied our philosophy: Forget what looks best. Forget what sells best. What works best?
Car makers scoffed.
Cars were expensive. The Beetle was economical. Cars were work to drive. Volkswagens were fun to drive. Cars were changed to look better.
Volkswagens were changed to work better. Cars were built to self-destruct. Volkswagens were built to last.
Volkswagens became popular. Car makers became nervous. Especially in 1975 when we introduced the Rabbit. Today, it's still being copied.
So, after 35 years of turning our backs on every popular notion known to the car business, what's next?
A lot. We have a growing passion for the most practical, best performing, personal transportation our German engineering can build and almost anyone's money can buy.
We're raising more than a few eyebrows with two new Volkswagens: The 1985 Jetta and Golf.
They reaffirm our philosophy. As do the Quantum, Scirocco, GTI, Cabriolet, Vanagon and Camper.
We could follow the crowd. We could go with the flow. But that would be like trying to fit a round peg in a round hole.

Volkswagen.

It's not a car. It's a Volkswagen.

25

25 Full-page ad for *Volkswagen*. This company's policy is to set itself apart from competitors in the automobile branch. "We could follow the crowd ... But that would be like trying to fit a round peg in a round hole." (USA)
26 Full-page advertisement for IBM small business computers. According to the advertisement these are only expensive in the customer's mind. Black text on skin-toned head, logo in blue. (USA)
27 "What good is a computer as fast as Einstein, if your printer is as slow as Gutenberg?" From a full-page advertisement for *Check* computer printers. (USA)
28 "What does a typical cruise passenger look like?" (All types are typical.) Ad for "ms Europa" cruises. (GER)
29, 29a "Hear no eagle, see no eagle." Illustration and complete advertisement for Barclays Bank. (USA)

25 Ganzseitiges Inserat für *Volkswagen*. Das Unternehmen will sich mit seiner Geschäftspolitik deutlich von der Konkurrenz absetzen: «Mit dem Strom zu schwimmen wäre so einfach, wie einen runden Pfahl in ein rundes Loch zu setzen.» (USA)
26 Ganzseitiges Inserat für kleine IBM-Geschäfts-Computer, die nach Aussage der Werbung nur in der Vorstellung, also im Kopf des Kunden, teuer sind. Schwarze Schrift in hautfarbenem Kopf, Markenzeichen blau. (USA)
27 «Was nützt ein Computer, der so schnell wie Einstein ist, wenn der Printer so langsam wie Gutenberg ist?» Aus einem ganzseitigen Inserat für *Check*-Printer. (USA)
28 Inserat für Kreuzfahrten mit der «ms Europa», die jedem Typ und jeder Altersgruppe etwas bieten. (GER)
29, 29a «Nichts hören und nichts sehen wollen.» Illustration und vollständiges Inserat der Barclays Bank. (USA)

25 Annonce pleine page de *Volkswagen*. Commercialement, l'entreprise veut se distinguer des concurrents. «Nous pourrions suivre le courant. Mais ce serait aussi simple que d'enfoncer un cylindre dans un trou rond.» (USA)
26 Annonce pleine page pour des petits ordinateurs IBM. La publicité suggère qu'ils ne sont chers que dans la tête du client. Texte noir inscrit dans la tête couleur chair, sigle bleu. (USA)
27 «A quoi vous sert un ordinateur qui est aussi rapide qu'Einstein si votre imprimante est aussi lente que Gutenberg?» D'une annonce pleine page pour *Check*-Printer. (USA)
28 Annonce de «ms Europa» proposant des croisières à chacun, quel que soit son âge ou sa personnalité. (GER)
29, 29a «Ne rien entendre et ne rien voir.» Illustration et annonce complète de Barclays Bank. (USA)

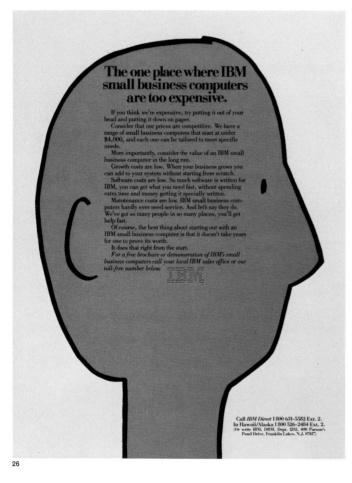

26

Advertisements
Inserate
Annonces

27

Wie sieht ein typischer Kreuzfahrer aus?

Eines sind sie alle, die Kreuzfahrer auf der ms Europa: verschieden! Da sind zum Beispiel abgeklärte Abenteurer und frische Hochzeitspärchen dabei, oder Manager, Hausfrauen, Akademiker, Privatiers, Handwerker, Angestellte, Freiberufler, ganze Familien, einzelne Damen, Bekannte und Unbekannte, welche mit 1 Dutzend Koffern und andere mit 1 Reisetasche.

Alle Altersgruppen kreuzen auf: Das Ergebnis von 2 Reisen, die wir kürzlich machten, wird jene überraschen, die meinen, das Kreuzfahren setze ein ziemlich gestandenes Alter voraus. 7 % sind bis 19 Jahre, 5 % sind 20–29 Jahre, 19 % sind 30–44 Jahre, 35 % sind 45–59 und 34 % sind darüber.

Das Interessante an Bord der Europa: Jeder ist aufgeschlossen, jeder akzeptiert den anderen, so wie er ist. Man macht zusammen Landausflüge, Malkurse, Tanzstunden; dreht Jogging-Runden auf den endlosen Decks; spielt Schach und Bridge, Golf und Tennis; geht gemeinsam in den Nachtclub, ins Kino, zur Frühgymnastik, zum Captains Dinner, zum Kostümball, ins Fitness Center. Oder man geht sich einfach aus dem Weg... denn alles ist auf der Europa möglich!

Wenn Sie ganz genau wissen wollen, wie ein typischer Kreuzfahrer aussieht, dann kommen Sie doch mal an Bord! Unsere Reisen bringen Sie zu den schönsten Plätzen, fernsten Inseln, weißesten Stränden und fremdesten Menschen. Sie dauern 7 bis 99 Tage und kosten von 2.310,– bis 94.510,– DM. Ihr Reisebüro sagt Ihnen gerne, wo wir in diesem Jahr noch aufkreuzen. Oder schreiben Sie uns. Hapag-Lloyd AG, Kreuzfahrten, Postfach 10 79 47, D-2800 Bremen 1.

ms Europa · Hapag-Lloyd AG

28

DESIGNER / GESTALTER / MAQUETTISTE:

25 Mark Hughes
26 Gary Goldsmith
28 Ursel Koch/Uli Weber
29 Norman Egelston

ART DIRECTOR / DIRECTEUR ARTISTIQUE:

25 Mark Hughes
26 Gary Goldsmith
27 Dean Hanson
28 Uli Weber
29 Norman Egelston

AGENCY / AGENTUR / AGENCE – STUDIO:

25, 26 Doyle Dane Bernbach
27 Fallon McElligot & Rice
28 Leonhardt & Kern
29 The Agency

29

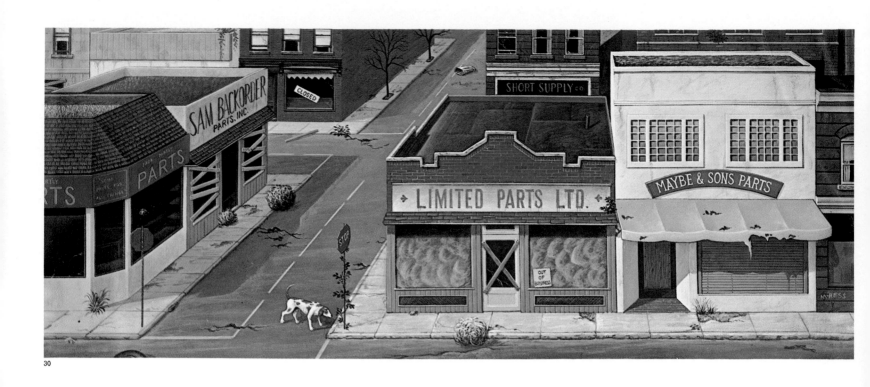

Advertisements/Inserate/Annonces

Divan Alanda. Rückenlehnen und Armlehnen verstellbar. Design Paolo Piva, 1980.

Seit zwei Tagen warte ich auf irgendjemanden, die Armlehnen und die Rückenlehnen des Alanda Divans sind zum Glück verstellbar, wenn es nur irgendjemand wäre, der neben mir sitzt, die Armlehnen und die Rückenlehnen sind zum Glück verstellbar, man ist nie so allein, wie wenn man die Rückenlehnen und die Armlehnen verstellen kann und man verstellt sie nur, weil niemand da ist, der die Armlehnen und/oder die Rückenlehnen verstellt haben möchte.

B&B ITALIA

34

ARTIST / KÜNSTLER / ARTISTE:

30, 31 Mark Hess
32, 33 Teresa Fasolino
34 Giovanni Mulazzani

ART DIRECTOR / DIRECTEUR ARTISTIQUE:

30, 31 Bob Akers
32, 33 Ann Prochazka
34 Fritz Tschirren

AGENCY / AGENTUR / AGENCE – STUDIO:

30, 31 N. W. Ayer
32, 33 Vansant Dugdale
34 STZ Srl

30, 31 "Bryant will make travelling all over town for parts a thing of the past." Illustration and complete ad for an air conditioning-systems manufacturer. (USA)
32, 33 Complete advertisement and illustration in actual size for *Westinghouse*. The emphasis is on preparedness in military missions in the present and in the future. (USA)
34 Double-spread advertisement in shades of brown and gold for versatile upholstered furniture from *B&B Italia*. (SWI)

30, 31 Illustration und vollständige Anzeige für einen Hersteller von Klimaanlagen: «*Bryant* macht die stadtweite Suche nach Teilen zu einem Ding der Vergangenheit.» (USA)
32, 33 Vollständiges Inserat und Illustration in Originalgrösse für *Westinghouse*, mit Anspielung auf die eigene Zuverlässigkeit im militärischen Nachschubwesen. (USA)
34 Doppelseitiges Inserat in Brauntönen für Einrichtungen von *B&B Italia*. (SWI)

30, 31 Illustration et annonce complète d'un fabricant des installations de climatisation: «Avec *Bryant*, chercher dans toute la ville des pièces détachées, c'est du passé.» (USA)
32, 33 Annonce complète et illustration grandeur nature pour *Westinghouse*; allusion à la fiabilité de l'entreprise dans le domaine du ravitaillement militaire. (USA)
34 Annonce double page pour des meubles rembourrés de *B&B Italia*, dans des tons bruns. (SWI)

REGARD D'EAU, JOUES CORAIL, BOUCHE FRUIT
PARASOL PACIFIQUE DE ROCHAS

ROUGE A
LÈVRES N° 3
FARD A
PAUPIERES
RIVAGE BLEU /
VAGUE DE CORAIL
VERNIS A
ONGLES N° 31

ROCHAS
PARIS

35

37

36

38

39

35 Double-spread advertisement for *Rochas* to promote their new range of make-up shades, here royal-blue eye-shadow, coral-toned rouge, and "fruit" lip colour. (FRA)
36 Advertisement for an estate agent group specializing in supermarket malls. The ad refers in particular to the ICSC Deal Making Convention at which this company are represented. (USA)
37 Illustration for tennis shoes, showing how and what to look for when purchasing a new pair. Greyish-white shoe against a blue sky, tennis court in dark blue-green tone. (USA)
38 From a series of ads for *Ellesse* aerobic shoes. Red tones, with shoe in greyish-white. (USA)
39 Full-page advertisement for the film-compositors Florian of Paris. (FRA)

35 Doppelseitiges Inserat für neue Make-up-Farben von *Rochas*, hier Wasserblau für die Augen, «Koralle» für die Wangen, «Frucht» für die Lippen. (FRA)
36 Anlässlich einer Tagung in New York veröffentlichtes Inserat für ein Immobilien-Unternehmen, das auf Einkaufszentren spezialisiert ist und interessante Angebote verspricht. In Farbe. (USA)
37 Illustration für die Tennisschuhwerbung der Kennex Corporation. Grau-weisser Schuh vor blauem Himmel, Spielfeld in dunklem Blaugrün. (USA)
38 Aus einer Inseratenkampagne für *Ellesse*-Aerobic-Schuhe. Rottöne, weiss-grauer Schuh. (USA)
39 Ganzseitiges Inserat für die Setzerei Florian in Paris. (FRA)

35 Annonce double page pour les nouvelles couleurs de maquillage de *Rochas*. Un collage de papiers déchirés aux couleurs contrastées met en valeur l'illustration. (FRA)
36 Annonce en couleurs publiée par une société immobilière à l'occasion d'un congrès à New York. Spécialisée dans les centres commerciaux, elle promet des offres intéressantes. (USA)
37 Illustration pour la publicité des chaussures de tennis de la Kennex Corporation. Chaussure gris blanc sur fond de ciel bleu, court de tennis bleu-vert foncé. (USA)
38 Annonce en couleurs figurant dans une campagne des chaussures *Ellesse*-Aerobic. (USA)
39 Annonce pleine page pour l'imprimerie Florian à Paris. (FRA)

突っかかるタイプ

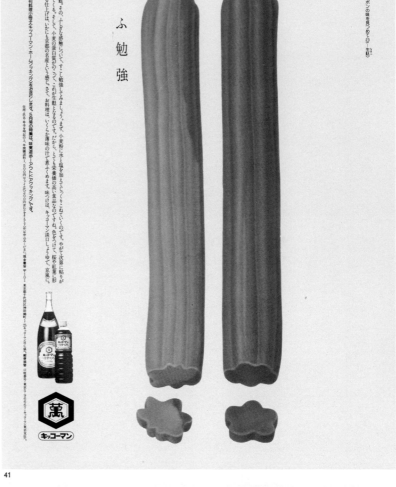

ふ勉強

40

41

Advertisements/Inserate/Annonces

ARTIST / KÜNSTLER / ARTISTE:

40, 41 Tadashi Ohashi
42, 43 Milton Glaser

DESIGNER / GESTALTER / MAQUETTISTE:

40, 41 Tadashi Ohashi
42, 43 Milton Glaser

ART DIRECTOR / DIRECTEUR ARTISTIQUE:

40, 41 Tadashi Ohashi
42, 43 Joe La Rosa

AGENCY / AGENTUR / AGENCE – STUDIO:

42, 43 Waring & La Rosa

40, 41 Examples from a long-running promotion campaign with full-page advertisements for products made by the spice and sauce manufacturer *Kikkoman*. The illustration in Fig. 40 is in tones of brown, in Fig. 41 in pale green and pink shades. (JPN)
42, 43 "Not manufactured but created by the earth when it was new." Full-page advertisements from a series to promote the mineral water *Perrier*, Fig. 43 in actual size. (USA)

40, 41 Beispiele aus einer langjährigen Pressekampagne mit ganzseitigen Inseraten für Produkte des Gewürz- und Saucenherstellers *Kikkoman*. Illustration in Abb. 40 in Brauntönen, in Abb. 41 in blassem Grün und Rosa. (JPN)
42, 43 Ganzseitige Inserate aus einer Kampagne für das Mineralwasser *Perrier*, «nicht hergestellt, sondern von der Erde geschaffen, als sie neu war». Abb. 43 in Originalgrösse. (USA)

40, 41 Exemples d'annonces pleine page conçues pour une campagne de presse visant à promouvoir les produits de la firme de condiments et sauces *Kikkoman*. L'illustration de la fig. 40 est réalisée dans des tons de bruns, celle de la fig. 41 en vert et rose. (JPN)
42, 43 Annonces pleine page figurant dans une campagne pour l'eau minérale *Perrier*. On y vante ses qualités naturelles d'eau de source. La fig. 43 est grandeur nature. (USA)

Earth's First Soft Drink.

Perrier. Not manufactured, but created by the earth when it was new.

42

Perrier. Earth's First Soft Drink.

Not manufactured
but created by the earth
when it was new.

44

46

ARTIST / KÜNSTLER / ARTISTE:

44–47 David Jemerson Young
48 Steven Guarnaccia

DESIGNER / GESTALTER / MAQUETTISTE:

44–47 David Jemerson Young
48 Bob Manley

ART DIRECTOR / DIRECTEUR ARTISTIQUE:

44–47 David Jemerson Young
48 Bob Manley

AGENCY / AGENTUR / AGENCE – STUDIO:

44–47 Young & Laramore
48 Altman & Manley

44, 45 Illustration and full-page advertisement for an accounting and professional services firm offering assistance to growing businesses. The textured background covers the whole advertisement. (USA)
46, 47 Illustration and full-page ad for an architect who "translates" the customer's lifestyle into the houses he remodels. Textured ground. (USA)
48 Newspaper advertisement for a medical insurance plan covering a fully comprehensive approach to medical care. (USA)

44, 45 Illustration und ganzseitige Anzeige einer Unternehmensberatungsfirma. Der Hintergrund zieht sich über die gesamte Anzeige. (USA)
46, 47 Illustration und ganzseitiges Inserat für einen Architekten, der auf die persönlichen Bedürfnisse seiner Auftraggeber eingeht. Das strukturierte Aquarellpapier zieht sich über das ganze Inserat. (USA)
48 Zeitungsinserat für ein Versicherungsprogramm, das die vielen Aspekte im Gesundheitswesen berücksichtigen soll. «Die medizinische Landschaft ist kein Ort, an dem man sich wie ein Tourist aufführt.» (USA)

44, 45 Illustration et annonce pleine page d'une firme de conseils d'entreprises. Le fond coloré s'étend sur toute la page. (USA)
46, 47 Illustration et annonce pleine page pour un architecte prêt à répondre aux besoins personnels de ses clients. La structure du papier aquarelle sert également de fond au texte. (USA)
48 Annonce pour une assurance offrant un programme varié en matière de santé. «Le paysage médical n'est pas un lieu de tourisme.» (USA)

45

47

Advertisements / Inserate / Annonces

DANKE, HERR DAIMLER.

Das Ding krachte, rauchte, stank und drohte jeden Moment zu explodieren. Aber es lief. Es hatte 4 Räder, transportierte vier nervöse Passagiere und war ein Triumph für Gottlieb Daimler: die erste erfolgreiche Verbrennungsmaschine.

Wir bei United Technologies bauen auch Verbrennungsmaschinen. Drei von vier Linienmaschinen der westlichen Welt fliegen z.B. mit

Triebwerken unserer Firma Pratt & Whitney Aircraft.

Sie laufen verlässlicher als Daimlers Ungetüm von 1885. Sie sind auch unauffälliger — niemand bleibt mehr stehen, um sie anzustaunen. Aber gerade deshalb halten wir gern mal inne, um des Mannes zu gedenken, mit dessen pferdelosem Antrieb die ganze Reiserei angefangen hat.

UNITED TECHNOLOGIES

`49`

DANKE, HERR HERTZ.

Als Heinrich Hertz unter dem großen Helmholtz studierte, war Elektrizität noch ein trappierendes, neues Spielzeug in der wissenschaftlichen Welt. Jeder hatte eine andere Theorie, was man damit anfangen könnte.

Es war Hertz, der dem Durcheinander ein Ende machte. In einem nicht geschlossenen Stromkreis produzierte er mit einem Funkeninduktor elektrische Wellen, die er dann mit einer Drahtschlinge aus der Luft holte. Das drama-

tische kleine Kunststück im Klassenzimmer ebnete den Weg zur weltweiten drahtlosen Kommunikation und zum Radar.

Heute sind die Himmel voller Hubschrauber, Flugzeuge und Raumfähren. Zu ihrem Orientierungssinn und ihrer Performance hat United Technologies eine Menge beigetragen. Wir haben ihnen Augen und Ohren gegeben. Aber ohne die grundlegende Arbeit von Hertz hätten wir auch nicht gewusst, wie.

UNITED TECHNOLOGIES

`50`

DANKE, HERR BUNSEN.

Völlig zu Recht erinnert sich jeder Student an den Bunsenbrenner im Chemielabor — Bunsen war Laborman durch und durch. Und ein Mann von Vision: wenn er etwas für ein Experiment brauchte, das es nicht gab, erfand er es einfach. Die Nassbatterie. Kalorimeter. Filterpumpe. Thermosäule.

Seine größte Errungenschaft aber bleibt sein Beitrag zur Spektroskopie. Diese Methode zur Bestimmung anorganischer Substanzen, himm-

lische eingeschlossen, half uns, das Universum besser zu verstehen.

Speziell auch uns bei United Technologies. Neben Düsentriebwerken für den modernen Reiseverkehr oder Flugcomputern bauen wir nämlich auch Brennstoffzellen für Raumfahrzeuge, die das Sonnensystem an der Nähe studieren.

Ohne Robert Wilhelm Bunsen wär's noch immer ziemlich geheimnisvoll an dem großen Himmelszelt.

UNITED TECHNOLOGIES

`51`

On Monday, March 19th, an animated version of Igor Stravinsky's The Soldier's Tale will be presented by "Great Performances" on PBS, produced by R.O. Blechman, director of The Ink Tank.

2 West 47th Street
New York, N.Y. 10036

`52`

49–51 From a series of advertisements for *United Technologies* with black-and-white portraits of famous inventors in branches of science where this company is also active. Shown here are Gottlieb Daimler, Heinrich Hertz and Robert Wilhelm Bunsen, the inventor of spectroscopy and the "burner". (GER)
52 Black-and-white advertisement for an animated version of Stravinsky's *The Soldier's Tale*, produced by R.O. Blechman. (USA)
53 Advertisement in black and white for furnishings by *Habitat*, on the occasion of the Trade Fair 85 in Japan. (JPN)
54 Ad for the synthetic fibre *Arnel* by *Celanese*. (USA)
55, 56 Two of four black-and-white ads relating to the seasons, here winter and autumn, for a shopping centre. (USA)

49–51 Aus einer Serie von Inseraten für *United Technologies* mit Schwarzweiss-Porträts berühmter Erfinder auf Gebieten, in denen auch dieses Unternehmen tätig ist. (GER)
52 Inserat in Schwarzweiss für die Ankündigung einer Zeichentrick-Version von Igor Strawinskys *Geschichte vom Soldaten*, produziert von R.O. Blechman. (USA)
53 Zur Expo 85 in Japan veröffentlichtes Inserat in Schwarzweiss für Möbel und Einrichtungsgegenstände von *Habitat*. (JPN)
54 Inserat für die Triacetatfaser *Arnel* von *Celanese*. Hier wird das Lob eines Kunden zitiert. (USA)
55, 56 Aus einer Reihe von Schwarzweiss-Inseraten eines Einkaufszentrums, die sich auf die verschiedenen Jahreszeiten beziehen, hier auf den Winter und den Herbst. (USA)

49–51 D'une série d'annonces pour *United Technologies*: portraits en noir et blanc d'inventeurs qui se sont illustrés dans des domaines que la firme exploite. (GER)
52 Annonce en noir et blanc pour la sortie d'une version en dessin animé de *L'Histoire du soldat* d'Igor Strawinsky, produite par R.O. Blechman. (USA)
53 Annonce en noir et blanc des meubles et objets d'*Habitat* publiée pour l'Expo 85 au Japon. (JPN)
54 Annonce pour la fibre synthétique *Arnel* de Celanese. On y cite l'éloge d'un client. (USA)
55, 56 Exemples d'une série d'annonces en noir et blanc d'un centre commercial, se rapportant aux saisons, en l'occurrence le printemps et l'automne. (USA)

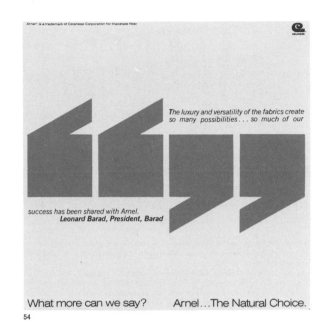

Arnel® is a trademark of Celanese Corporation for triacetate fiber.

The luxury and versatility of the fabrics create so many possibilities... so much of our

success has been shared with Arnel.
Leonard Barad, President, Barad

What more can we say? Arnel...The Natural Choice.

54

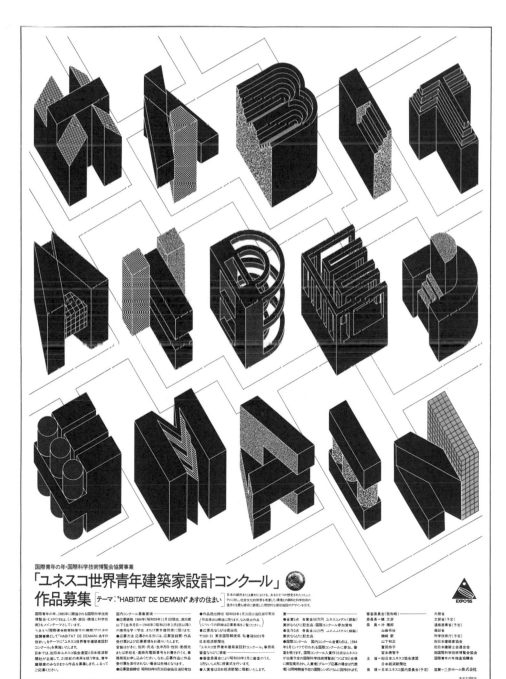

国際青年の年・国際科学技術博覧会協賛事業
「ユネスコ世界青年建築家設計コンクール」
作品募集 テーマ：“HABITAT DE DEMAIN” あすの住まい

53

Winter. It's the season for rain and umbrellas. And bundling up. It's a great time for discovering the cozy hospitality of Victoria Court. You'll find sweaters and boots, posters and stationery. And much more. Plus restaurants to relax in.

Victoria Court
For any season
Over 36 shops and restaurants at the corner
of State and Victoria in downtown Santa Barbara

55

Fall. It's the season for apples and books. And back-to-school. It's a wonderful time for experiencing the Old World feeling of Victoria Court. You'll find tote bags and notebooks, toys and candy. And much more. Plus restaurants to fit any budget.

Victoria Court
For any season
Over 36 shops and restaurants at the corner
of State and Victoria in downtown Santa Barbara.

56

45

Take me to the theatre.

For routes and information, call MTD at 962-7682

57

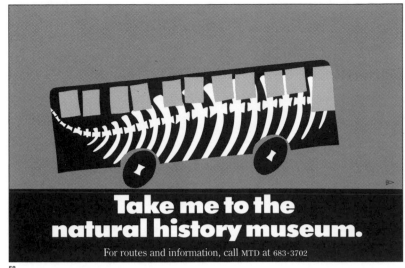

Take me to the natural history museum.

For routes and information, call MTD at 683-3702

58

57, 58 Examples from a series of small format, black-and-white advertisements placed in newspapers to promote a bus service. Each advertisement emphasizes one of the destinations which can be reached on the service route. (USA)
59, 60 Black-and-white advertisements for a business bank which helps with loans and makes regular adjustments to the customer's needs without "putting the squeeze on". (USA)
61–63 Complete advertisement and two illustrations from a press campaign for a new Dutch reference work, "Grote Van Dale". Dutch words, with their various meanings, are illustrated. The words shown here, translated, mean: Meerschaum (pipe of Venus), Novice-brothers (monks who tended the cattle) and Potboy (messenger boy), respectively. (NLD)

57, 58 Beispiele aus einer Serie von kleinformatigen Zeitungsanzeigen in Schwarzweiss für eine Buslinie. Die verschiedenen Ziele, wie hier das Theater und das Naturgeschichtliche Museum, sind jeweils Gegenstand der Illustrationen. (USA)
59, 60 Inserate in Schwarzweiss für eine Handelsbank, die veranschaulichen will, wie es dem Kunden ergeht, wenn seine Bank seinen Kreditbedürfnissen nicht gerecht werden kann. (USA)
61–63 Vollständiges Inserat und zwei Illustrationen aus einer Pressekampagne für ein neues holländisches Nachschlagewerk. Hier werden Begriffe aus der holländischen Sprache illustriert (wörtlich übersetzt: Schaumgöttin, Kalbsbruder, Topfjunge), deren richtige Bedeutung im «Grote Van Dale» zu finden ist. (NLD)

59

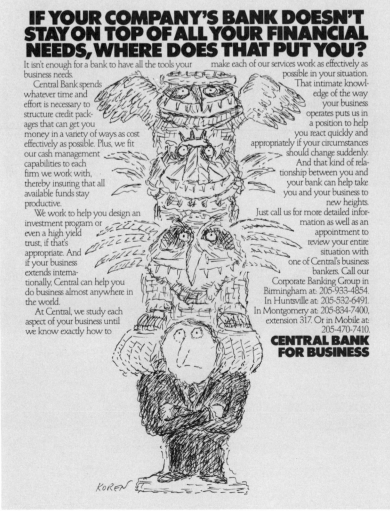

60

61

Advertisements
Inserate
Annonces

57, 58 Exemples tirés d'une série d'annonces de journaux petit format en noir et blanc pour une ligne d'autobus. Les diverses stations fournissent le thème de chaque illustration, comme ici le théâtre et le Muséum d'histoire naturelle. (USA)

59, 60 Annonces en noir et blanc pour une banque d'affaires. Les illustrations montrent ce qui arrive au client lorsque sa banque ne peut pas répondre à ses besoins en crédit. (USA)

61–63 Annonce complète et deux illustrations qui figurent dans une campagne de presse pour un nouveau dictionnaire hollandais. Les dessins illustrent des expressions de la langue hollandaise dont la signification exacte est donnée dans le «Grote Van Dale» (traduction littérale des mots illustrés ici: déesse de l'écume, frère de veau, gamin de pot). (NLD)

ARTIST / KÜNSTLER / ARTISTE:

57, 58 Sandra Higashi
59, 60 Edward Koren
61–63 J. C. Suarès

DESIGNER / GESTALTER / MAQUETTISTE:

57, 58 Marty Neumeier
61–63 Tom Vergouw

ART DIRECTOR / DIRECTEUR ARTISTIQUE:

57, 58 Marty Neumeier
59, 60 Jerry Sullivan
61–63 Tom Vergouw

AGENCY / AGENTUR / AGENCE – STUDIO:

57, 58 Neumeier Design Team
59, 60 Sullivan Haas Coyle
61–63 J. Walter Thompson

62

63

64

65

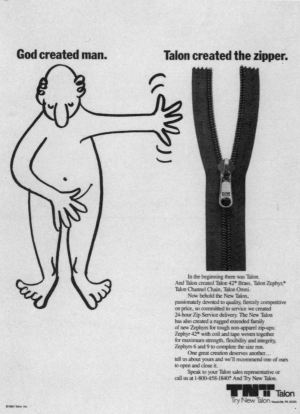

66

67

Genius & | **Applied systems No.3**

Salmon P. Chase had a system we can bank on. Perhaps of Salmon Chase's portrait were on the $20 bill instead of the $10,000 bill, more would know of his important contributions to America as a lawyer, statesman, senator, chief justice, and secretary of the treasury. For instance, during the Civil War, the U.S. government was in dire need of credit. Chase spearheaded a new system in 1863 to permit banks to organize and to issue notes up to the amount of their capital, secured by government bonds deposited with the Treasury. Chase's national banking system grew from a particular need—his country needed capital, and a system he could call his own assured it ...an applied system so strong, it began the system we can all depend upon today.

CCI is just as solution driven. Computer Consoles, Incorporated is the applied computer systems company which offers unique solutions to specific industry needs. We're not generic product oriented, nor do we serve all market segments. Our ability to apply computer systems to particular problems separates us from the crowd of traditional data processing companies. We've been perfecting applied computer systems for years, beginning with the telephone industry. Our TELEPOWER® products keep CCI as the world's #1 supplier of Directory Assistance Systems. And today, we've expanded our capabilities to the office with OFFICEPOWER™ systems. By understanding how people work in specific office applications, we can apply a system which works the way they need it to. Like Salmon Chase, we are able to focus on the real problem and offer the best solution. CCI doesn't follow other computer companies ...we follow the great geniuses who knew how to get things done. Maybe we can do the same for you. Call us at 800-833-7477 (In New York State call 716-482-5000). Or write us at Dept. WC, 97 Humboldt Street, Rochester, NY 14609. You may not get your picture on a Treasury Note. But you will get a system that's yours and yours alone.

A limited supply of Salmon Chase poster prints is available. Request on your letterhead.

CCI COMPUTER CONSOLES INCORPORATED®

CCI.
Systems you can call your own.

69

Genius & | **Applied systems No.2**

Eli Whitney put his system on the line. It's hard to believe, but the cotton gin was one of Eli Whitney's biggest failures. His machine was stolen and copied, his patent was infringed, and he didn't make a cent on it. Yet, thanks to a federal contract to build 10,000 muskets, Whitney was able to invent a system which would make up for early America's lack of skilled machinists ...an applied system which permitted an unskilled man to turn out a product as good as one made by someone experienced. Whitney's own concept of standardized parts, along with his planning of divided labor, made him a success, and the father of the assembly line...a system he could call his own.

CCI is also a pioneer problem-solver. Computer Consoles, Inc. is the applied computer systems company...an integrator of hardware, software and communications technologies which is oriented to total solutions. We're by no means a traditional data processing company. Nor are we a "me too" product company simply following the markets we serve. CCI offers selective expertise applying special systems to specific needs.

We're well known in the telephone industry and are today the leading supplier of Directory Assistance Systems. Our new TELEPOWER® products offer telephone companies new sources of revenue and improved productivity. We also have studied the ways today's office workers function. And just as Eli Whitney realized that everyone can produce like an expert, we realize that every worker should have access to information and contribute to greater productivity. Therefore, we have developed OFFICEPOWER™ systems which respond specifically to particular applications. We've even employed Whitney's idea of standardization to our own computer components. At CCI we've followed history's great geniuses to devise applied computer systems. And now, we invite you to get some of this thinking working for you. Call us at 800-833-7477 (In New York State, call 716-482-5000). Or write us at Dept. WW, 97 Humboldt Street, Rochester, NY 14609. With us, you can have a system that's truly all yours.

A limited supply of Eli Whitney poster prints is available. Request on your letterhead.

CCI COMPUTER CONSOLES INCORPORATED®

CCI.
Systems you can call your own.

70

Shouldn't your polyester yarn be as versatile as the new technology?

Introducing Fortrel D-210 polyester. Has an outdated yarn left you years behind the times? Well, imagine a polyester staple so versatile it can be used with any spinning process. We did. And the result is Celanese Fortrel® D-210 polyester. A 1.2 denier per filament, high modulus fiber that combines enhanced aesthetics with superb performance. And it works with *air-jet, ring, and open-end spinning methods.* Versatility is just one of its strengths. D-210 offers improved weaving and knitting efficiency, *higher tenacity,* increased yarn elongation, and a 10% *improvement in yarn uniformity.* Which means, of course, less worrying about breakdowns and lost downtime. That's not all. The lower denier per filament of Fortrel D-210 offers improved fabric aesthetics. It also *blends beautifully with cotton in all spinning systems.* Fabrics come out with a soft, natural hand and look. Try it for shirting, sleepwear, and sheeting, and you'll see the difference. We think it'll leave the competition hanging by a thread. For more information, give your account representative a call. Look what polyester is doing now.

CELANESE FIBERS OPERATIONS.

IT'S FORTREL

71

Invitation til alle med øjne og ører.

I morgen holder vi åbent hus for alle, der har lyst til en oplevelse i lyd og billede. Vi strækker lukketiden helt til kl. 15.00 og vil indtil da lukke op for Bang & Olufsens spændende nyhedspakke.

De vil kunne se og opleve det nye Link system, der giver Dem mulighed for at få Hi-Fi lyd over hele huset - fra et centralt anlæg. De vil kunne lytte til de nye spændende Red Line højtalere. Og De vil blive præsenteret for musik, der kan hænge på væggen. Nemlig Beosystem 3000 og Beosystem 10. Og sidst, men ikke mindst, blænder vi op for de nye farve-TV fra Bang & Olufsen og den nye VHS videobåndoptager.

Vi starter denne rejse ind i en verden af lyd og billede i morgen kl. 9.00. De kan glæde Dem til en herlig oplevelse. Kom og hils på os i morgen.

dragsbæk
Tlf. (08) 13 19 44   Vingaardsgade 16-20, 9000 Aalborg
- når det drejer sig om Bang & Olufsen

74

69, 70 Newspaper advertisements for an applied computer-systems company who prepare systems to individual needs—as the two geniuses portrayed here: Salmon P. Chase who pioneered a national banking system, and Eli Whitney who introduced a system of standardized parts for the machine industry. (USA)
71 Ad for the introduction of *Fortrel* polyester fibre by *Celanese*. (USA)
72, 73 From a press campaign for *Apple* computers in Japan. The circle by Hakuin (18th century) symbolizes the universe. (JPN)
74 "For all who have eyes and ears." Newspaper advertisement for hi-fi, TV and video apparatus from *Bang & Olufsen*. (DEN)
75, 76 Newspaper ads for *Cerberus* safety systems, in which the firm's detectors are likened to the highly-sensitive detecting organs of certain animals. (SWI)

72

73

75

76

69, 70 Zeitungsinserate für ein Computer-Unternehmen, das bahnbrechende, spezifischen Bedürfnissen angepasste Systeme anbieten will, wie sie seinerzeit von den hier porträtierten Salmon P. Chase für das Bankwesen und Eli Whitney für den Maschinenbau erfunden wurden. (USA)
71 Inserat für die Einführung von *Fortrel*-Polyester von *Celanese*. (USA)
72, 73 Aus einer Zeitungskampagne für *Apple*-Computer in Japan. Der Kreis von Hakuin (18. Jahrhundert) bedeutet das Universum. (JPN)
74 «Für alle, die Augen und Ohren haben.» Zeitungsinserat für Musik- und TV-Anlagen von *Bang & Olufsen*. (DEN)
75, 76 Zeitungsanzeigen für *Cerberus*-Sicherheitssysteme, deren Detektoren hier mit der Sensorik gewisser Tierarten verglichen werden. (SWI)

69, 70 Annonces de journaux pour une entreprise d'informatique qui propose des systèmes inédits adaptés aux besoins spécifiques, ainsi que le firent en leur temps Salmon P. Chase pour les banques et Eli Whitney dans la construction de machines. (USA)
71 Annonce pour la promotion du polyester *Fortrel* de *Celanese*. (USA)
72, 73 Inspiration zen pour une campagne des ordinateurs *Apple* au Japon. Le cercle de Hakuin (18e siècle) symbolise l'univers. (JPN)
74 «Pour tous ceux qui ont des yeux et des oreilles.» Annonce de journal pour les appareils radio, phono, TV de *Bang & Olufsen*. (DEN)
75, 76 Annonces de journaux pour les systèmes de sécurité *Cerberus*. Les détecteurs sont comparés aux sens de certains animaux. (SWI)

2

Booklets

Folders

Catalogues

Programmes

Broschüren

Faltprospekte

Kataloge

Programme

Brochures

Dépliants

Catalogues

Programmes

77

78

77 Portrait of Edgar Allan Poe on a self-promotion postcard from Pancho. (FRA)
78 Front of an invitation card (in approximately the actual size) to an exhibition in Frankfurt of posters and graphic works by Celestino Piatti. In black with soft violet. (GER)
79 Black-and-white illustration as self-promotion piece for Barbara Klunder. (CAN)
80 An announcement of shoe creations by *Andrea Pfister*. (ITA)
81 Cover of a large-format prospectus for a radio station appealing to the younger listener. Illustration in green, light blue and yellow on black, on cream stock. (JPN)
82, 83 Double spread and cover of a catalogue for platinum jewellery. All the illustrations are in tones of russet, grey and blue with black, on pale grey stock. (GER)

77 Porträt Edgar Allan Poes auf einer Eigenwerbungskarte von Pancho. (FRA)
78 Vorderseite einer Einladungskarte der Stiftung Buchkunst zu einer Ausstellung der Arbeiten von Celestino Piatti in Frankfurt. In Schwarz mit sanftem Violett. (GER)
79 Als Eigenwerbung verwendete Illustration in Schwarzweiss von Barbara Klunder. (CAN)
80 Hier werden Schuhkreationen von *Andrea Pfister* angekündigt. (ITA)
81 Vorderseite eines grossformatigen Prospekts, der für einen Radiosender für junge Leute wirbt. Illustration grün, hellblau, gelb und schwarz, Papier chamois. (JPN)
82, 83 Doppelseite und Umschlag eines Katalogs für Platinschmuck. Für alle Illustrationen wurden warme Rotbraun-, Grau- und Blautöne mit Schwarz verwendet. (GER)

77 Portrait d'Edgar Allan Poe décorant une carte d'autopromotion de Pancho. (FRA)
78 Recto d'une carte d'invitation de la Fondation Buchkunst (Art du Livre) à une exposition des travaux de Celestino Piatti à Francfort. Noir, avec du violet assourdi. (GER)
79 Illustration noir et blanc pour l'autopromotion de l'artiste Barbara Klunder. (CAN)
80 Annonce des créations de chaussures d'*Andrea Pfister*. (ITA)
81 Recto du dépliant publicitaire au grand format d'une station de radio s'adressant aux jeunes. Illustration vert, bleu clair, jaune, noir, papier chamois. (JPN)
82, 83 Double page et couverture d'un catalogue de bijoux en platine. Toutes les illustrations sont exécutées en tons chauds – roux, gris, bleu, avec du noir. (GER)

79

80

82

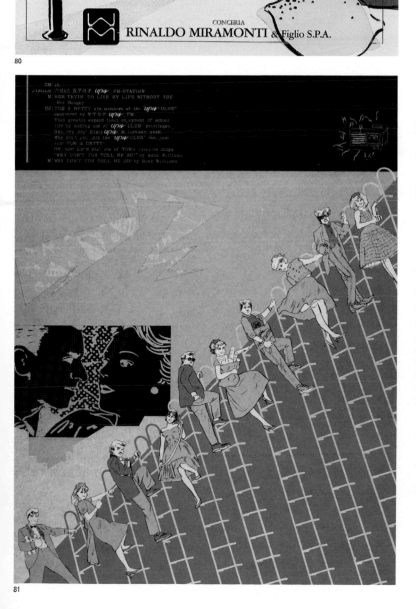

81

83

ARTIST / KÜNSTLER / ARTISTE:

84 Tomislav Spikic
85 Titti Garelli
86 Santo Alligo
87, 88 Max Casalini

ART DIRECTOR:
84–88 Francesco Gioana

84

85

84–88 Full-page illustrations and example of a double spread from a concertina-fold, hard-cover publication, bound with tapes, containing 17th century recipes. Fig. 84 illustrates a dish of lamb chops with nut and herb sauce; Fig. 85 is for lasagne with cream of hops, nuts and rosemary; Fig. 86 relates to a terrine of goose with stinging nettles; Fig. 87, 88 illustrate a dish of scampi tails, cooked in an enriched chicken broth. (ITA)

84–88 Ganzseitige Illustrationen und Beispiel einer Doppelseite aus einer Publikation mit Kochrezepten aus dem 17. Jahrhundert. Abb. 84 illustriert ein Gericht mit Hammel-koteletts an einer Nuss-Kräuter-Sauce, Abb. 85 Lasagne mit einer Paste aus Nüssen und Hopfen zubereitet, Abb. 86 betrifft ein Rezept für eine Gänse-Terrine, zu dem auch Brennesseln gehören, Abb. 87, 88 gehören zu einem Gericht aus Garnelen, in Hühner-brühe gekocht. (ITA)

84–88 Illustrations pleine page et double page-type d'un carnet de recettes du 17e siècle. La fig. 84 illustre un mets de côtelette de mouton en sauce aux noix et aux herbes, la fig. 85: des lasagnes préparées avec une pâte de noix et de houblon. La fig. 86 concerne une terrine de pâté d'oie aromatisée aux orties. Les fig. 87 et 88 se rapportent à un plat de crevettes cuites dans du bouillon de poule. (ITA)

86

**Booklets
Prospekte
Brochures**

87

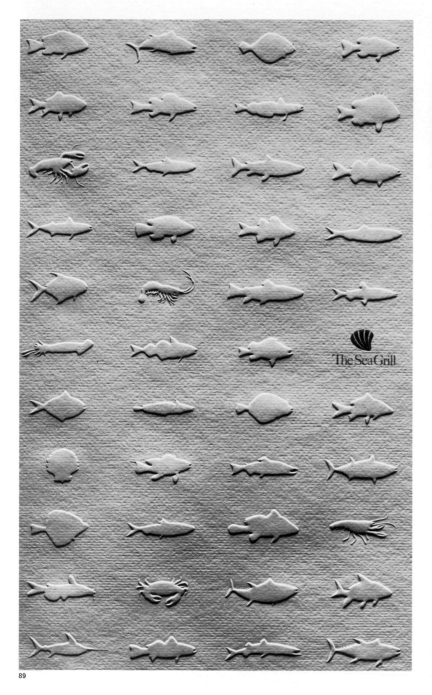

89

90

ARTIST / KÜNSTLER / ARTISTE:

90 Terry Speer
93, 94 Nina Duran
95 Andy Warhol

DESIGNER / GESTALTER / MAQUETTISTE:

89 Tom Geismar
90 David Bartels
91, 92 Kenzo Nakagawa/Hiro Nobuyama/Satch Morikama
93–95 J. C. Suarès

ART DIRECTOR / DIRECTEUR ARTISTIQUE:

89 Tom Geismar
91, 92 Kenzo Nakagawa
93–95 J. C. Suarès

93

94

91

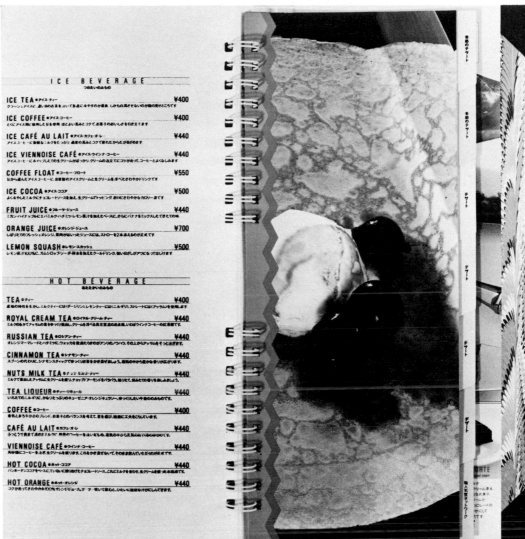

92

AGENCY / AGENTUR / AGENCE – STUDIO:

89 Chermayeff & Geismar Associates
90 Bartels & Company, Inc.
91, 92 Bolt & Nuts Studio

95

89 Blind-embossed cover of a menu for a high-class fish restaurant.
Off-white card, golden shell and gold-toned lettering. (USA)
90 Gaily-coloured cover of a menu. (USA)
91, 92 Cover of a dessert menu for a Japanese restaurant, and the
menu opened showing the spiral binding and illustration. (JPN)
93–95 Illustrations and double spread from a publication on the
history of the mineral water Perrier. Fig. 93: Arena of Nîmes; Fig. 94:
Perrier—"Just what the doctor ordered." (USA)

89 Blindgeprägte Vorderseite einer Speisekarte für ein exklusives
Fischspezialitätenrestaurant. Karton chamois, Schrift und Emblem
goldfarben. (USA)
90 Farbenfroher Umschlag für eine Menu-Karte. (USA)
91, 92 Vorderseite, in verhaltenen Farbtönen, und geöffnete, ringge-
heftete Dessert-Karte eines japanischen Restaurants. (JPN)
93–95 Illustrationen und Doppelseite aus einer Publikation über die
Geschichte des Mineralwassers Perrier. Abb. 93: Arena von Nîmes,
Abb. 94: Perrier als Kurmittel. (USA)

89 Recto (gaufré à sec) du menu d'un restaurant de spécialités de
poisson. Carton chamois, texte et emblème or. (USA)
90 Couverture haute en couleur pour un menu. (USA)
91, 92 Recto aux teintes adoucies de la carte des desserts à reliure
spirale d'un restaurant japonais, montrée ouverte. (JPN)
93–95 Illustrations et double page d'une publication consacrée à
l'historique de l'eau minérale Perrier. Fig. 93: les arènes de Nîmes;
fig. 94: le Perrier en cure thermale. (USA)

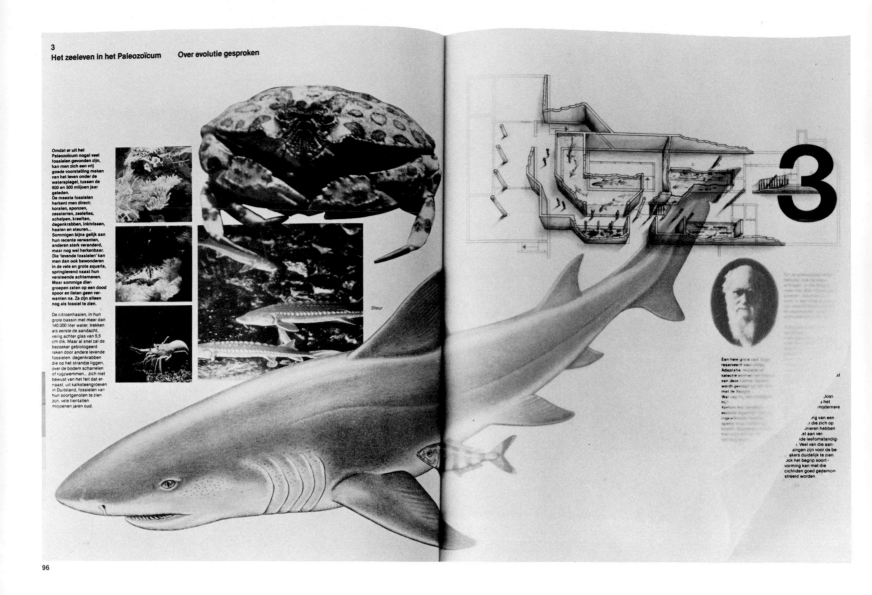

Het zeeleven in het Paleozoïcum   Over evolutie gesproken

96

---

96 Double spread with transparent overlay, partly printed, from a catalogue for a new natural history museum at the zoological gardens in the Dutch town of Emmen. The catalogue forms part of the comprehensive documentation for both museum and zoo (see also Fig. 99, 100). The subject of the spread shown here is sea life in the Paleozoic era of evolution. (NLD)
97, 98 Double spreads with polychrome illustrations from a brochure offering a world cruise by the Holland America Line. (USA)
99, 100 Cover with punched-out butterflies and a complete spread from a brochure devoted to the life-cycle of butterflies, for the 50th anniversary of the zoological gardens in Emmen. (NLD)

96 Doppelseite mit transparentem, teilweise bedrucktem Einlageblatt aus einem Katalog für ein neues naturhistorisches Museum im Tierpark der holländischen Stadt Emmen. Der Katalog ist Teil einer umfangreichen Dokumentation zum fünfzigjährigen Jubiläum des Zoos (siehe auch Abb. 99, 100). Das Thema der hier gezeigten Doppelseite ist die Evolution im Wasser. (NLD)
97, 98 Doppelseiten mit mehrfarbigen Abbildungen aus einer Broschüre für den Verkauf einer von der Holland–America-Linie angebotenen Weltreise per Schiff. (USA)
99, 100 Umschlag mit ausgestanzten Schmetterlingen und Doppelseite aus einer anlässlich der Eröffnung des Schmetterling-Pavillons im Tierpark Emmen herausgegebenen Broschüre. (NLD)

96 Double page avec un encart transparent, partiellement imprimé, dans le catalogue d'un nouveau muséum d'histoire naturelle au jardin zoologique de la ville hollandaise d'Emmen. Ce catalogue fait partie d'une importante documentation publiée à l'occasion du cinquantenaire du zoo (cf. les fig. 99, 100). Sujet de cette double page: l'évolution née de la mer. (NLD)
97, 98 Doubles pages illustrées en polychromie, dans une brochure de vente pour les tours du monde en paquebot offerts par la compagnie de navigation Holland–America. (USA)
99, 100 Couverture aux papillons en découpe, et page double d'une brochure du jardin zoologique d'Emmen éditée à l'occasion de l'inauguration du pavillon consacré aux papillons. (NLD)

Booklets / Prospekte / Brochures

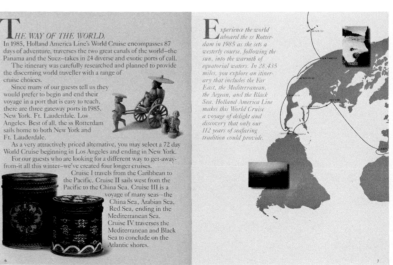

97   98

60

ARTIST / KÜNSTLER / ARTISTE:

96 Richard Orr/Rijkent Vleeshouwer/
    John Stoel (Photo)
99, 100 Hilde Wolters

DESIGNER / GESTALTER / MAQUETTISTE:

96, 99, 100 Koos Staal
97, 98 Gretchen Goldie/Kimberlee Kewsick

ART DIRECTOR / DIRECTEUR ARTISTIQUE:

96, 99, 100 Koos Staal
97, 98 Keith Bright/Noreen Young

AGENCY / AGENTUR / AGENCE – STUDIO:

96, 99, 100 Koos Staal
97, 98 Bright & Associates

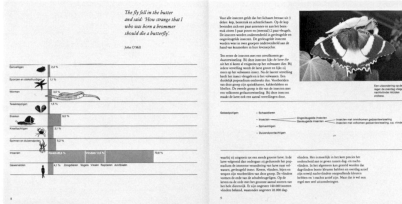

100

Wie van vlinders houdt.

101–103 Cover and double spreads from a 120-page booklet publicizing the design of the Danish state railways. Fig.102 shows that good basic design can still be applied even for unconventional wagons; Fig.103 shows the table of contents and accompanying illustration. Text in Danish and English. (DEN)
104–107 Cover, double spreads and a single page from a city guidebook for Tokyo, one of a series on various cities, all in handy, tall-pocket size, published by the *Access Press*. (USA)

101–103 Vorderseite und Doppelseiten aus einer Broschüre des Dänischen Designrats über das Design der dänischen Eisenbahn. Abb.102 zeigt am Beispiel verschiedener Transportmittel, wie das Grundprinzip des Designs angewendet wurde; Abb.103 ist die einführende Doppelseite mit Inhaltsverzeichnis. (DEN)
104–107 Umschlag, Doppelseiten und eine einzelne Seite aus einem Stadtführer für Tokio in handlichem Buchformat, aus einer Reihe über verschiedene Städte, herausgegeben von *Access Press*. (USA)

101–103 Première page de couverture et doubles pages d'une brochure du Conseil national du design danois consacrée à l'esthétique des chemins de fer danois. Fig.102: application des principes de design retenus à divers véhicules; fig.103: page double initiale avec le sommaire. (DEN)
104–107 Couverture, doubles pages et page simple d'un guide de la ville de Tōkyō au format pratique, dans une collection *Access Press* décrivant diverses villes du monde. (USA)

101

Dansk Designråd
Danish Design Council

102

ARTIST / KÜNSTLER / ARTISTE:
104–107 Reven T. C. Wurman (Photo)

DESIGNER / GESTALTER / MAQUETTISTE:
101–103 Jens Nilsen
104–107 Richard Saul Wurman

ART DIRECTOR / DIRECTEUR ARTISTIQUE:
104–107 Richard Saul Wurman

104

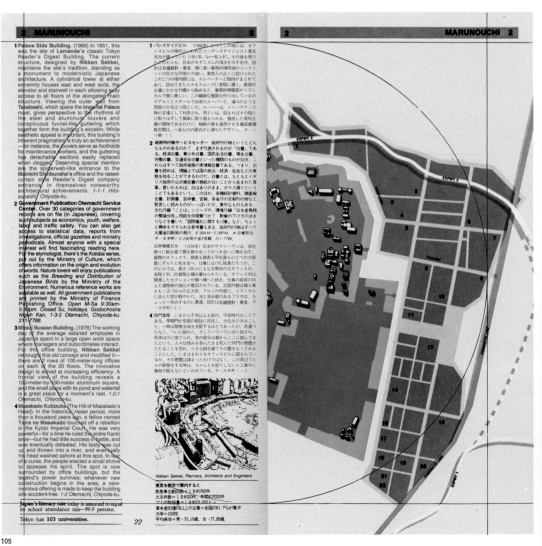

105

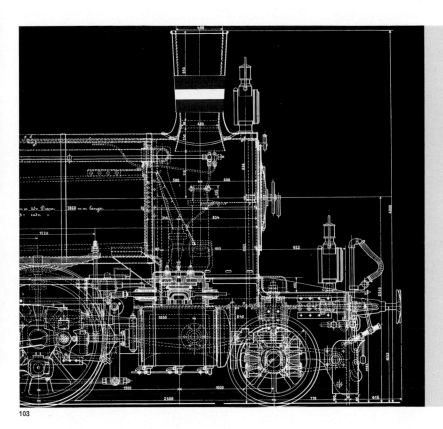

Booklets/Prospekte/Brochures

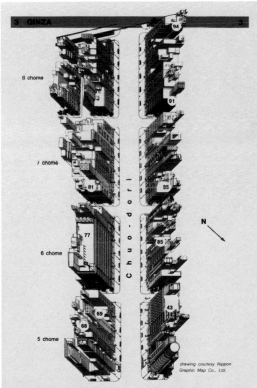

3 GINZA

8 chome

7 chome

Chuo-dori

6 chome

N

5 chome

drawing courtesy Nippon
Graphic Map Co., Ltd.

45 Itoya. Established in 1904 as a stationery store, this is a favorite stop for everyone, from kids looking for crayons to professional designers and draftsmen. A quick rundown on their stock gives us the following list: **Basement 1**—typewriters, rubber stamps; **Basement 2**—wrapping paper, gift boxes, notes; **1st floor**—cards and fashionable notepaper; **Mezzanine**—fountain pens, desk accessories, quality stationery; **2nd floor**—files, ballpoint pens, office supplies; **3rd floor**—desks, lighting, file cabinets; **4th floor**—hobby floor stocking computer games, radio-controlled models, games; **5th floor**—paper goods, both Japanese and imported, and a selection of wallpaper; **6th floor**—art and graphic design products; **7th floor**—press type, offset printing service, color copies; **8th floor**—picture frames and framing service; **9th floor**—tearoom and gallery exhibiting the works of different illustrators every week. Anything the artist

45 伊東屋 和菓子系文具用品として、1904年（明治37年）の
創業である。子供から何でのデザイナーまで、様々な客層
で賑わいにもにぎわっている。では、各フロアー毎の
売り場構成を順不同ようし、地下1、2、タイプライター、印
刷関係、印鑑、印刷、中地下は包装紙、ギフトボックス、ノー
トなど紙製品も豊富にある。1階はカード、ノートなどの
ファンシー商品のフロアー、ここにいつも女の子や小さい子
であふれている。中地下は万年筆さいふなど高級ステイ
ショナリー、2階には、ファイル、ボールペンなど事
務用品が揃っている。3階は机、照明などインテリア用
品。4階はホビーのフロアー。7階は、文字に加
陳列調され、デザイン用品のフロアー。7階は、文字に加
エサービス、オフセット印刷やカラーコピーも出来る。8
階は額縁加工、9階はギャラリーといういし。1週間ごと
にものの変わり、特に若手イラストレーターの作品展を
定に人気がある。文具用品として便利だけではない
伊東屋の使い方を知って戴きたいものである。〒中・銀座2-7-15、561-8311。

40

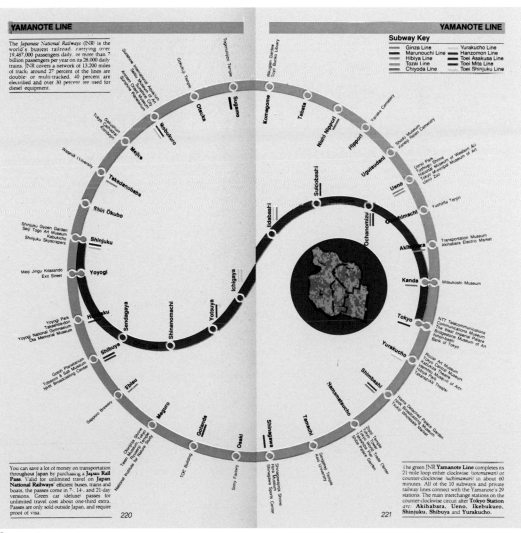

YAMANOTE LINE · YAMANOTE LINE

The *Japanese National Railways* (JNR) is the world's busiest railroad, carrying over 19,487,000 passengers daily, or more than 7 billion passengers per year on its 28,000 daily trains. JNR covers a network of 13,200 miles of track; around 27 percent of the lines are double- or multi-tracked, 40 percent are electrified and over 30 percent are used for diesel equipment.

Subway Key

- Ginza Line
- Marunouchi Line
- Hibiya Line
- Tozai Line
- Chiyoda Line
- Yurakucho Line
- Hanzomon Line
- Toei Asakusa Line
- Toei Mita Line
- Toei Shinjuku Line

You can save a lot of money on transportation throughout Japan by purchasing a **Japan Rail Pass.** Valid for unlimited travel on **Japan National Railways'** efficient buses, trains and boats, the passes come in 7-, 14-, and 21-day versions. Green car (deluxe) passes cost about one-third extra. Passes are only sold outside Japan, and require proof of visa.

220

The green JNR **Yamanote Line** completes its 21-mile loop either clockwise (*sotomawari*) or counter-clockwise (*uchimawari*) in about 60 minutes. All of the 10 subways and private railway lines connect with the Yamanote's 29 stations. The main interchange stations on the counter-clockwise circuit after **Tokyo Station** are: **Akihabara, Ueno, Ikebukuro, Shinjuku, Shibuya** and **Yurakucho.**

221

106

107

108 Front cover of a gatefold prospectus for a printer and a designer. The initials in the form of birds stand for the designer's name, also for the AGI (of which he is the Swedish president) and for the (royal) printer, *Björkmans*. (SWE)
109–111 Examples from the copiously-compiled, boxed graphic project to advertise papers from *Mohawk* Paper Mills. The whole forms a graphic essay on mazes and labyrinths, and offers an illustrated historical account—plus a die-cut, ball-in-the-maze game to construct (complete with steel balls). Figs. 109, 110 show the cover and double spread from a large-format brochure and Fig. 111 shows a gatefold prospectus with a staple-bound inserted booklet. (USA)
112 Double spread from a booklet for the International Paper Co. on the subject of book printing; red and black text on ivory vellum. (USA)

108 Vorderseite eines aufklappbaren Prospekts einer Druckerei und eines Designers. Die Anfangsbuchstaben in Vogelform stehen für den Namen des Designers und für die AGI, deren Präsident er in Schweden ist, sowie für jenen der Druckerei *Björkmans*. (SWE)
109–111 Beispiele aus einer reich ausgestatteten Werbe-Schachtel des Papierherstellers *Mohawk*, deren zentrales Thema das Labyrinth ist. Geschichtliches bis zur Gegenwart ist illustriert und kommentiert und mit austrennbaren Labyrinth-Spielen aufgelockert. Abb. 109 zeigt den Umschlag einer grossformatigen Broschüre, Abb. 110 eine Doppelseite daraus, und Abb. 111 ist ein Faltprospekt mit eingeheftetem Büchlein. (USA)
112 Doppelseite aus einer zum Thema der Buchdruckerkunst konzipierten Broschüre der International Paper Co. Roter und schwarzer Druck auf Velin. (USA)

108 Recto du prospectus bipartite d'une imprimerie et d'un designer. Les initiales en forme d'oiseau sont celles du designer et de l'AGI dont il préside la section suédoise, ainsi que de l'imprimerie *Björkmans*. (SWE)
109–111 Echantillons du contenu d'une boîte publicitaire du papetier *Mohawk* dont le riche assortiment est axé sur le thème du labyrinthe. L'aperçu historique est illustré et commenté, des jeux de labyrinthe détachables donnant de la variété à l'exposé. Fig. 109: couverture d'une brochure au grand format. La fig. 110 montre une page double tirée de cette brochure, la fig. 111 un dépliant avec un cahier encarté. (USA)
112 Double page d'une brochure de l'International Paper Co. traitant de l'art typographique. Impression en rouge et noir sur vélin. (USA)

ARTIST / KÜNSTLER / ARTISTE:

108 Olle Eksell
109–111 Seymour Robins

DESIGNER / GESTALTER / MAQUETTISTE:

108 Olle Eksell
109–111 Seymour Robins
112 Lucille Tenazas

ART DIRECTOR / DIRECTEUR ARTISTIQUE:

108 Olle Eksell
109–111 Seymour Robins
112 Marshall Harmon

AGENCY / AGENTUR / AGENCE – STUDIO:

108 Olle Eksell Design
109–111 Seymour Robins Design
112 Harmon Kemp Inc.

109

108

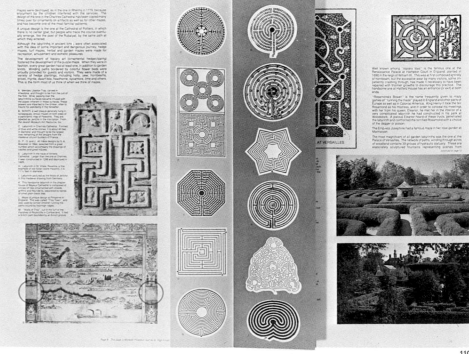

110

This is Mohawk Artemis
Cover, 80 lb. Blue.

THREADING
THE
LABYRINTH
OF
DESIGN

Labyrinth-Logo typography © 1984 by Seymour Robins

Booklets
Prospekte
Brochures

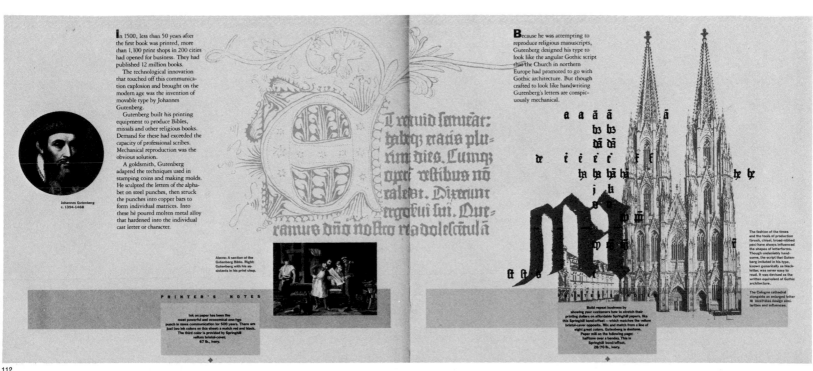

In 1500, less than 50 years after the first book was printed, more than 1,100 print shops in 200 cities had opened for business. They had published 12 million books.

The technological innovation that touched off this communication explosion and brought on the modern age was the invention of movable type by Johannes Gutenberg.

Gutenberg built his printing equipment to produce Bibles, missals and other religious books. Demand for these had exceeded the capacity of professional scribes. Mechanical reproduction was the obvious solution.

A goldsmith, Gutenberg adapted the techniques used in stamping coins and making molds. He sculpted the letters of the alphabet on steel punches, then struck the punches into copper bars to form individual matrices. Into these he poured molten metal alloy that hardened into the individual cast letter or character.

Johannes Gutenberg
c. 1394-1468

Above: A section of the Gutenberg Bible. Right: Gutenberg with his assistants in his print shop.

P R I N T E R ' S   N O T E S

Ink on paper has been the most powerful and economical one-two punch in mass communication for 500 years. There are just two ink colors on this sheet: a match red and black. The third color is provided by Springhill vellum bristol-cover, 67 lb., Ivory.

Because he was attempting to reproduce religious manuscripts, Gutenberg designed his type to look like the angular Gothic script that the Church in northern Europe had promoted to go with Gothic architecture. But though crafted to look like handwriting Gutenberg's letters are conspicuously mechanical.

The fashion of the times and the tools of production (brush, chisel, broad-nibbed pen) have always influenced the shapes of letterforms. Though undeniably handsome, the script that Gutenberg imitated in his type, known generically as blackletter, was never easy to read. It was devised as the written equivalent of Gothic architecture.

The Cologne cathedral alongside an enlarged letter M illustrates design similarities and influences.

Build repeat business by showing your customers how to stretch their printing dollars on affordable Springhill papers, like this Springhill hand-crafted — which matches the vellum bristol-cover opposite. Mix and match from a line of eight great colors. Gutenberg in doctrine. Paper mill on the following page: halftone over a bendey. This is Springhill bond-offset, 28/70 lb., Ivory.

ARTIST / KÜNSTLER / ARTISTE:

114, 115 Robert Cunningham
116 Frank Deras
118, 119 Kathleen Toelke

DESIGNER / GESTALTER / MAQUETTISTE:

113 Michael R. Abramson/Claire Hess
114, 115 Bruce Blackburn
116 Sandra Koenig
117 Christof Gassner
118, 119 Sandy Runnion/Jeff Runnion

ART DIRECTOR / DIRECTEUR ARTISTIQUE:

113 Larry Wolson
114, 115 Bruce Blackburn
116 Don Bartels/Greg Silveria
118, 119 Sandy Runnion/Jeff Runnion

AGENCY / AGENTUR / AGENCE – STUDIO:

114, 115 Danne & Blackburn, Inc.
116 Landor Associates
118, 119 Runnion Design

113

Child
Care
Referral
Service

IBM

114

What if I'm dissatisfied with my initial choice of provider? Can I get additional advice?
Yes. The referral organization will assist you in trying to find another provider.

Does the CCRS visit the providers they'll refer me to?
Although the CCRS staff is familiar with the local child care providers, they may not have visited the providers who list their services with the CCRS. In those states that have child care regulations for the form of care you are seeking, providers must demonstrate that they comply with the law prior to referral by the CCRS staff. However, no system of regulation or visitation should be taken by parents as a guarantee of quality child care. Only parental observation and ongoing monitoring can give you this assurance.

Can I use this service for temporary child care—say, if I'm ill or away on business and unable to take care of my child?
Yes, although the emphasis is on furnishing information about providers for dependable long-term arrangements.

Can the CCRS help in finding care for children with special needs, è.g., handicapped children?
The CCRS generally can provide information on child care programs which have accommodations for children with special needs. However, they cannot provide specialized advice on the most appropriate educational plan or treatment for a particular child. The CCRS should be able to refer you to a community resource where such advice is available.

Why is IBM providing this referral service instead of day care centers at company locations?
The principle behind this program is to give those eligible a wide range of options so they can decide which one is best-suited for their needs. That kind of flexibility—in terms of proximity to home or work, form of care, and ages of children served—would be impossible to achieve in day care centers at company locations. In addition, the placement of such day care centers near all major IBM plants and offices would lead to inequities in those areas where the IBM population density would not warrant such a facility.

115

113 Box and contents—sales-promotion samples of *Formica* brand laminate with naturally-coloured metal surfaces. The metal colours shown are: aluminium, pewter, brass and copper. (AUS)
114, 115 Cover and double spread from an IBM brochure informing its parental staff about the child-care service offered. (USA)
116 Cover of a corporate-identity manual. (USA)
117 Opened box which contains small cardboard cubes, as mailer for *Chromolux* by *Zanders Feinpapiere* (paper manufacturers). (GER)
118, 119 Separate cards each informing on a specific social benefit for the staff of *Keane*. Fig. 119: folder shown opened. (USA)

113 Schachtel mit Inhalt, eine Werbesendung für *Formica*-Schichtstoffplatten mit echten Metalloberflächen. Die Schachteln in den Metallfarben Aluminium, Zinn, Messing und Kupfer. (AUS)
114, 115 Umschlag und Doppelseite aus einer IBM-Broschüre, die über Vermittlungen von Kinderhütediensten informiert. (USA)
116 Umschlag für ein Corporate-Identity-Handbuch. (USA)
117 Geöffnete Schachtel mit kleinen Kartonwürfeln, als Werbesendung für *Chromolux* von *Zanders Feinpapiere* konzipiert. (GER)
118, 119 Aus einzelnen Karten bestehende Information über die Sozialleistungen von *Keane*. Abb. 119: geöffneter Umschlag. (USA)

113 Boîte publicitaire et son contenu, une réalisation publicitaire pour les panneaux stratifiés *Formica* surfacés de métal. Boîtes aux couleurs métalliques alu, étain, laiton, cuivre. (AUS)
114, 115 Couverture et page double d'une brochure IBM consacrée aux services de garderies d'enfants. (USA)
116 Couverture d'un manuel d'identité globale de marque. (USA)
117 Boîte ouverte garnie de petits cubes en carton: envoi publicitaire *Chromolux* du papetier *Zanders Feinpapiere*. (GER)
118, 119 Information multicartes sur les prestations sociales de *Keane*. Fig. 119: la couverture présentée ouverte. (USA)

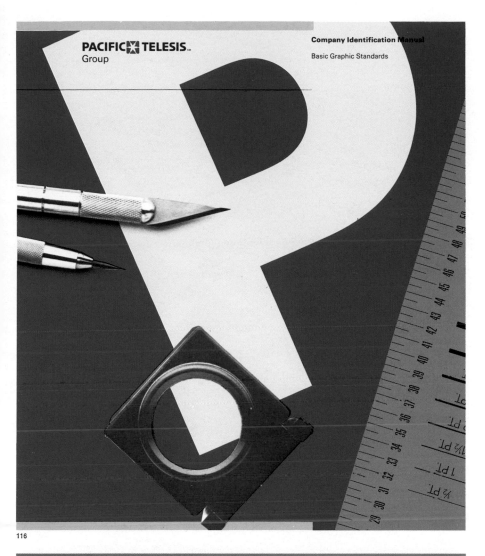

116

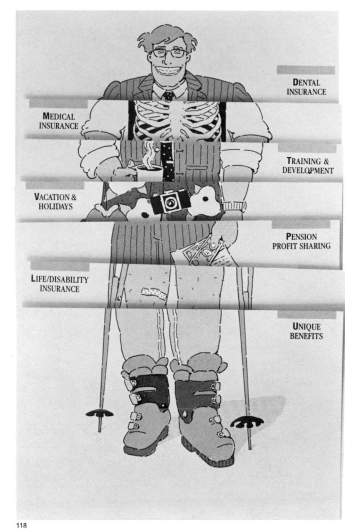

118

117

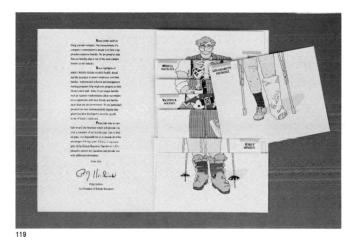

119

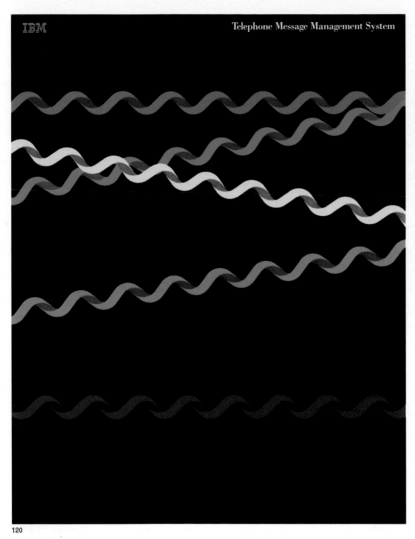

120

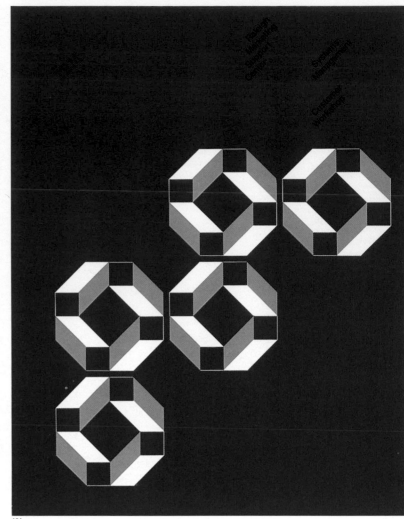

121

**Booklets
Prospekte
Brochures**

124

125

122

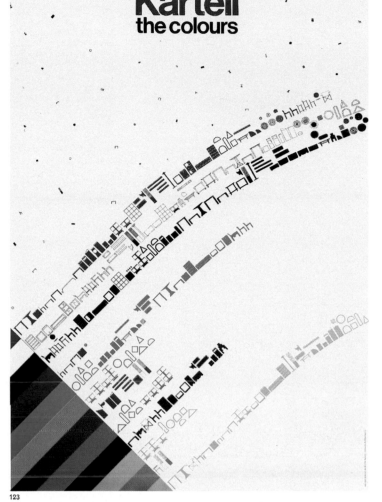

123

120–122, 124 Covers of brochures on various business systems produced by IBM. Shown here are the telephone system, the systems management, the IBM 9000 (for the engineer and scientist) and the technical co-ordinator programme. (USA)
123 Single page from a spiral-bound catalogue for *Kartell* utility furniture. (ITA)
125 Front cover of a catalogue for bathroom and kitchen fixtures and fittings. Green apple, green leaves, yellow fruit on white ground. (JPN)
126, 127 Samples of the introductory double spreads to the chapters in a hard-cover catalogue for *Sunar* office furniture. Black reading text, white display text, thin line in gold, on backgrounds printed in various tints. (USA)

120–122, 124 Umschläge für Broschüren über verschiedene Geschäftsbereiche der IBM, hier Telephontechnik, Computersysteme für den kaufmännischen und die technisch-wissenschaftlichen Bereiche sowie für ein Koordinationsprogramm. (USA)
123 Seite aus einem Katalog für das *Kartell*-Möbelsystem. (ITA)
125 Umschlagvorderseite eines Katalogs für Badezimmer- und Kücheneinrichtungen. Grüner Apfel, grüne Blätter, gelbe Fruchte auf weissem Grund. (JPN)
126, 127 Einleitende Doppelseiten zu verschiedenen Kapiteln eines Katalogs für *Sunar*-Büromöbel. Weiss und schwarz mit Gold auf farbig bedrucktem Papier. (USA)

120–122, 124 Couvertures de diverses brochures consacrées chacune à un domaine d'activité déterminé d'IBM: technologie du téléphone, systèmes informatiques pour les services commerciaux, d'une part, les services techniques et scientifiques, de l'autre, ainsi que pour un programme de coordination. (USA)
123 Page de catalogue pour le système d'ameublement *Kartell*. (ITA)
125 Première page de couverture d'un catalogue d'équipements pour cuisines et salles de bains. Pomme et feuilles vertes, fruits jaunes, fond blanc. (JPN)
126, 127 Doubles pages initiales de divers chapitres d'un catalogue des meubles de bureau *Sunar*. Blanc et noir, avec de l'or, sur papier couleur. (USA)

ARTIST/KÜNSTLER/ARTISTE:

125 Masahiko Fujii

DESIGNER/GESTALTER:

120, 121 Antonia Goldmark
122 Jack Reich
123 Centrokappa
124 Jon Craine
125 Jun Yoshida/Toshinori Nozaki/
   Motokazu Uchida/Jun Murase
126, 127 Bill Bonnell

ART DIRECTOR:

120 Al Hollworth
121, 124 Jon Craine
122 Jack Reich
125 Shozo Murase
126, 127 Bill Bonnell

AGENCY/AGENTUR/AGENCE:

120, 121 Antonia Goldmark
   Design, Inc.
122, 124 IBM
123 Centrokappa
125 Pure Planning Design Office
126, 127 Bonnell Design Associates

126

127

ARTIST / KÜNSTLER / ARTISTE:

128, 129 Alan E. Cober
130 Lonni Sue Johnson
131 Robert Heindel

128–131 Double spread and three examples of illustrations (Fig.129 in actual size) from a brochure featuring pieces of furniture from the *Herman Miller* Collection, portrayed by nine different artists; here, walnut stools and two versions of loungers by Charles Eames. (USA)

128–131 Vollständige Doppelseite und drei Beispiele der Illustrationen (Abb.129 in Originalgrösse) aus einer Broschüre für Möbel aus der *Herman-Miller*-Kollektion, die von insgesamt neun Künstlern interpretiert wurden. Die Themen sind hier die Nussbaum-Stühle und zwei verschiedene Sessel-Modelle von Charles Eames. (USA)

128–131 Double page complète et trois exemples des illustrations (la 129 au format original) d'une brochure pour les meubles de la collection *Herman Miller* interprétés par neuf artistes différents. Les thèmes sont ici les suivants: les sièges en noyer et deux différents modèles de fauteuils créés par Charles Eames. (USA)

DESIGNER / GESTALTER / MAQUETTISTE:

128–131 Barbara Loveland

ART DIRECTOR / DIRECTEUR ARTISTIQUE:

128–131 Barbara Loveland

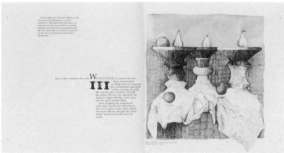

128

129

70

130

131

132

135

ARTIST / KÜNSTLER / ARTISTE:

132–134 Fred Otnes

DESIGNER / GESTALTER / MAQUETTISTE:

132–134 Bill Duevell
135, 136 Jeremy Perrott

ART DIRECTOR / DIRECTEUR ARTISTIQUE:

132–134 Henry Epstein
135, 136 Jeremy Perrott

AGENCY / AGENTUR / AGENCE – STUDIO:

132–134 ABC Corporate Art Department
135, 136 Optimus Graphic Design

132–134 Full-page illustrations and double spread from a brochure entitled "Commentary" issued by the US television network ABC. Two news commentators, known for their witty oratory, are presented, along with their various commentaries. Here, humorously speaking out on the topics of "Baltimore City" and "Tights for Men". (USA)
135, 136 Cover and its illustration in actual size for a catalogue listing the educational software available from *Acorn* Computers, Britain's leading educational computer manufacturer. (GBR)

132–134 Ganzseitige Illustrationen und Doppelseite aus einer Broschüre des amerikanischen Fernsehsenders ABC. Es werden zwei Nachrichtenkommentatoren vorgestellt, die ihr Können hier mit humoristischen Beiträgen zu verschiedenen Themen unter Beweis stellen. Die Themen sind die Stadt Baltimore und Strumpfhosen für Männer. (USA)
135, 136 Umschlag und Illustration in Originalgrösse für einen Katalog über *Acorn* (Eichel) Computer Software. (GBR)

132–134 Illustrations pleine page et double page d'une brochure de la chaîne de télévision américaine ABC. On y présente deux commentateurs de l'actualité qui témoignent de leur savoir-faire en fournissant des commentaires teintés d'humour sur deux thèmes: la ville de Baltimore et les collants pour messieurs. (USA)
135, 136 Couverture et illustration au format original d'un catalogue des logiciels *Acorn* (le nom de la marque veut dire «gland de chêne», d'où l'image choisie). (GBR)

133

134

137 Cover of a documentation folder for the special services of the American finance company SEI. (USA)
138 Brochure cover for a firm of consultants. (USA)
139–141 Double spreads from brochures for the ISC Computer Systems. Fig. 139 relates to software, Fig. 140 to the advantages for bank tellers, Fig. 141 to the company's field service. (USA)
142 Graphic data (in actual size) showing profit ratios, from a brochure aimed at retailers, for 9-Lives cat food producers. (AUS)
143 Concertina-fold prospectus for a bank. Wine-red title. (USA)

137 Umschlag einer Dokumentationsmappe für spezielle Dienstleistungen der amerikanischen Finanzgesellschaft SEI. (USA)
138 Umschlag für die Broschüre einer Beraterfirma. (USA)
139–141 Doppelseiten aus Broschüren des ISC-Computer-Herstellers. Abb. 139 bezieht sich auf die Software, Abb. 140 auf die Vorteile im Bankwesen, Abb. 141 auf den Kundendienst. (USA)
142 Illustration einer Umsatzstatistik aus einem Prospekt für Katzenfutter-Konserven der Marke 9-Lives. (AUS)
143 Leporello-Prospekt einer Bank. Weinroter Titel. (USA)

137 Couverture d'une documentation sur les services spéciaux offerts par la société financière américaine SEI. (USA)
138 Couverture de la brochure d'une société-conseil. (USA)
139–141 Doubles pages de diverses brochures du fabricant d'ordinateurs ISC. La fig. 139 se rapporte aux logiciels, la fig. 140 à l'informatique bancaire, la fig. 141 au service après-vente. (USA)
142 Illustration d'une statistique sur le chiffre d'affaires dans un dépliant des conserves pour chats 9-Lives. (AUS)
143 Dépliant bancaire en accordéon. Titre bordeaux. (USA)

139

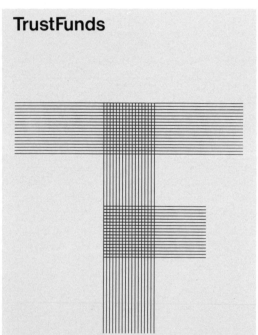

137

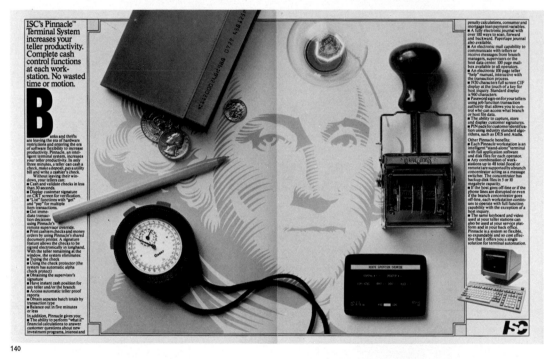

140

138

141

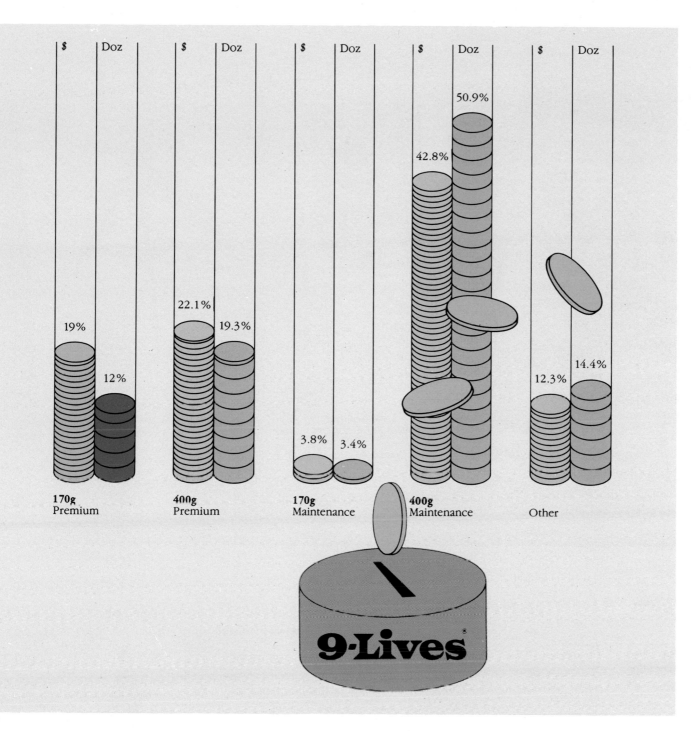

	$	Doz	$	Doz	$	Doz	$	Doz	$	Doz
	19%	12%	22.1%	19.3%	3.8%	3.4%	42.8%	50.9%	12.3%	14.4%

170g
Premium

400g
Premium

170g
Maintenance

400g
Maintenance

Other

9·Lives®

142

DESIGNER:

137, 138 George Tscherny
139–141 Nicolas Sidjakov
142 Flett Henderson
& Arnold
143 David Franek

ART DIRECTOR:

137, 138 George Tscherny
139–141 Jerry Leonhart

AGENCY:

137, 138 George
Tscherny, Inc.
139–141 Livingston/
Sirutis Advertising
142 Flett Henderson
& Arnold
143 Invisions Ltd.

ARTIST / KÜNSTLER / ARTISTE:

139–141 David Stevenson/Nicolay Zurek (Photo)

143

144

Booklets/Prospekte/Brochures

145

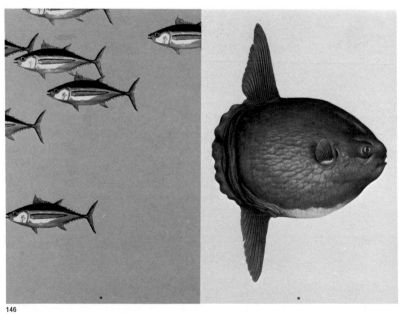

146

144 Direct-mailer for the Champion Paper Co. in the form of a boxed set of herb seeds. (USA)
145, 146 From an advertising brochure about fish, in full colour, for a paper manufacturer. (USA)
147 Polychrome cover of a prospectus offering giant inflatable cans for promotional purposes. (USA)
148 Double spread from a prospectus for a rentable film-and-photo studio in Cologne. (GER)
149 Illustration from a catalogue for *Stubbies* sports articles. (USA)

144 Direktwerbung einer Papierfabrik in Form einer dreiteiligen Mappe mit Schuber. (USA)
145, 146 Aus einer Werbebroschüre über Fische, für eine Papierfabrik. In Farbe. (USA)
147 Mehrfarbiger Umschlag für einen Prospekt über riesige Plastikversionen von Bierdosen. (USA)
148 Doppelseite aus einem Prospekt für das Photo-Mietstudio Robinson. Braun und Gelb mit Rot. (GER)
149 Illustration aus einem Katalog für Sportartikel der Marke *Stubbies*. (USA)

144 Publicité directe d'un papetier sous forme d'un album tripartite sous emboîtage. (USA)
145, 146 Brochure publicitaire d'un fabricant de papier, en couleur; sujet: les poissons. (USA)
147 Couverture polychrome d'un prospectus sur des boîtes de bière géantes en plastique. (USA)
148 Double page d'un prospectus de l'atelier photo Robinson à louer. Brun, jaune, rouge. (GER)
149 Illustration d'un catalogue d'articles de sport *Stubbies*. (USA)

147

Stern-Titel werden im Studio Robinson fotografiert. Die Nadorf 1601 hier fotografieren. Ford fährt komplette neue Modellreihen auf der 25 Meter Endlos-Horizont des Studios. Der WDR dreht hier Filme und Henkel produziert Videos. Bekannte Fotografen fotografieren bei Robinson – manchmal auch für Robinson.

Das Stammteam bei Robinson besteht aus erfahrenen Fotografen, Assistenten, Stylisten und Set-Bauern, die Ihnen als Fotograf, Werbeagentur oder Industrieunternehmen zur Verfügung stehen (Kundenschutz, das versteht sich von selbst, ist gewährleistet). Unser Team kann Ihnen bei Castings behilflich sein und die Requisiten besorgen – wenn Sie wollen, auch King Kong. Die Studiomiete ist je nachdem. Ob Sie nur einen Raum und z. B. die Hohlkehle mieten. Ob Sie Licht brauchen oder zwei Fotoassistenten möchten. Ob Sie nur eine kleine Ecke oder das ganze Studio wollen.

Hollywood in Köln zu vermieten

148

ARTIST / KÜNSTLER / ARTISTE:

147 Bill Mayer
148 Heinz Edelmann
149 Sandra Higashi

DESIGNER / GESTALTER / MAQUETTISTE:

144 Peter Good
145, 146 Adrian Pulfer
147 Bill Kumke/Bill Mayer
149 Mark Oliver

ART DIRECTOR / DIRECTEUR ARTISTIQUE:

144 Peter Good
145, 146 Marty Pedersen/Adrian Pulfer
149 David Bartels
148 Robert Pütz
149 Mark Oliver

AGENCY / AGENTUR / AGENCE – STUDIO:

145, 146 Jonson Pedersen Hinrichs & Shakery
147 Bartels & Company, Inc.
148 Robert Pütz GmbH
149 Mark Oliver, Inc.

149

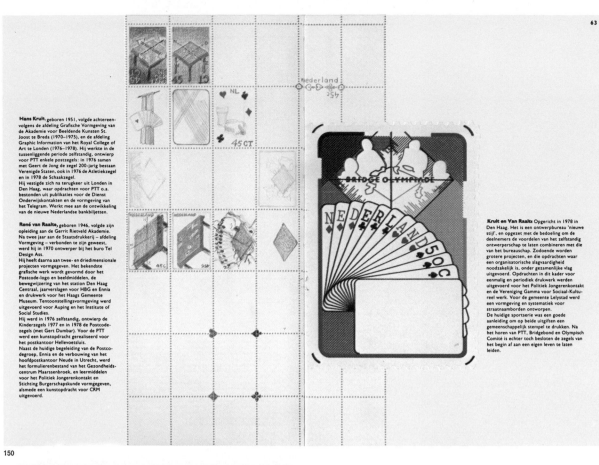

Hans Krult, geboren 1951, volgde achtereenvolgens de afdeling Grafische Vormgeving van de Akademie voor Beeldende Kunsten St. Joost te Breda (1970–1975), en de afdeling Graphic Information van het Royal College of Art te Londen (1976–1978). Hij werkte in de tussenliggende periode zelfstandig, ontwierp voor PTT enkele postzegels: in 1976 samen met Geert de Jong de zegel 200-jarig bestaan Verenigde Staten, ook in 1976 de Atletiekzegel en in 1978 de Schaakzegel.
Hij vestigde zich na terugkeer uit Londen in Den Haag, waar opdrachten voor PTT o.a. bestonden uit publikaties voor de Dienst Onderwijskontakten en de vormgeving van het Telegram. Werkt mee aan de ontwikkeling van de nieuwe Nederlandse bankbiljetten.

René van Raalte, geboren 1946, volgde zijn opleiding aan de Gerrit Rietveld Akademie. Na twee jaar aan de Staatsdrukkerij – afdeling Vormgeving – verbonden te zijn geweest, werd hij in 1970 ontwerper bij het buro Tel Design Ass.
Hij heeft daarna een twee- en driedimensionale projecten vormgegeven. Het bekendste grafische werk wordt gevormd door het Postcode-logo en beeldmiddelen, de bewegwijzering van het station Den Haag Centraal, jaarverslagen voor HBG en Ennia en drukwerk voor het Haags Gemeente Museum. Tentoonstellingsvormgeving werd uitgevoerd voor Auping en het Institute of Social Studies.
Hij werd in 1976 zelfstandig, ontwierp de Kinderzegels 1977 en in 1978 de Postcodezegels (met Gert Dumbar). Voor de PTT werd een kunstopdracht gerealiseerd voor het postkantoor Hellevoetsluis.
Naast de huidige begeleiding van de Postcodegroep, Ennia en de verbouwing van het hoofdpostkantoor Neude in Utrecht, werd het formulierenbestand van het Gezondheidscentrum Haarssenbroek, en leermiddelen voor het Politiek Jongerenkontakt en Stichting Burgerschapskunde vormgegeven, alsmede een kunstopdracht voor CRM uitgevoerd.

Krult en Van Raalte Opgericht in 1978 in Den Haag. Het is een ontwerpbureau 'nieuwe stijl', en opgezet met de bedoeling om de deelnemers de voordelen van het zelfstandig ontwerperschap te laten combineren met die van het bureauschap. Zodoende worden grotere projecten, en de opdrachten waar een organisatorische slagvaardigheid noodzakelijk is, onder gezamenlijke vlag uitgevoerd. Opdrachten in dit kader voor eenmalig en periodiek drukwerk werden uitgevoerd voor het Politiek Jongerenkontakt en de Vereniging Gamma voor Sociaal-Kultureel werk. Voor de gemeente Lelystad werd een vormgeving en systematiek voor straatnaamborden ontworpen.
De huidige sportserie was een goede aanleiding om op beide uitgiften een gemeenschappelijk stempel te drukken. Na het horen van PTT, Bridgebond en Olympisch Comité is echter toch besloten de zegels van het begin af aan een eigen leven te laten leiden.

150

**Booklets
Prospekte
Brochures**

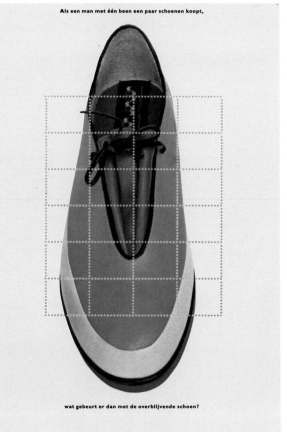

152

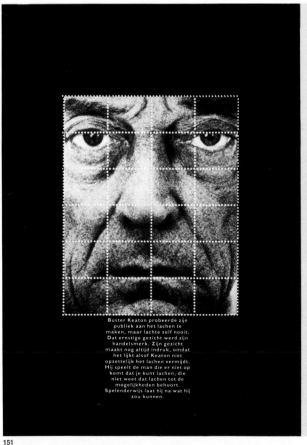

151

ARTIST / KÜNSTLER / ARTISTE:

150–154 Anthon Beeke
157, 158 Lonni Sue Johnson

DESIGNER / GESTALTER / MAQUETTISTE:

150–154 Anthon Beeke
155, 156 Mike Schroeder
157, 158 Karyn Voldstad

ART DIRECTOR / DIRECTEUR ARTISTIQUE:

150–154 Anthon Beeke
155, 156 Woody Pirtle
157, 158 Barry Bomzer

AGENCY / AGENTUR / AGENCE – STUDIO:

150–154 Anthon Beeke
155, 156 Pirtle Design
157, 158 Bomzer Associates

150–154 Double spreads and cover from a brochure about Dutch stamps issued in 1980. Fig. 150 refers to a Bridge Olympiad, Figs. 151, 153, 154 are from the general section on stamps, Fig. 152 shows the yellow cover. (NLD)
155, 156 Double spreads from a small-size brochure for a Dallas hospital. The text inside the pastel-coloured speech balloons relates to the various medical and community services this non-profit-making hospital offers. (USA)
157, 158 Full-page illustrations from a booklet issued by a company to promote its sales-training programme. (USA)

150–154 Doppelseiten und gelber Umschlag aus einer Broschüre über die 1980 herausgegebenen holländischen Briefmarken. Abb. 151, 153, 154 gehören zum allgemeinen Kapitel über Briefmarken, mit perforierten Farbillustrationen; Abb. 150 bezieht sich auf eine Marke zur Erinnerung an eine Bridge-Olympiade. (NLD)
155, 156 Doppelseiten aus einer kleinformatigen Broschüre für ein medizinisches Universitätszentrum in Texas. Der Text in pastellfarbigen Sprechblasen betrifft die Dienstleistungen. (USA)
157, 158 Ganzseitige Illustrationen aus einer Broschüre über ein Verkaufs-Schulungsprogramm. (USA)

150–154 Doubles pages et couverture jaune d'une brochure où figurent les émissions de timbres néerlandais en 1980. Les fig. 151, 153, 154 illustrent des généralités sur les timbres-poste (reproductions perforées); la fig. 150 représente le timbre avion émis pour une olympiade du bridge. (NLD)
155, 156 Doubles pages de la brochure au petit format d'un centre médical universitaire texan. Le texte des bulles pastel concerne les services offerts. (USA)
157, 158 Illustrations pleine page dans la brochure explicative d'un programme de techniques de vente. (USA)

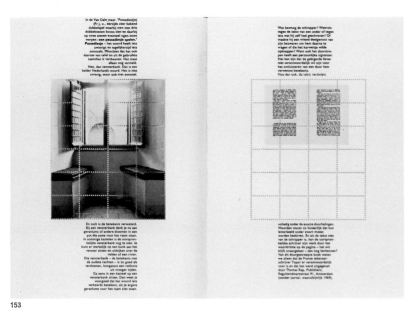

153

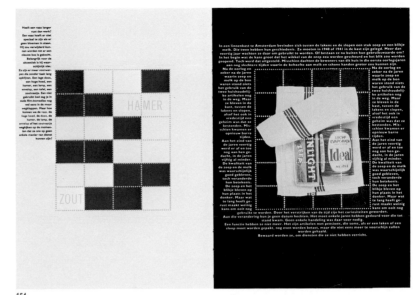

154

155

156

157

158

79

159

The Network Serving The Profession

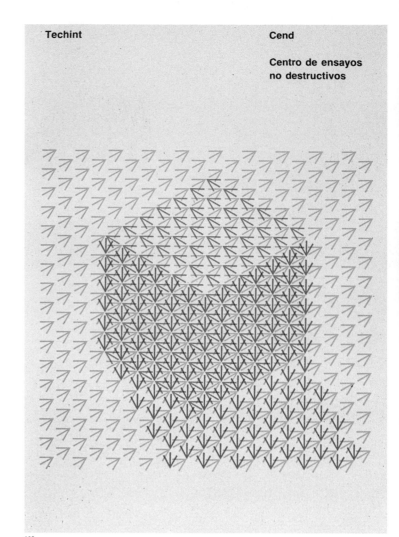

160

Cend

Centro de ensayos
no destructivos

162

BETTER MADE IN BRITAIN

guide

*Private companies purchasing
their own shares.*

163

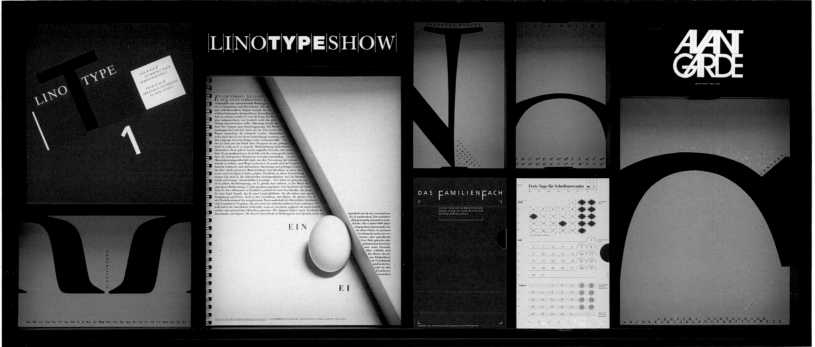

161

159 Cover of a brochure for the American Institute of Architects aimed at recruiting new members. Dull bordeaux and olive green, on beige. (USA)
160 Cover of a brochure for a non-destructive test centre. (ARG)
161 Wooden box with interchangeable typographic elements as three-dimensional "magazine" which can be bought on subscription from Mergenthaler Linotype GmbH. All typographic information material is sent free of charge at irregular intervals. (GER)
162 Part of the information material for a sales-promotion exhibition of British goods. (GBR)
163–165 Covers (watercolour) from booklets and a spread, for a firm of management consultants. (GBR)

164

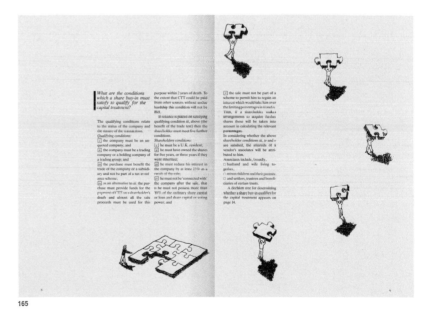

165

159 Vorderseite des Umschlags einer Broschüre für das American Institute of Architects, die der Mitgliederwerbung für diese Vereinigung dienen soll. Mattes Bordeaux und Oliv auf Beige. (USA)
160 Umschlag der Broschüre eines Testzentrums für zerstörungsfreies Verfahren. (ARG)
161 Dreidimensionale Direktwerbung für die Mergenthaler Linotype GmbH, in Form eines Holzkastens mit auswechselbaren typographischen Elementen, die im Abonnement bezogen werden können. (GER)
162 Für Informationsmaterial über eine verkaufsfördernde Ausstellung britischer Waren. (GBR)
163–165 Umschläge (Aquarelle) und eine Doppelseite für zwei Broschüren einer Betriebsberatungs-firma, die auf verschiedene Fragen eingeht – daher die Fragezeichen und das Puzzle. (GBR)

159 Première page de couverture d'une brochure de l'American Institute of Architects destinée au recrutement de nouveaux membres. Bordeaux mat et olive sur beige. (USA)
160 Couverture d'une brochure consacrée à un centre d'essais non destructifs. (ARG)
161 Publicité directe tridimensionnelle pour Mergenthaler Linotype. Il s'agit d'une boîte en bois; les éléments typo interchangeables se commandent en abonnement. (GER)
162 Documentation pour une exposition de produits britanniques destinés à l'exportation. (GBR)
163–165 Couvertures (aquarelles) et une page double de deux brochures où une société de conseils aux entreprises examine divers problèmes, d'où le point d'interrogation et le puzzle. (GBR)

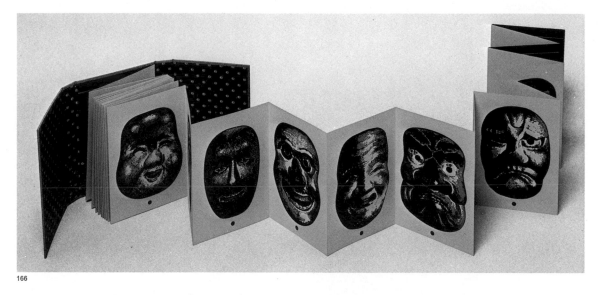

166

167

HBJ
CHILDREN'S
BOOKS
1984 **HBJ** 1985

HARCOURT BRACE JOVANOVICH
A GRADED LIST FOR PRESCHOOL THROUGH HIGH SCHOOL

168

169

ARTIST / KÜNSTLER / ARTISTE:

166, 167 Shigeru Akizuki
168 Roseanne Litzinger
169 Lonni Sue Johnson
170, 171 Karen Barbour

DESIGNER / GESTALTER / MAQUETTISTE:

166, 167 Shigeru Akizuki/Yoshio Hara
168 Roseanne Litzinger
169 Steve Phillips
170, 171 Ellen Kier

ART DIRECTOR / DIRECTEUR ARTISTIQUE:

166, 167 Shigeru Akizuki
168 Rubin Pfeffer
169 Steve Phillips
170, 171 Ellen Kier

AGENCY / AGENTUR / AGENCE – STUDIO:

168 R. Litzinger Illus. & Design
169 Steve Phillips Design

Booklets / Prospekte / Brochures

166, 167 Concertina-folder opened out (dark brown on light brown) and closed, showing the cover (dark blue, red and yellow on grey), for an exhibition of Japanese masks. (JPN)
168 Cover of a children's book catalogue; the book "faces" express various children's moods: happy, sad, inquisitive and frightened. (USA)
169 Polychrome illustration for a Christmas card for the *Venture* magazine. (USA)
170, 171 Illustration in original size and complete cover for a folder to promote the new "Health Check" advertising supplement in the Sunday edition of the *New York Times*. (USA)

166, 167 Leporello (Dunkelbraun auf Hellbraun) und Vorderseite davon (Dunkelblau mit Rot und Gelb auf Grau) für eine Ausstellung japanischer Masken. (JPN)
168 Umschlag-Vorderseite eines Katalogs für Kinderbücher, die hier ein glückliches, trauriges, forschendes und ängstliches «Gesicht» machen. (USA)
169 Mehrfarbige Illustration für eine Weihnachtskarte der Zeitschrift *Venture*. (USA)
170, 171 Illustration in Originalgrösse und vollständige Vorderseite eines Prospekts der *New York Times* über eine spezielle Werbebeilage für Fitness-Produkte. (USA)

166, 167 Dépliant en accordéon (brun foncé sur brun clair) et son recto (bleu foncé avec du rouge et du jaune sur gris). Exposition de masques folkloriques japonais. (JPN)
168 Première page de couverture d'un catalogue de livres d'enfants aux quatre expressions caractéristiques: bonheur, tristesse, recherche, anxiété. (USA)
169 Illustration polychrome pour une carte de vœux de Noël du magazine *Venture*. (USA)
170, 171 Illustration au format original et recto complet d'un prospectus du *New York Times* consacré à un encart publicitaire spécial de produits pour garder la forme. (USA)

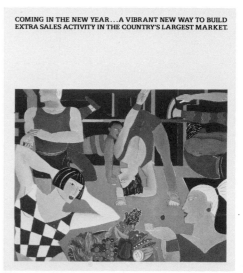

COMING IN THE NEW YEAR...A VIBRANT NEW WAY TO BUILD EXTRA SALES ACTIVITY IN THE COUNTRY'S LARGEST MARKET.

171

170

172

Booklets/Prospekte/Brochures

175

176

177

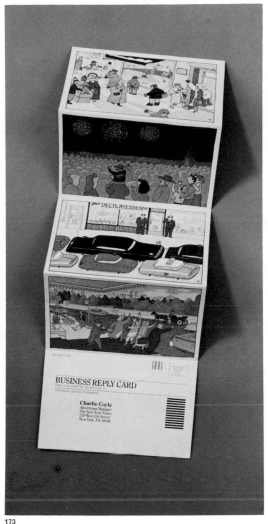

173

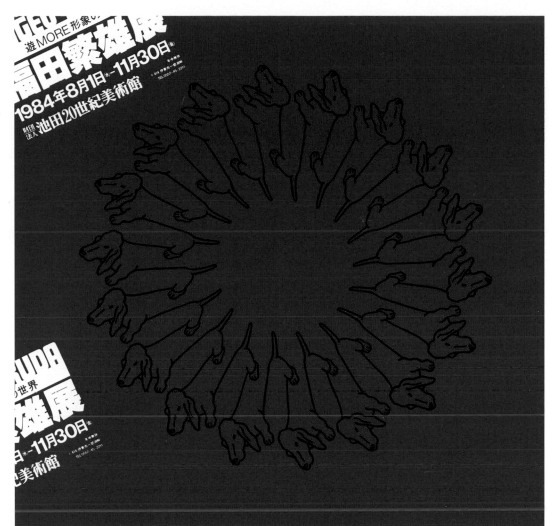

174

178

172, 173 Illustration in actual size and complete concertina-folder aimed at advertisers for "The World of New York"—a supplement in the Sunday edition of the *New York Times*. (USA)
174 Cover of a catalogue for an exhibition of the works of Shigeo Fukuda in the Ikeda Museum of 20th Century Art. (JPN)
175–177 Examples of direct mail articles sent by *Life* magazine. The lifebelt and the thermos flask were sent in summer, the giant salt-cellar at the end of the year. (USA)
178 Cover of the spring/summer catalogue of the New York book publishers Carroll & Graf, Inc. (USA)

172, 173 Illustration in Originalgrösse und vollständiges Leporello, mit dem die *New York Times* um Inserate in einer der Stadt New York gewidmeten Beilage wirbt. (USA)
174 Vorderseite eines Katalogs für eine Ausstellung der Arbeiten von Shigeo Fukuda im Ikeda Museum of 20th Century Art. (JPN)
175–177 Beispiele der für die Zeitschrift *Life* versandten Direkt-werbe-Artikel. Der Rettungsring und die Thermosflasche wurden im Sommer, der Riesen-Salzstreuer zum Jahresende verschickt. (USA)
178 Umschlag für den Frühjahr/Sommer-Katalog eines New Yorker Buchverlags. (USA)

172, 173 Illustration au format original et dépliant en accordéon où elle figure. Le *New York Times* s'y adresse aux annonceurs potentiels (supplément consacré à la ville de New York). (USA)
174 Première page de couverture du catalogue d'une exposition des œuvres de Shigeo Fukuda au Ikeda Museum of 20th Century Art à Tōkyō. (JPN)
175–177 Echantillons des articles de publicité directe distribués par le magazine *Life*: la bouée de sauvetage et le thermos en été, la salière géante en fin d'année. (USA)
178 Couverture du catalogue de printemps et d'été d'une maison d'édition newyorkaise. (USA)

ARTIST / KÜNSTLER / ARTISTE:

172, 173 Tom Blum
174 Shigeo Fukuda
178 Burkey Belser

DESIGNER / GESTALTER / MAQUETTISTE:

172, 173 Peter Schaefer
174 Shigeo Fukuda
175–177 Gilbert Lesser
178 Burkey Belser

ART DIRECTOR / DIRECTEUR ARTISTIQUE:

172, 173 Peter Schaefer
175–177 Gilbert Lesser
178 Burkey Belser

AGENCY / AGENTUR / AGENCE – STUDIO:

178 Burkey Belser, Inc.

179

180

ARTIST / KÜNSTLER / ARTISTE:

179 Paul Hogarth
180 Jözef Sumichrast
182 Michael David Brown
184 Dagmar Frinta

DESIGNER / GESTALTER / MAQUETTISTE:

179 Clare Boam
181, 182 Domenica Genovese
183 Dennis Tabor
184 Tom Papadimoulis

ART DIRECTOR / DIRECTEUR ARTISTIQUE:

179 Keren House
180 David Lawrence
181, 182 Domenica Genovese
183 Dennis Tabor
184 Tom Papadimoulis

AGENCY / AGENTUR / AGENCE – STUDIO:

179 The Partners
180 David Lawrence Design
181, 182 North Charles Street Design Organzization
183 Pihas, Schmidt, Westerdahl Co.
184 Marschalk Group

179 Double spread with portraits (watercolour/pencil) of some of the staff, from the portfolio of one of London's oldest-established commodity brokers. (GBR)
180 Illustration from a brochure for the State of Illinois. (USA)
181, 182 Covers from course catalogues for the Oberlin College. Fig. 181: Black text, red exclamation mark on deep turquoise; Fig. 182: A montage from the worlds of art, literature and the sciences. (USA)
183 Green and white cardboard box revealing a rose made of black pinstripe suiting; sent by the Chamber of Commerce, Portland, the "City of Roses", to attract industry. (USA)
184 Illustration from a brochure to promote a bank's trust fund. Four artists were asked to interpret the word "trust". (USA)

179 Doppelseite mit mehrfarbigen Porträts der Mitarbeiter, aus der Broschüre einer Londoner Börsenmaklerfirma. (GBR)
180 Illustration aus einer Broschüre des Staates Illinois. (USA)
181, 182 Umschläge von Broschüren für das Oberlin College mit dem Studienprogramm. Abb. 181: Schwarze Schrift, rotes Ausrufezeichen auf Grün; Abb. 182: Die Künste, Literatur, Natur- und Sozialwissenschaften sind Thema der farbigen Montage. (USA)
183 Geöffneter Karton mit grünem Deckel, grüner Einlage und Rose aus schwarzem Nadelstreifenstoff, eine an potentielle Investoren gerichtete Werbesendung für die Stadt Portland. (USA)
184 Illustration aus der Broschüre einer Bank, die Künstler aufgefordert hatte, das Wort «Vertrauen» zu interpretieren. (USA)

179 Page double d'une brochure où une société d'agents de change présente ses collaborateurs en polychromie. (GBR)
180 Illustration dans une brochure de l'Etat d'Illinois. (USA)
181, 182 Couvertures de brochures contenant les programmes de l'Oberlin College. Fig. 181: texte noir, point d'exclamation rouge sur vert; fig. 182: montage polychrome illustrant les arts, les lettres, les sciences physiques et sociales. (USA)
183 Carton au couvercle vert présenté ouvert. Intérieur vert, rose en tissu noir à fines rayures. Envoi publicitaire de la ville de Portland destiné aux investisseurs potentiels. (USA)
184 Illustration d'une brochure bancaire où des artistes livrent leur interprétation du mot «confiance». (USA)

Demetrius Vikelas
Grèce
1894-1896

Le Comité International Olympique (CIO) dirige
Mouvement et met les Jeux sur pied, mais son rôle
plus large: il est chargé de stimuler l'activité sportiv
dans le monde entier.

L'une de ses premières tâches est le patronage d'
Académie olympique (à Olympie, justement, dans l
Péloponnèse grec): c'est un centre de formation des
tiné aux futurs éducateurs sportifs. Une deuxième e
l'animation de la Solidarité olympique: c'est un orga
nisme qui soutient, grâce aux droits que les chaînes
de télévision paient pour diffuser les Jeux, le développement général des sports. Et le Musée olympiqu
à Lausanne? Depuis le 23 juin 1982, il renseigne le
public sur l'histoire des Jeux Olympiques. Une bibli
thèque spécialisée y est adjointe.

L'Espagnol Juan Antonio Samaranch préside le C
depuis 1980. Il a pris à cette date la succession de
l'Irlandais Lord Killanin, qui lui-même avait rempla
l'Américain Avery Brundage. Depuis les débuts du
Mouvement olympique, en 1894, sept présidents o
assumé cette fonction.

Baron
Pierre de Coubertin
France
1896-1925

Comte Henri
de Baillet-Latour
Belgique
1925-1942

J. Sigfrid Edström
Suède
1946-1952

Avery Brundage
Etats-Unis
d'Amérique
1952-1972

The Lord Killanin
Irlande
1972-1980

S.E.M.
Juan Antonio
Samaranch
Espagne 1980

185

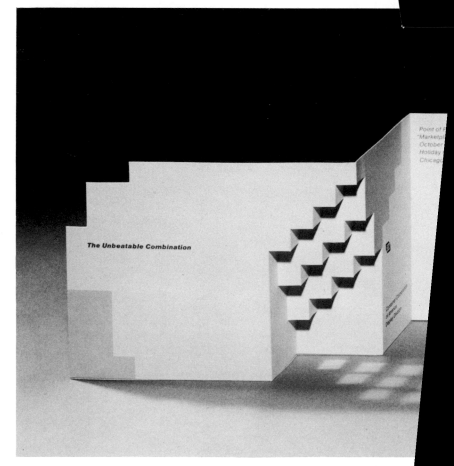

The Unbeatable Combination

88

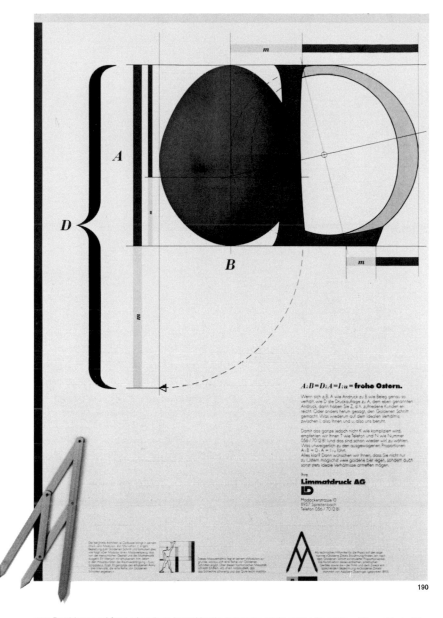

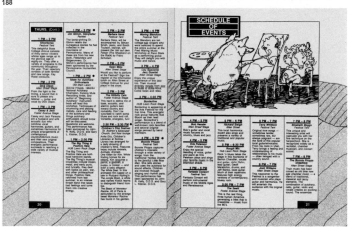

185 Double spread from a brochure issued by the International Olympics Committee. The subject of the illustration is the sports togetherness of young people from five continents. (SWI)
186 Three-dimensional invitation to a display exhibition by the *Container Corporation*. (USA)
187–189 Cover and double spreads from a programme for an arts festival in Pennsylvania. (USA)
190 Large-format mailer sent at Easter by the Limmatdruck AG (printers). The customer also receives a real pair of "golden compasses" constructed according to the golden section. (SWI)

185 Doppelseite aus einer Broschüre des Internationalen Olympischen Komitees. Das Thema der Illustration ist das sportliche Zusammensein der Jugend aus fünf Kontinenten. (SWI)
186 Dreidimensionale Einladung zu einer Display-Ausstellung der *Container Corporation*. (USA)
107–109 Umschlag und Doppelseiten einer Broschüre für ein Kunst-Festival in Pennsylvania. (USA)
190 Grossformatige Direktwerbung der Limmatdruck AG, die zu Ostern verschickt wurde. Als Zubehör erhält der Kunde einen nach dem Goldenen Schnitt konstruierten Proportionszirkel. (SWI)

185 Double page d'une brochure du Comité international olympique. L'illustration symbolise la rencontre sportive de la jeunesse de cinq continents. (SWI)
186 Invitation tridimensionnelle à une exposition de la *Container Corporation*. (USA)
187–189 Couverture et doubles pages de la brochure d'un festival d'art en Pennsylvanie. (USA)
190 Publicité directe au grand format de l'imprimerie Limmatdruck SA pour Pâques. Le cadeau qui l'accompagne consiste en un compas de précision construit d'après la section d'or. (SWI)

ARTIST / KÜNSTLER / ARTISTE:

185 Monique Félix/Michel Charrier/
    Georges Lemoine/Etienne Delessert
187–189 Lanny Sommese

DESIGNER / GESTALTER / MAQUETTISTE:

186 Kerry Grady/Joyce Culkin
187–189 Greg Klee/Ann Murdock/Lynne Smyers
190 Marc Locatelli

ART DIRECTOR / DIRECTEUR ARTISTIQUE:

185 Rita Marshall/Etienne Delessert
186 Kerry Grady
187–189 Lanny Sommese
190 Ernst Schadegg

AGENCY / AGENTUR / AGENCE – STUDIO:

186 CCA Coop. Design
187–189 Lanny Sommese Design
190 Schadegg & Wenzl

191

192

193

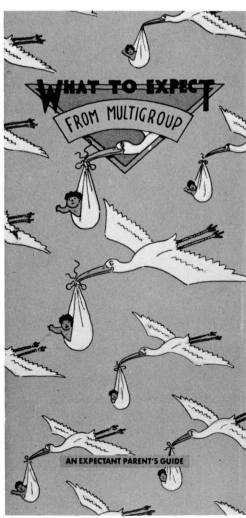

194

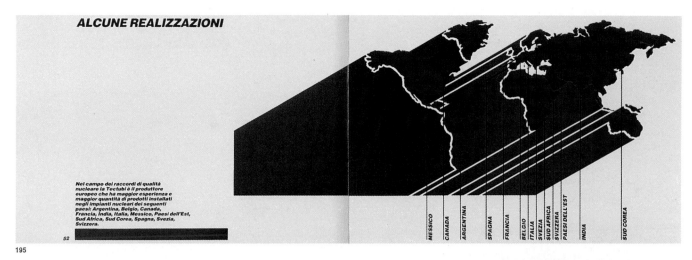

191 Double spread from a brochure for *Kromekote* paper from *Champion*. (USA)
192 Cover of a brochure for a bank providing credit for the film industry. (ITA)
193 Illustration from a brochure for a Wall Street brokerage firm. White, black, red on blue. (USA)
194 Cover of a handbook for an insurance group. White storks on a blue sky. (USA)
195, 196 Illustrations from a brochure as part of the corporate identity for a finance firm. (ITA)
197 Double spread from a publication to mark the 100th anniversary of the Zurich tram. (SWI)

191 Double page d'une brochure consacrée au *Kromekote* du papetier *Champion*. (USA)
192 Première page de couverture d'une brochure bancaire: crédits pour les cinéastes. (ITA)
193 Illustration noir, blanc, rouge sur bleu pour la brochure d'un groupe de boursiers. (USA)
194 Couverture du manuel d'une compagnie d'assurances destiné aux futurs parents. (USA)
195, 196 Diagrammes tirés d'une brochure de la société financière *Castek*. (ITA)
197 Double page d'une publication de la Régie des transports zurichois: le métro express. (SWI)

191 Doppelseite aus einer Broschüre für die Papierqualität *Kromekote* von *Champion*. (USA)
192 Vorderseite der Broschüre einer Bank über Kredite für Filmschaffende. (ITA)
193 Illustration aus der Broschüre einer Börsenmakler-Firma. Weiss, Schwarz, Rot auf Blau. (USA)
194 Umschlag eines für werdende Eltern bestimmten Handbuchs einer Versicherung. (USA)
195, 196 Darstellungen aus einer Broschüre der Finanzierungsgesellschaft *Castek*. (ITA)
197 Doppelseite aus einer Publikation der Zürcher Verkehrsbetriebe, hier zur geplanten S-Bahn. (SWI)

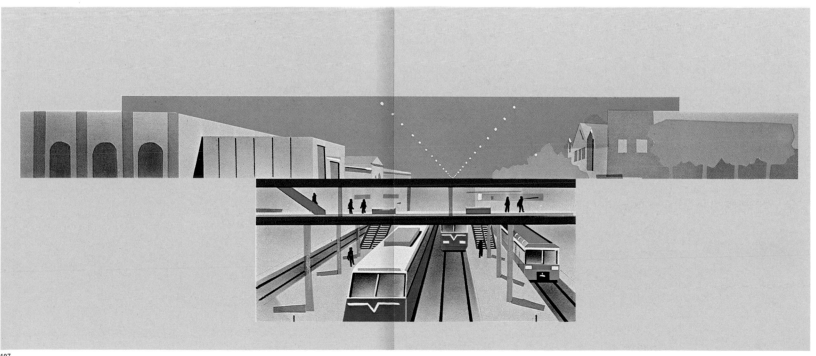

197

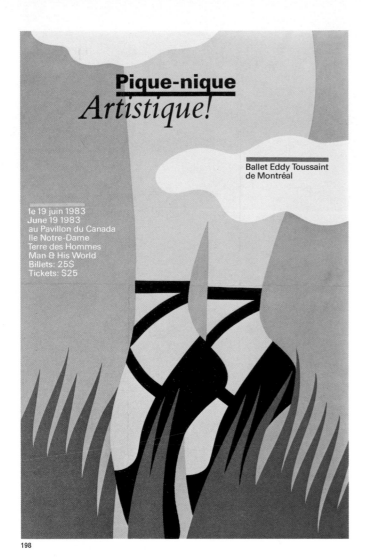

Pique-nique
Artistique!

Ballet Eddy Toussaint
de Montréal

le 19 juin 1983
June 19 1983
au Pavillon du Canada
Ile Notre-Dame
Terre des Hommes
Man & His World
Billets: 25S
Tickets: S25

198

Barber of Seville. November 29 - December 1, 1984

Barber of Seville
by Gioacchino Rossini

Grand Opera Series
November 29 & December 1, 1984

Popular Opera Series
November 30, 1984

Love triumphs over all thanks to an astonishing whirlwind of schemes contrived by that busy-body barber, Figaro. Gifted young Metropolitan Opera baritone Allan Glassman showcases his singing and acting talents as the irrepressible Barber with New York

City Opera mezzo-soprano Susanne Marsee portraying the flirtatious Rosina. Exciting new tenor Joseph Evans debuts as Almaviva, while bassos Thomas Hammons and Irwin Densen as Bartolo and Basilio keep the plot jumping.

199

ARTIST / KÜNSTLER / ARTISTE:

199, 200 Bob Appleton

DESIGNER / GESTALTER / MAQUETTISTE:

198 Susan Scott
199, 200 Bob Appleton
201, 202 Kenzo Nakagawa/Satch Morikami
203, 204 Bill Duevell

198 Announcement of a ballet evening, with picnic basket and wine provided. Yellow tights, blue shoes, green grass, pale blue background. (CAN)
199, 200 The operas these illustrations relate to are: *The Barber of Seville* and *La Traviata*; from a programme of the Connecticut Opera. (USA)
201, 202 Season's greetings on the covers of advertising folders, each of which also includes four perforated postcards; for the paper company *Takao*. (JPN)
203, 204 Embossed cover and double spread from a brochure issued by ABC television network on the occasion of the 1984 Olympics. (USA)

198 Ankündigung eines Ballett-Abends, hier «künstlerisches Picknick» genannt. Gelbe Beine in blauen Schuhen, grünes Gras, hellblauer Hintergrund. (CAN)
199, 200 *Der Barbier von Sevilla* und *La Traviata* sind die Themen dieser Seiten aus einem Programmheft der Connecticut Opera. (USA)
201, 202 Neujahrsglückwünsche auf den Vorderseiten von Werbeprospekten für den Papierhersteller *Takeo*. Abb. 202: Schwarz, Grau- und Brauntöne auf Weiss. (JPN)
203, 204 Umschlag (geprägt) und Doppelseite aus einer Broschüre, die anlässlich der Olympiade 1984 von dem Fernsehsender ABC herausgegeben wurde. (USA)

198 Annonce d'une soirée de ballet baptisée «pique-nique artistique». Jambes jaunes, chaussons bleus, herbe verte, fond bleu clair. (CAN)
199, 200 *Le Barbier de Séville* et *La Traviata* sont les thèmes choisis pour ces pages d'un programme du Connecticut Opera sous forme de brochure. (USA)
201, 202 Vœux de Nouvel An figurant au recto de dépliants publicitaires du papetier *Takeo*. Fig. 202: divers noirs, gris et bruns sur blanc. (JPN)
203, 204 Couverture gaufrée et double page d'une brochure de la chaîne de télévision ABC publiée à l'occasion des Jeux Olympiques de 1984. (USA)

La Traviata. March 28-30, 1985

La *Traviata*
by Giuseppe Verdi

Grand Opera Series
March 28 & 30, 1985

Popular Opera Series
March 29, 1985

Amid the glittering gaiety of 19th century Parisian society, the courtesan and the aristocrat pour out their love for each other. Scene after scene of Verdi's tragic masterpiece overflows with drama and pathos as Violetta and Alfredo sing of their love. Enjoy it all: hear the Italian while a simultaneous

English translation is projected onto a screen above the stage. Making her debut as Violetta is internationally renowned soprano Elena Mauti-Nunziata. Icelandic tenor Kristian Johannsson, makes his East Coast debut as Alfredo with baritone Norman Phillips as Germont.

200

201

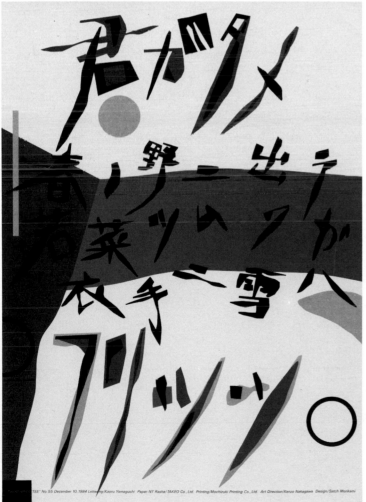

TEE" No. 55 December 10, 1984 Lettering/Kaoru Yamaguchi Paper/NT Rasha/TAKEO Co., Ltd. Printing/Mochizuki Printing Co., Ltd. Art Direction/Kenzo Nakagawa Design/Satch Morikami

202

203

204

ART DIRECTOR / DIRECTEUR ARTISTIQUE:

198 Susan Scott
199, 200 Bob Appleton
201, 202 Kenzo Nakagawa
203, 204 Henry Epstein

AGENCY / AGENTUR / AGENCE – STUDIO:

198 Susan Scott
199, 200 Appleton Design
203, 204 ABC Corporate Art Dept.

205 Illustration in actual size as self promotion for Selçuk Demirel. The same illustration also appears in a portfolio created for an exhibition of works by this artist in the Turkish gallery Nev. (FRA)
206 Self-promotional piece with the title "Stamp Dinner". (CAN)
207 Double-spread illustration from a brochure of a creative marketing team. (IRE)
208, 209 Two double spreads from a small-format catalogue, which accompanied a poster exhibition at the new Paris headquarters of IBM Europe. Black and white with grey. (GBR)

205 Illustration in Originalgrösse als Eigenwerbung für Selçuk Demirel. Die gleiche Illustration ist auch Bestandteil einer Mappe, die anlässlich einer Ausstellung dieses Künstlers in der türkischen Galerie Nev konzipiert worden ist. (FRA)
206 Als Eigenwerbung verwendete Illustration mit dem Titel «Briefmarken-Mahl». (CAN)
207 Doppelseitige Illustration aus der Broschüre eines international tätigen Werbeteams. (IRE)
208, 209 Zwei Doppelseiten aus einem kleinformatigen Katalog, der für eine Plakatausstellung von IBM Europa in Paris konzipiert worden ist. Schwarzweiss-Illustrationen mit warmem Grauton. (GBR)

205 Illustration grandeur nature servant d'autopromotion à l'artiste Selçuk Demirel. Elle figure également dans le portefeuille conçu à l'occasion de l'exposition des œuvres de l'artiste à la galerie turque Nev. (FRA)
206 Illustration autopromotionnelle intitulée «Repas philatélique». (CAN)
207 Illustration double page dans la brochure d'une équipe publicitaire internationale. (IRE)
208, 209 Deux pages doubles d'un catalogue au petit format réalisé pour une exposition d'affiches organisée à Paris par IBM-Europe. Illustrations noir et blanc avec un gris chaud. (GBR)

ARTIST / KÜNSTLER / ARTISTE:

205 Selçuk Demirel
206 Marie-Louise Cusack
207 Heinz Edelmann
208 Jacques Benoît
209 R. O. Blechman/Cassandre

DESIGNER / GESTALTER / MAQUETTISTE:

205 Selçuk Demirel
208, 209 Alan Fletcher/Paul Anthony/Tessa Boomitford

205

206

207

ART DIRECTOR / DIRECTEUR ARTISTIQUE:

207 Robert Pütz
208, 209 Alan Fletcher

AGENCY / AGENTUR / AGENCE – STUDIO:

207 Robert Pütz GmbH
208, 209 Pentagram

**Booklets
Prospekte
Brochures**

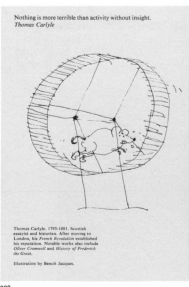

Nothing is more terrible than activity without insight.
Thomas Carlyle

Thomas Carlyle. 1795-1881. Scottish
essayist and historian. After moving to
London, his *French Revolution* established
his reputation. Notable works also include
Oliver Cromwell and *History of Frederick
the Great.*

Illustration by Benoit Jacques.

The quality of life is fuelled
by our productive wealth.
Edward de Bono

Edward de Bono. Contemporary English
writer and lecturer. Born 1933. Books
include *The Use of Lateral Thinking,
Greatest Thinkers, Future Positive.* Lecturer
in Medicine, Cambridge. Television
broadcaster on 'thinking'.

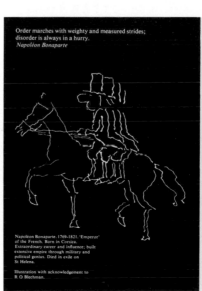

Order marches with weighty and measured strides;
disorder is always in a hurry.
Napoléon Bonaparte

Napoléon Bonaparte. 1769-1821. 'Emperor'
of the French. Born in Corsica.
Extraordinary career and influence; built
extensive empire through military and
political genius. Died in exile on
St Helena.

Illustration with acknowledgement to
R O Blechman.

It is not the men in your life
it's the life in your men that counts.
Mae West

Mae West. 1892-1981. American
Hollywood film star of the golden era.
Famous for her roles opposite W C Fields,
and her risqué wit. Films include *I'm No
Angel, Diamond Lil, My Little Chickadee.*

Illustration adapted from a French poster
design by Cassandre.

208   209

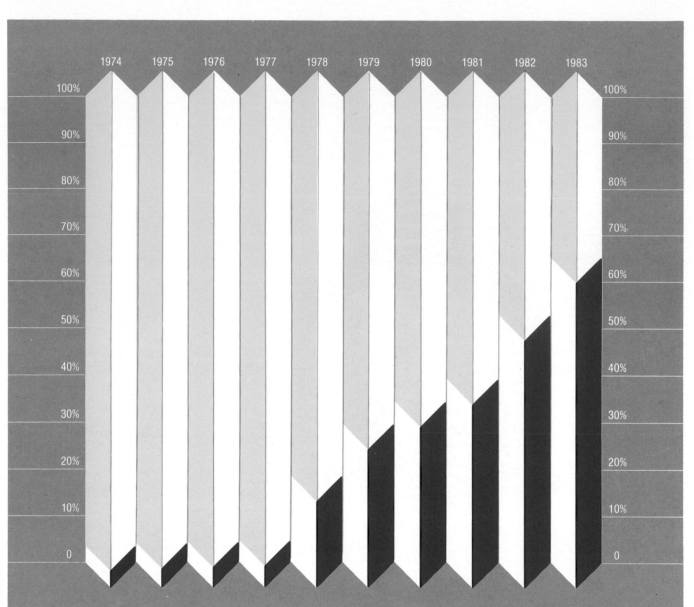

1974 1975 1976 1977 1978 1979 1980 1981 1982 1983

100% 100%

90% 90%

80% 80%

70% 70%

60% 60%

50% 50%

40% 40%

30% 30%

20% 20%

10% 10%

0 0

210

ARTIST / KÜNSTLER / ARTISTE:

210 Harri Boller
 Boller/Coates/Spadaro
211 Cross Assoc./
 Harri Boller
213 Folon
214 Lonal Harding/
 Phil Marco (Photos)
215 Nicolas Sidjakov/
 Michael Mabry/
 Gregory Heisler (Photo)
216 Richard Hess

DESIGNER / GESTALTER:

210–216 Kit Hinrichs/
 Lenore Bartz

ART DIRECTOR:

210–216 Kit Hinrichs

AGENCY / AGENTUR / AGENCE:

210–216 Jonson Pedersen
 Hinrichs & Shakery

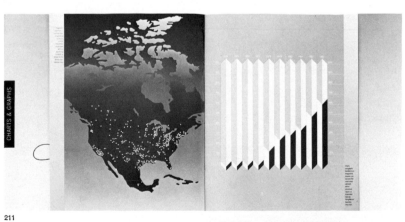

211

212

213 214

210–216 Single page and double spreads from an advertising brochure for the paper manufacturer Potlatch Corp. entitled "The Art of Annual Reports". Richly illustrated, it carries text and comments appertaining to the conception, graphic presentation, ideals and appeal of the annual report. Fig. 215 (left) shows a heavy drilling rig in bold geometric shapes; (right) a satellite test-chamber photograph resembles a scene from an outer-space thriller. Fig. 216 (left) demonstrates that the viewer's curiosity is aroused when a familiar product is placed in a surrealistic setting. (USA)

210–216 Einzelseite und Doppelseiten aus einer für den Papierhersteller Potlatch Corp. gestalteten Werbebroschüre mit dem Titel «Die Kunst der Jahresberichte». Gezeigt werden Beispiele aus verschiedenen Jahresberichten und Kommentare von zahlreichen Persönlichkeiten. Abb. 215 links veranschaulicht einen riesigen Drillbohrer in graphischer Umsetzung, rechts daneben ist eine Satelliten-Testkammer zu sehen. Abb. 216 links beweist, dass unter anderem surrealistische Szenen – gerade in einem Jahresbericht – die Aufmerksamkeit des Betrachters auf sich ziehen. (USA)

210–216 Page simple et doubles pages d'une brochure publicitaire conçue pour le papetier Potlatch Corp. sous le titre de «L'art du rapport annuel». On y présente divers exemples de rapports agrémentés des commentaires d'un grand nombre de personnalités. Fig. 215: à gauche, la transposition graphique d'une perceuse géante; à droite, une chambre d'essais pour satellites. L'illustration de la fig. 216 entend souligner le fait que le recours à des scènes surréalistes par exemple est un moyen ingénieux de capter et de fixer l'attention du lecteur feuilletant son rapport annuel. (USA)

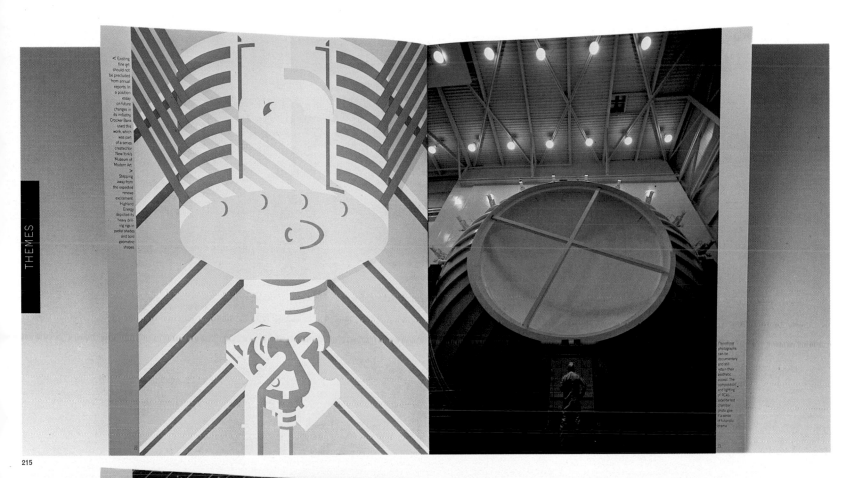

215

216

217 Illustration for self-promotion purposes. (USA)
218 Front of an invitation card, in actual size, for an exhibition of fashion graphics covering four decades by artist René Gruau at the Bartsch & Chariau gallery, Munich. (GER)
219, 220 Complete cover and introductory page from the catalogue to an exhibition by Japanese artist Kiyoshi Awazu. Fig. 219: Violet-blue figures, black text on white background; Fig. 220: Wine-red background with white lettering. (JPN)

217 Für Eigenwerbungszwecke verwendete Illustration. (USA)
218 Vorderseite (Originalgrösse) der Einladungskarte zu einer Ausstellung von René Gruau mit dem Titel «Modegraphik aus vier Jahrzehnten» in der Galerie Bartsch & Chariau, München. (GER)
219, 220 Vollständiger Umschlag des Katalogs zu einer Ausstellung des Japaners Kiyoshi Awazu und einleitende Seite. Abb. 219: Gestalten violett auf Weiss, Schrift schwarz; Abb. 220: Hintergrund in hellem Weinrot, Schrift weiss. (JPN)

217 Illustration servant à la promotion de l'artiste. (USA)
218 Recto (format original) de la carte d'invitation à une exposition des œuvres de René Gruau à la galerie munichoise Bartsch & Chariau: «Quatre décennies de publicité mode». (GER)
219, 220 Couverture complète du catalogue d'une exposition des œuvres du Japonais Kiyoshi Awazu, et page initiale. Fig. 219: figures violettes sur blanc, texte noir; fig. 220: le fond est exécuté en bordeaux clair, le texte en blanc. (JPN)

ARTIST / KÜNSTLER / ARTISTE:

217 Stanislaw Fernandes
218 René Gruau
219, 220 Kiyoshi Awazu

217

218

DESIGNER / GESTALTER / MAQUETTISTE:

217 Stanislaw Fernandes
218 Bartsch & Chariau
219. 220 Kiyoshi Awazu

ART DIRECTOR / DIRECTEUR ARTISTIQUE:

217 Stanislaw Fernandes

AGENCY / AGENTUR / AGENCE – STUDIO:

217 Stanislaw Fernandes Design

Booklets
Prospekte
Brochures

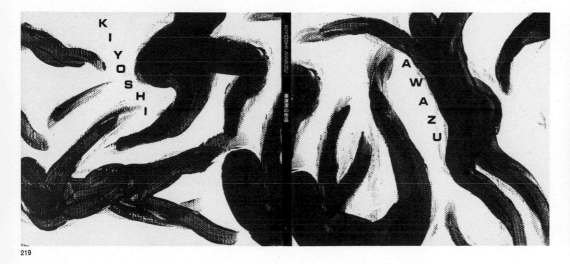

219

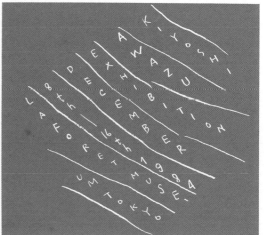

220

99

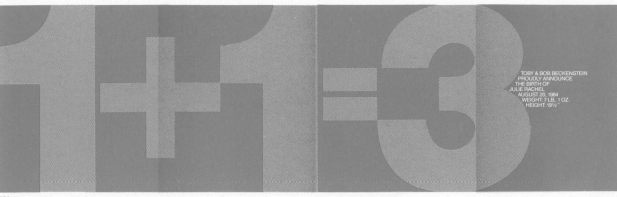

TOBY & BOB BECKENSTEIN
PROUDLY ANNOUNCE
THE BIRTH OF
JULIE RACHEL
AUGUST 20, 1984
WEIGHT: 7 LB., 1 OZ.
HEIGHT: 19½"

221

222

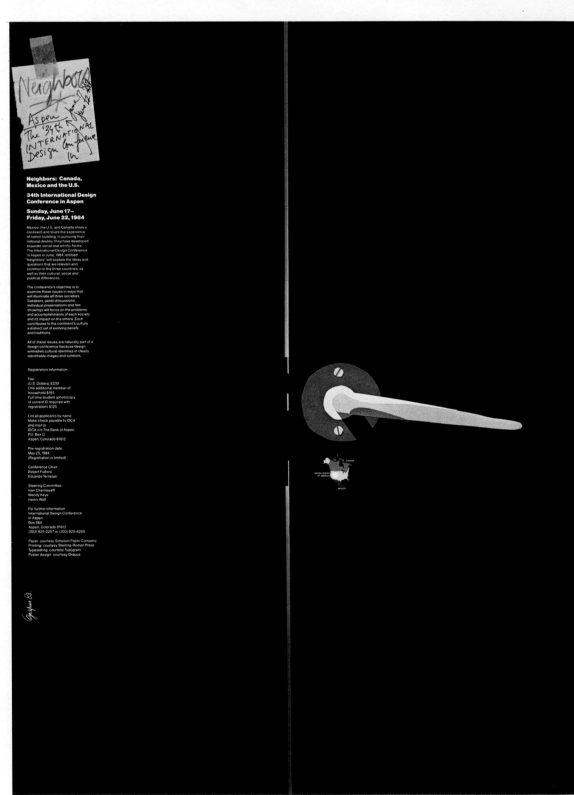

223

ARTIST / KÜNSTLER / ARTISTE:

223 Grapus
224 Halas & Batchelor

DESIGNER / GESTALTER / MAQUETTISTE:

221 Arthur Beckenstein
222 David Brier
223 Grapus
224 Garth Bell
225, 226 Katherine & Michael McCoy

**Booklets
Prospekte
Brochures**

100

224

225

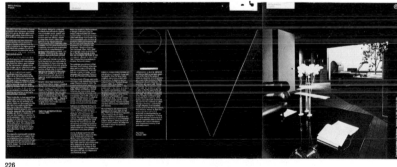

226

221 Concertina-fold birth announcement card shown opened out and closed. (USA)
222 Cover of a large-format brochure for a graphic designer on the subject of typography. (USA)
223 Invitation poster to the 34th International Design Conference in Aspen. (USA)
224 Black cover—closed and open—showing hexagonal brochure for an animation film studio. (GBR)
225, 226 Green gatefold cover with slit initials and cover opened to reveal white text on black ground and first page of the catalogue for designers McCoy & McCoy. (USA)

221 Auseinander- und zusammengefaltete Geburtsanzeige für Julie Rachel Beckenstein. (USA)
222 Vorderseite der grossformatigen Broschüre eines Graphikers zum Thema Typographie. (USA)
223 Einladung zur International Design Conference in Aspen. Thema: Kanada, USA, Mexiko. (USA)
224 Schwarzer Umschlag mit Broschüre für einen Hersteller von Zeichentrickfilmen. (GBR)
225, 226 Grüner Umschlag mit Auslegeseite und eingeschnittenen Initialen, geöffneter Umschlag mit weissem Text auf Schwarz sowie erste Seite eines Katalogs der Gestalter McCoy & McCoy. (USA)

221 Faire-part de naissance (déplié et plié) pour Julie Rachel Beckenstein. (USA)
222 Première page de couverture de la brochure au grand format d'un graphiste sur la typo. (USA)
223 Invitation à l'International Design Conference d'Aspen. Sujet: Canada, E.-U., Mexique. (USA)
224 Enveloppe noire – fermée et ouverte – avec la brochure d'un producteur de films d'animation. (GBR)
225, 226 Couverture verte (deux pages repliées), initiales incisées, présentée fermée et ouverte – texte blanc sur noir, et première page d'un catalogue des designers McCoy & McCoy. (USA)

227–230 Spreads from a tall-format programme for the National Theatre Mannheim, with information on forthcoming productions. Fig. 227 relates to a comedy by Lessing; Fig. 229 to "The Exception and the Rule" and *Timmi*; Fig. 230 is for a play by Gorki and "Flirtation". (GER)
231, 232 Illustration and cover with transparent overlay for the invitation to participate in the competitions and celebrations of the Olympic Games in Los Angeles. (USA)
233 Spread from a programme for *The Nutcracker* danced by the Arizona Dance Theatre. The illustrations refer to the dance of the dolls, the gift-wrapped rat—and the nutcracker. (USA)

227–230 Doubles pages du programme du Théâtre National de Mannheim. Toutes les doubles pages (noir et blanc, fig. 230 avec du rouge) renseignent sur les pièces jouées. (GER)
231, 232 Illustration et couverture complète avec papier transparent pour l'invitation à participer aux Jeux Olympiques de Los Angeles. (USA)
233 Double page d'une brochure annonçant une représentation du ballet *Casse-noisette*. Les illustrations évoquant des bouts de papier couleur déchirés se rapportent au prologue et à la première scène où l'on voit les poupées, Marie, le cadeau renfermant un rat et le casse-noisette. (USA)

227–230 Doppelseiten aus dem Programmheft des Nationaltheaters Mannheim. Alle Doppelseiten (in Schwarzweiss, Abb. 230 mit Rot) informieren über die angekündigten Stücke. (GER)
231, 232 Illustration und vollständiger Umschlag mit Transparentpapier für die Einladung zur Teilnahme an den Olympischen Spielen in Los Angeles. (USA)
233 Doppelseite aus einer Broschüre für eine Ballettaufführung des *Nussknackers*. Die Illustrationen (wie aus gerissenen, farbigen Papierstreifen) beziehen sich auf den Prolog und die erste Szene, in der Marie eine als Geschenk verpackte Ratte und den Nussknacker bekommt. (GER)

227

228

229

230

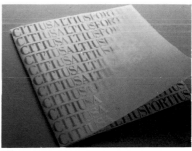

231

SYNOPSIS

PROLOGUE A huge book stands on stage, dimly lit by a nearby candle. Herr Drosselmeyer is busy preparing himself, while his three animated dolls, Harlequin, Pierrot and Columbine, frolic around the stage, dancing, kissing and fighting. They finally convince Drosselmeyer to open the book and reveal the story of Marie and the Nutcracker. **ACT I, SCENE 1: THE PARTY** It is Christmas Eve early in the Nineteenth Century. Marie's parents are giving a holiday party for their friends and children. Herr Drosselmeyer arrives bearing gifts and amusing the crowd with his conjuring tricks. He also brings three dolls, who we recognize as Harlequin, Pierrot and Columbine, that delight the crowd with

their dancing. Drosselmeyer fills Marie's head with fantasy as she dances along with the three dolls. Her mischievous brother, Fritz, disrupts the entire party by presenting Marie with a gift wrapped rat! But soon order is restored and Drosselmeyer gives Marie one last gift – a Nutcracker, his favorite toy. Marie immediately falls under the Nutcracker's spell, and she hardly notices that the party ends and the guests depart. Herr Drosselmeyer leaves smiling, for he is preparing Marie for a wondrous fairytale of love, growth, and maturity.

233

ARTIST / KÜNSTLER / ARTISTE:

233 Karen Swearingen

DESIGNER / GESTALTER / MAQUETTISTE:

227–230 Christof Gassner
231, 232 Arnold Schwartzman
233 Steve Ditro / Karen Swearingen

ART DIRECTOR / DIRECTEUR ARTISTIQUE:

231, 232 Arnold Schwartzman
233 Steve Ditro

AGENCY / AGENTUR / AGENCE – STUDIO:

227–230 Christof Gassner
231, 232 James Robie Design
233 SHR Communications

Booklets
Prospekte
Brochures

234

ARTIST / KÜNSTLER / ARTISTE:

235, 236 Jim Jacobs
237 Cathy Hull
238 Michael Vanderbyl
239 Greg MacNair

DESIGNER / GESTALTER / MAQUETTISTE:

234 Bob Appleton
235, 236 Jim Jacobs
237 Cathy Hull
238 Michael Vanderbyl
239 David Bartels
240, 241 Paula Scher/Terry Koppel/
Richard Mantel

ART DIRECTOR / DIRECTEUR ARTISTIQUE:

234 Bob Appleton
235, 236 Jim Jacobs
237 Cathy Hull
239 David Bartels

AGENCY / AGENTUR / AGENCE – STUDIO:

234 Appleton Design
235, 236 Jim Jacobs'Studio, Inc.
238 Vanderbyl Design
239 Bartels & Co., Inc.
240, 241 Mantel, Koppel & Scher

235

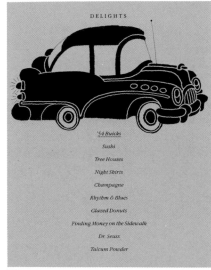

236

237

234 Announcement of a new address; brown paper tied like a parcel with real cord. (USA)
235, 236 Double spread and cover of a brown paper booklet, printed in black and red, for a firm presenting the products of novelty manufacturers to trade buyers. (USA)
237 Computer-aided self-portrait on a self-promotional piece for the artist. (USA)
238 Cover of a catalogue containing full-colour reproductions of some of the exhibits; for an exhibition in San Francisco of the New York school of figurative expressionism. (USA)
239 Self-promotion mailer for an illustrator. In black and white, with text fields in blue. (USA)
240, 241 From an advertising brochure for the design studio Mantel, Koppel & Scher. (USA)

234 Annonce de changement d'adresse. Sur papier d'emballage brun, vraie ficelle blanche. (USA)
235, 236 Double page et recto d'un prospectus imprimé en noir et en rouge sur papier d'emballage pour une exposition-vente de divers articles de consommation nouveaux. (USA)
237 Autoportrait réalisé avec l'assistance de l'ordinateur par une illustratrice, qui s'en sert pour sa promotion. (USA)
238 Couverture du catalogue d'une exposition d'expressionistes figuratifs. (USA)
239 Publicité directe pour un illustrateur. Noir et blanc, blocs de textes en bleu. (USA)
240, 241 Pages d'une brochure publicitaire de l'atelier de design Mantel, Koppel & Scher. (USA)

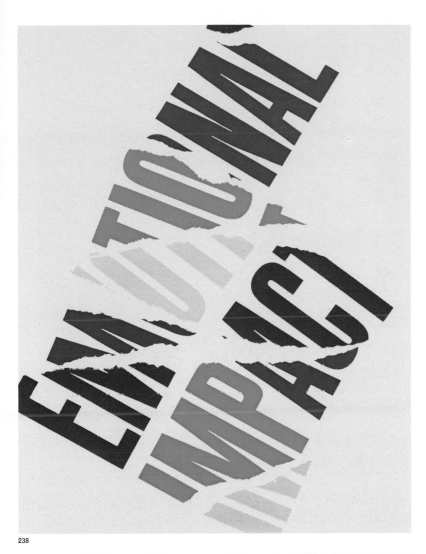

238

239

240

241

234 Bekanntgabe einer neuen Adresse. Aus braunem Packpapier mit richtiger weisser Kordel. (USA)
235, 236 Doppelseite und Vorderseite eines Prospekts aus schwarz und rot bedrucktem Packpapier für eine Verkaufsausstellung verschiedener neuer Konsumartikel. (USA)
237 Mit dem Computer produziertes Selbstporträt, als Eigenwerbung einer Illustratorin. (USA)
238 Umschlag eines Katalogs für eine Ausstellung figurativer Expressionisten. (USA)
239 Direktwerbung für einen Illustrator. In Schwarzweiss, Textfelder blau. (USA)
240, 241 Aus einer Werbebroschüre für das Design-Studio Mantel, Koppel & Scher. (USA)

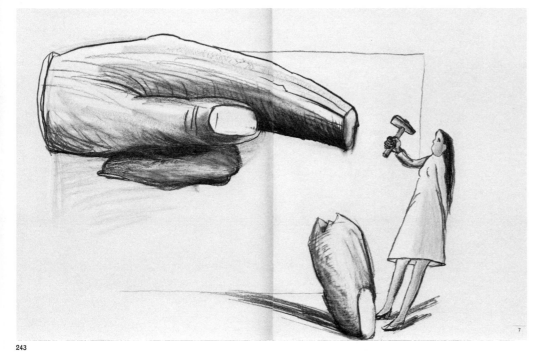

243

ANTISTROPHEN

246

Booklets/Prospekte/Brochures

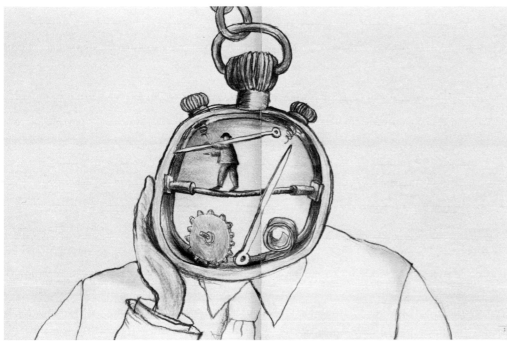

244

ARTIST / KÜNSTLER / ARTISTE:
242–246 Christian Lang

DESIGNER / GESTALTER / MAQUETTISTE:
242–246 Christian Lang/Marcel Berlinger

ART DIRECTOR / DIRECTEUR ARTISTIQUE:
242–246 Christian Lang

AGENCY / AGENTUR / AGENCE – STUDIO:
242–246 Werbung Ciba-Geigy

245

242–246 Illustration in actual size, double spreads and cover of a picture-story book illustrated with coloured pencil drawings to promote the anti-depressive, medicinal drug *Ludiomil* by *Ciba-Geigy*. The artist attempts to show how a depressive patient, with correct therapy, can eventually loosen the shackles of depression and emerge from his dark, self-constrained world to a new meaningful life which seems to him more bearable. (SWI)

242–246 Illustration in Originalgrösse, Doppelseiten und Umschlag eines von *Ciba-Geigy* für das Anti-Depressivum *Ludiomil* herausgegebenen Bildbands mit Farbstiftzeichnungen. Der Künstler versucht aufzuzeigen, dass sich die Fesseln der Depression lösen lassen, dass ein Heraustreten aus Dunkelheit und Einengung in ein neu bewegtes Leben, das langsam, aber stetig wieder Konturen und Formen annimmt, möglich ist. (SWI)

242–246 Illustration au format original, doubles pages et couverture d'un album illustré de dessins au crayon couleur publié par *Ciba-Geigy* pour son antidépresseur *Ludiomil*. L'artiste a cherché à en visualiser l'effet: les liens de la dépression tombent, le patient sort de l'obscurité et du confinement, sa vie se fait plus dynamique et reprend lentement mais progressivement des contours et une forme déterminés. (SWI)

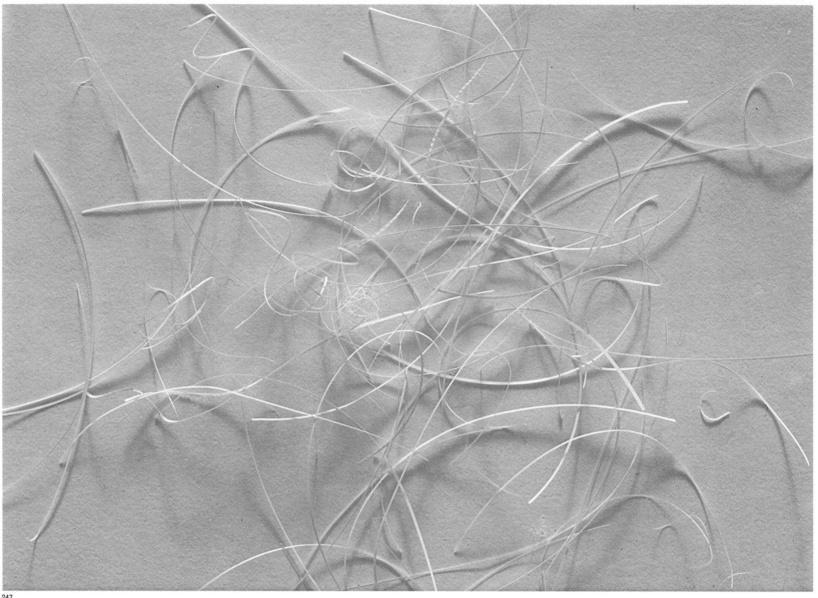

247

251

Gba
Locasalen
Salbe · Tinktur

Aktuell und adäquat auch bei Affektionen auf behaarter und exponierter Haut

Fachärzte empfehlen oft Tinktur und Salbe kombiniert

248

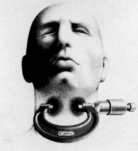

un diagnóstico preciso:
Amigdalitis

252

ARTIST / KÜNSTLER / ARTISTE:

247, 248 Arthur Samuel
249, 250 Christian Lang
251 Miloslav Kolář
252–254 Joan Marquès

DESIGNER / GESTALTER:

247, 248 Arthur Samuel
249, 250 Christian Lang
251 Miloslav Kolář
252–254 Joan Marquès

ART DIRECTOR:

247, 248 Arthur Samuel
249, 250 Christian Lang
251 Zdeněk Rohlík
252–254 Joan Marquès

AGENCY / AGENTUR / AGENCE:

247–250 Werbung Ciba-Geigy
251 Chemapol Advertising
252–254 Joan Marquès

Booklets
Prospekte
Brochures

249

247, 248 Detail of the illustration and complete cover (with toning background) of a prospectus for *Locasalen* ointment and tincture. (SWI)
249, 250 Full-page illustration and inside spread of a prospectus relating to social phobias and to the anti-depressive medical drug *Anafranil*. (SWI)
251 Illustration in pastel pinks, violet and grey for a medicinal preparation administered to reduce internal haemorrhage. (CSR)
252, 253 Complete cover and illustration from a prospectus for *Eupen*, a medical substance for the treatment of tonsilitis. Head in black crayon, throat with two red spots, clamp in natural metal colours. (SPA)
254 Illustration in yellow/brown tones for the influenza remedy *Dolmen*. (SPA)

247, 248 Detail der Illustration und vollständige Vorderseite (mit einheitlichem Hintergrund) eines Prospektes für *Locasalen*-Salbe und -Tinktur. (SWI)
249, 250 Ganzseitige Illustration zum Thema Zwangskrankheiten und vollständige Innenseite eines Prospektes für das Antidepressivum *Anafranil*. (SWI)
251 Illustration in sanftem Rosa, Violett und Grau für ein Medikament, das bei inneren Blutungen angewendet wird. (CSR)
252, 253 Vollständige Vorderseite und Illustration eines Prospektes für *Eupen*, ein Medikament gegen Mandelentzündungen. Mit schwarzem Stift gemalter Kopf, Hals mit zwei leuchtend roten Flecken, Gerät in Metallfarben. (SPA)
254 Illustration in Gelb- und Brauntönen für das Grippemittel *Dolmen*. (SPA)

247, 248 Détail de l'illustration et recto complet (au fond uniforme) d'un prospectus réalisé pour la pommade et la teinture *Locasalen*. (SWI)
249, 250 Illustration pleine page sur les névroses obsessionnelles et page intérieure complète du prospectus de l'antidépresseur *Anafranil*. (SWI)
251 Illustration aux tons rose adouci, violet et gris pour un remède des hémorragies internes. (CSR)
252, 253 Recto complet et illustration d'un prospectus pour l'*Eupen*, un remède des amygdalites. Tête dessinée au crayon noir, cou garni de deux taches rouges lumineuses, appareil aux couleurs métallisées. (SPA)
254 Illustration en divers jaunes et bruns pour l'antigrippal *Dolmen*. (SPA)

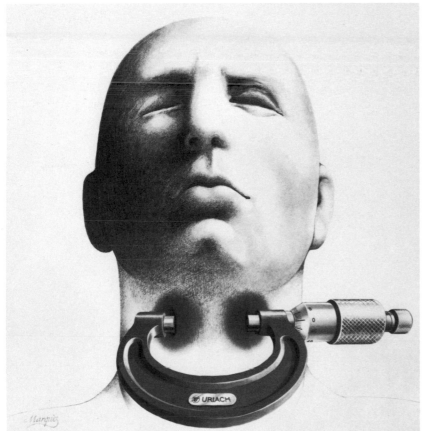

253

254

3

Newspaper Illustrations

Magazine Covers

Magazine Illustrations

Weekend Supplements

Trade Magazines

House Organs

Annual Reports

Book Covers

Zeitungs-Illustrationen

Zeitschriften-Umschläge

Zeitschriften-Illustrationen

Wochenendbeilagen

Fachzeitschriften

Hauszeitschriften

Jahresberichte

Buchumschläge

Illustrations de journaux

Couvertures de périodiques

Illustrations de périodiques

Suppléments dominicaux

Revues professionnelles

Journaux d'entreprise

Rapports annuels

Couvertures de livres

255

The New York Times

255–261 Illustrations and one complete page from the *New York Times*. The subject of the article for Figs. 255, 256 is computerized telephone calls that victimize the recipient—he cannot hang up. Fig. 257 illustrates an article about the economic status of black male parents; where have they gone? Fig. 258 belongs to an article on Israel's territorial expansion. Fig. 259 relates to a reader's question about pimentos and sweet peppers. Figs. 260, 261 are illustrations for the Op-Ed page, entitled "What the democrats must do to recover" and "Again, succession and soviet policy". (USA)

255–261 Illustrationen und eine vollständige Seite aus der *New York Times*. Das Thema des zu Abb. 255, 256 gehörenden Artikels sind Telephonanrufe durch Computer, denen der Empfänger ausgeliefert ist. Abb. 257 illustriert einen Beitrag über die wirtschaftliche Lage der schwarzen, männlichen Bevölkerung der USA. Abb. 258 gehört zu einem Artikel über Israels Territorial-Politik. Abb. 259 bezieht sich auf eine Leserfrage über Paprika- und Pfefferschoten. Abb. 260, 261 gehören zu Leitartikeln: «Was die Demokraten für ihre Stärkung tun müssen», und «Schon wieder, Nachfolge und sowjetische Politik». (USA)

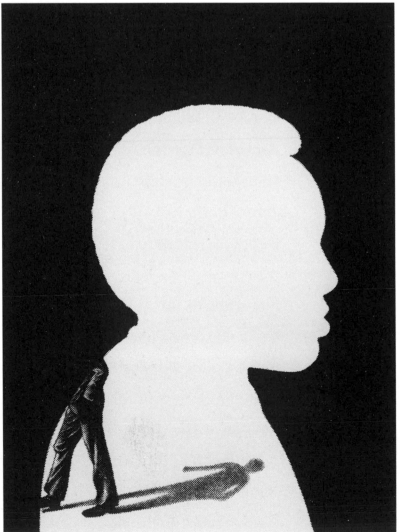

257

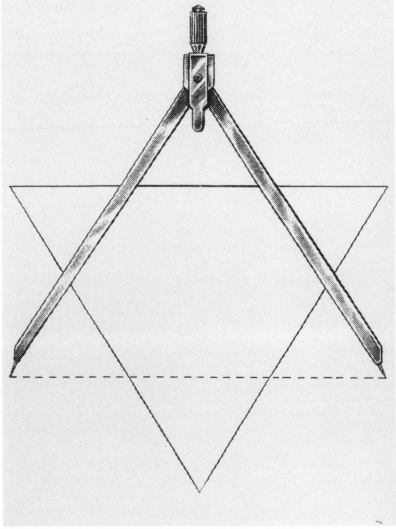

258

ARTIST / KÜNSTLER / ARTISTE:

255–258 Cathy Hull
259 Randall Enos
260, 261 Rafal Olbinski

DESIGNER / GESTALTER / MAQUETTISTE:

255–258, 260, 261 Jerelle Kraus

ART DIRECTOR / DIRECTEUR ARTISTIQUE:

255–258, 260, 261 Jerelle Kraus
259 Nancy Kent

PUBLISHER / VERLEGER / EDITEUR:

255–261 The New York Times

256

259

255–261 Illustrations et page complète du *New York Times*. L'article illustré en fig. 255 et fig. 256 traite des appels téléphoniques par ordinateur qui peuvent être casse-pieds. La fig. 257 accompagne un article sur la situation économique de la partie masculine de la population noire aux Etats-Unis. La fig. 258 fait partie d'un article sur la politique qu'Israël poursuit dans les territoires annexés. La fig. 259 se rapporte à un article où il est question de gousses de paprika et de poivre. Fig. 260, 261: «Ce que les Démocrates doivent faire pour revenir au pouvoir»; «Une fois de plus, le problème de la succession et la politique en U.R.S.S.» (USA)

260

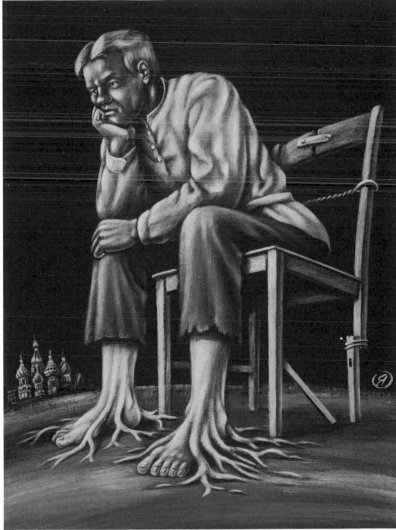

261

262

262–267 Black-and-white illustrations from the *New York Times*. Fig. 262 relates to an article entitled "America in the Age of Enlitenment", about the "lite" trend in American consumer goods and society. Fig. 263 relates to a humorous notice on the Reptile House in the Bronx zoo. Fig. 264 concerns a critical article about the sharp practices of some investors. Figs. 265 and 266 relate to book reviews. Fig. 267 illustrates the article "The people on economic recovery's scrapheap". (USA)
268 Illustration to one of the articles in an Iranian newspaper. This article is entitled "Bureaucracy System". (IRN)

262–267 Illustrationen in Schwarzweiss aus der *New York Times*. Abb. 262 gehört zu einem Beitrag über den Trend zur Leichtigkeit in den Vereinigten Staaten, angefangen bei den Nahrungsmitteln bis zum Substanzverlust der Werte der Gesellschaft. Abb. 263 illustriert eine humorvolle Notiz über das Reptilien-Haus im Zoo des New Yorker Stadtteils Bronx. Abb. 264 betrifft einen kritischen Artikel über einige fragwürdige Investitionspraktiken an der Wall Street. Abb. 265 und 266 gehören zu Buchbesprechungen. Abb. 267 illustriert einen Artikel mit dem Titel «Das Volk auf dem Schrotthaufen des wirtschaftlichen Aufschwungs». (USA)
268 Illustration zu einem in einer iranischen Zeitung erschienenen Artikel mit dem Titel «System der Bürokratie». (IRN)

262–267 Illustrations noir et blanc pour le *New York Times*. La fig. 262 illustre la perte des valeurs typiquement américaines, la fig. 263 un reportage humoristique sur le vivarium du zoo de Bronx, quartier de New York. La fig. 264 critique certaines méthodes en usage à Wall Street. Les fig. 265 et 266 se rapportent à des comptes rendus de livres. La fig. 267 accompagne un article intitulé «Le peuple et l'essor économique». (USA)
268 Illustration d'un article paru dans un journal iranien sous le titre de «Système de la bureaucratie». (IRN)

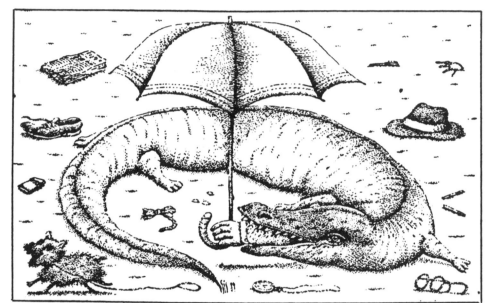

263

264

ARTIST / KÜNSTLER / ARTISTE:

262 Carolyn Gowdy
263–266 Peter Sis
267, 268 Ardeshir Mohasses

DESIGNER / GESTALTER / MAQUETTISTE:

262 Jerelle Kraus

ART DIRECTOR / DIRECTEUR ARTISTIQUE:

262, 264, 267 Jerelle Kraus
263, 265, 266 Steve Heller

PUBLISHER / VERLEGER / EDITEUR:

262–267 The New York Times
268 Kayhan

268

265

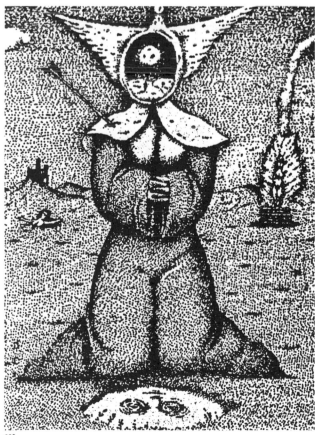

266

267

115

269

ARTIST / KÜNSTLER / ARTISTE:

269 Sean Kelly
270, 271 Kent Barton
272 Marcia Staimer Dugan

DESIGNER / GESTALTER / MAQUETTISTE:

269 Craig Black
270, 271 Richard Bard
272 Marcia Staimer Dugan

ART DIRECTOR / DIRECTEUR ARTISTIQUE:

269–271 Kent Barton
272 Marcia Staimer Dugan

PUBLISHER / VERLEGER / EDITEUR:

269–272 The Miami Herald

269–272 Black-and-white illustrations from the newspaper *The Miami Herald*. Fig. 269 relates to an article about the business status of dental hygienists; Fig. 270 concerns teacher problems; Fig. 271 accompanies an excerpt of the lecture given by Nobel Peace Prizewinner, the South African Bishop Tutu, on apartheid. Fig. 272 illustrates a girl's Halloween story about the real terrors for children today—child molesters. (USA)

269–272 Schwarzweiss-Illustrationen aus der Zeitung *The Miami Herald*. Abb. 269 bezieht sich auf einen Artikel über die berufliche Situation der Dentalhygienikerinnen; Abb. 270 betrifft Lehrerprobleme; Abb. 271 gehört zu einem Auszug der Rede des Friedensnobelpreisträgers Bischof Tutu über die Apartheid-Politik; Abb. 272 illustriert eine Geschichte über «Halloween», den Abend vor Allerheiligen, an dem die Kinder, möglichst furchterregend verkleidet, von Tür zu Tür ziehen. (USA)

269–272 Illustrations noir et blanc pour le journal *The Miami Herald*. La fig. 269 se réfère à un article sur la situation professionnelle des hygiénistes dentaires femmes. La fig. 270 concerne les problèmes des maîtres. La fig. 271 illustre un extrait du discours de l'évêque Desmond Tutu, prix Nobel de la paix, sur la politique de l'apartheid. La fig. 272 accompagne un article sur Halloween, la veille de la Toussaint, où les enfants se déguisent en monstres. (USA)

270

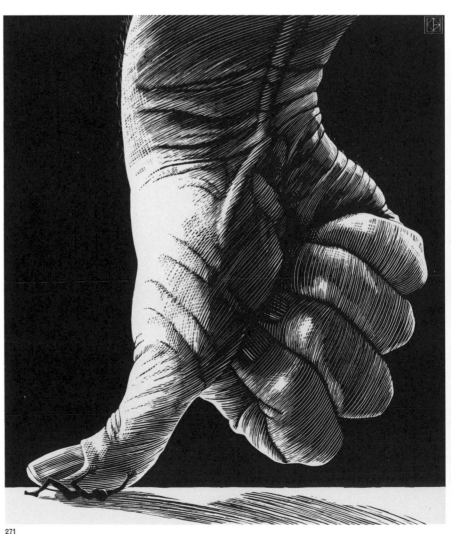

271

272

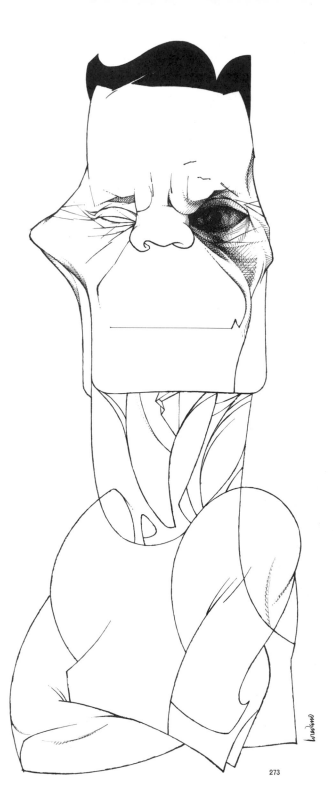

273

274

275

273 Illustration in actual size to an "Elegy for Pasolini" which appeared in the music publication *Troja*. (GER)
274 "Peace on Earth." Illustration from the *Boston Globe*. (USA)
275 Illustration to an article about the Gulf of Tonkin incident which led to the US intervention in the war in Vietnam. From the *New York Times*. (USA)
276, 277 Illustrations from *de Volkskrant* for an article about the Russian boycott of the Olympics and for a review of autobiographical books. (NLD)

273 Illustration in Originalgrösse zu einer «Elegie für Pasolini», erschienen in der Musikpublikation *Troja*. (GER)
274 «Friede auf Erden.» Illustration aus dem *Boston Globe*. (USA)
275 Illustration für einen Artikel über die Umstände, die zur Einmischung der USA in Vietnam führten. Aus der *New York Times*. (USA)
276, 277 Illustrationen aus *de Volkskrant* zum Olympia-Boykott der Russen und für eine Besprechung von autobiographischen Büchern. (NLD)

273 Illustration au format original pour une «Elégie pour Pasolini» publiée dans la revue musicale *Troja*. (GER)
274 «Paix sur terre.» Illustration pour le *Boston Globe*. (USA)
275 Illustration d'un article discutant des circonstances qui amenèrent les Etats-Unis à intervenir au Viêt-nam, dans le *New York Times*. (USA)
276, 277 Illustrations dans *de Volkskrant* sur le boycottage des Jeux Olympiques par les Soviétiques et pour des comptes rendus de mémoires. (NLD)

Newspaper Illustrations
Zeitungs-Illustrationen
Illustrations de journaux

ARTIST / KÜNSTLER / ARTISTE:

273 Loredano Silva
274 Barbara Nessim
275 George F. Kocar
276, 277 Waldemar Post

DESIGNER / GESTALTER:

274 Ronn Campisi
275 Jerelle Kraus

ART DIRECTOR:

274 Ronn Campisi
275 Jerelle Kraus
276, 277 Waldemar Post

AGENCY / AGENTUR / AGENCE:

274 Nessim & Associates
275 Kocar Art Inc.

PUBLISHER / VERLEGER / EDITEUR:

273 Falk Burhenne
274 Boston Globe
275 The New York Times
276, 277 de Volkskraut

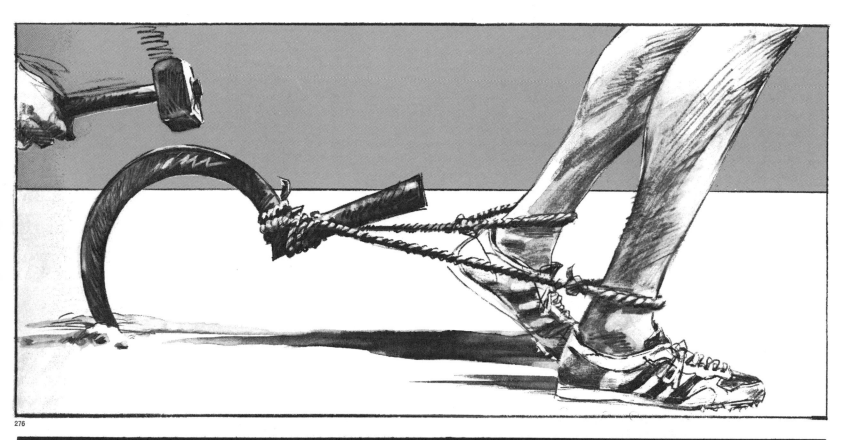

276

277

The Denver Post / Bonnie Timmons

Bonnie Timmons
Denver Post illustrator

Before coming to Denver, I lived in East Africa which looked like this:

Before that, I dissected cadavers in Toronto, which looked like this:

Before that, I won some ribbons for the 400-meter breast stroke, which looked like this:

I have been very happy:

Newspaper Illustrations
Zeitungs-Illustrationen
Illustrations de journaux

278 Page from *The Sunday Denver Post*; several illustrators were asked to draw their view of Denver and offer a short autobiography to accompany it. (USA)
279 Portrait of Henry Kissinger (as Henry Strangelove) from the newspaper *The Village Voice*. (USA)
280 Illustration from the *New York Times* for an article about the US economy and relating in particular to Lord Keynes "bottleneck" theory of inflation. (USA)
281 Caricature from the *International Herald Tribune*: "the secret" of Reagan's success. (USA)

278 Seite aus *The Sunday Denver Post*, die verschiedene Illustratoren beauftragte, Denver aus ihrer Sicht darzustellen, begleitet von kleinen biographischen Notizen. (USA)
279 Porträt Henry Kissingers («Henry Strangelove») aus der Zeitung *The Village Voice*. (USA)
280 Illustration für einen Artikel in der *New York Times* über den Zustand der Wirtschaft in den USA, mit speziellem Bezug auf die «Flaschenhals-Theorie» der Inflation von Lord Keynes. (USA)
281 Illustration aus *International Herald Tribune*: «Das Erfolgsgeheimnis» Ronald Reagans. (USA)

278 Page du *Denver Sunday Post*, où divers illustrateurs ont été invités à donner leur vision de Denver accompagnée de petites notices biographiques. (USA)
279 Portrait d'Henry Kissinger (dit «Henry Strangelove») dans le journal *The Village Voice*. (USA)
280 Illustration d'un article du *New York Times* sur l'état de l'économie américaine, avec une référence particulière à la théorie de Lord Keynes sur l'inflation. (USA)
281 Illustration de l'*International Herald Tribune*: «le secret du succès» de Ronald Reagan. (USA)

279

280

281

282

283

ARTIST / KÜNSTLER / ARTISTE:
282–284 Rubem Campos Grilo

PUBLISHER / VERLEGER / ÉDITEUR:
282, 283 Retrato do Brasil
284 Revista do Brasil

282–284 Examples of the stirring woodcuts by the Brazilian illustrator Rubem Campos Grilo which mostly appear in small opposition newspapers in Brazil. The trained agriculturist who, in his youth, experienced the worst period of the Brazilian dictatorship (1964 the coup d'état by the generals), was able to turn his hobby into art—through which he could join the side of the freedom fighters. The subjects of the illustration shown here are: "Military State" and "Human Rights", published by the *Retrato do Brasil*, and a story entitled "The Carriage of Holy Week", which appeared in the *Revista do Brasil*. (BRA)

282–284 Beispiele der aufrüttelnden Holzschnitte des Brasilianers Rubem Campos Grilo, die vor allem in kleinen brasilianischen Oppositionszeitungen erschienen sind. Der gelernte Agronom, der in seiner Jugend die schlimmste Periode der braslianischen Diktatur erlebte (1964 Staatsstreich durch die Generale), beschloss, sich mit seiner aus einem Hobby entwickelten Kunst auf die Seite der Freiheitskämpfer zu stellen. Die Themen der hier gezeigten Illustrationen: «Militärdiktatur» und «Menschenrechte», veröffentlicht in *Retrato do Brasil*, und eine Geschichte mit dem Titel «Die Kutsche in der Heiligen Woche», die in *Revista do Brasil* erschien. (BRA)

282–284 Exemples des bois saisissants de l'artiste brésilien Rubem Campos Grilo publiés en majeure partie dans des petits journaux d'opposition au Brésil. Agronome de formation, Campos Grilo a connu dans sa jeunesse toutes les horreurs de la dictature instituée par le coup d'Etat des militaires fomenté en 1964. Il décida un jour de mettre son talent de dessinateur au service des combattants pour la liberté. On voit ici «Dictature militaire» et «Droits de l'homme», deux illustrations publiées dans *Retrato do Brasil*, et un récit en images intitulé «La calèche de la Semaine sainte», paru dans la *Revista do Brasil*. (BRA)

Newspaper Illustrations
Zeitungs-Illustrationen
Illustrations de journaux

285

287

286

288

289

290

Newspaper Illustrations
Zeitungs-Illustrationen
Illustrations de journaux

ARTIST / KÜNSTLER / ARTISTE:

285–291 Loredano Silva

ART DIRECTOR / DIRECTEUR ARTISTIQUE:

285 Helmut Morell
286 Alain Dietlin

PUBLISHER / VERLEGER / EDITEUR:

285 Vorwärts Verlag
286 Journal Révolution
287–291 Frankfurter Allgemeine Zeitung GmbH

285 Portrait of Friedhelm Farthmann, Minister of Labour, Health and Welfare, of Nordrheinwestfalen (Westphalia) accompanying an interview in the SPD party organ *Vorwärts*. (GER)
286 Jacques Chirac's caricature in *Révolution*. (FRA)
287–291 Henri Beyle (alias Stendhal); Peter Weiss; Heinrich Böll; Jorge-Luis Borges and Alfred Andersch, drawn by Loredano (see also Figs. 285, 286) for corresponding articles in the literature pages of the *Frankfurter Allgemeine Zeitung*. (GER)

285 Porträt des Ministers für Arbeit, Gesundheit und Soziales in Nordrheinwestfalen, Friedhelm Farthmann, für ein Interview im SPD-Parteiorgan *Vorwärts*. (GER)
286 Karikatur Jacques Chiracs in der Zeitung *Révolution*. (FRA)
287–291 Henri Beyle alias Stendhal, Peter Weiss, Heinrich Böll, Jorge Luis Borges und Alfred Andersch, gezeichnet von Loredano (s. auch Abb. 285, 286) für entsprechende Beiträge im Literaturteil der *Frankfurter Allgemeine Zeitung*. (GER)

285 Portrait du ministre du travail, de la santé et des affaires sociales du Land allemand de Rhénanie du Nord-Westphalie, Friedhelm Farthmann, pour une interview parue dans le journal du parti socialiste allemand *Vorwärts*. (GER)
286 Caricature de Jacques Chirac, dans *Révolution*. (FRA)
287–291 Henri Beyle dit Stendhal, Peter Weiss, Heinrich Böll, Jorge Luis Borges, Alfred Andersch, par Loredano (cf. les fig. 285, 286), pour le *Frankfurter Allgemeine Zeitung* littéraire. (GER)

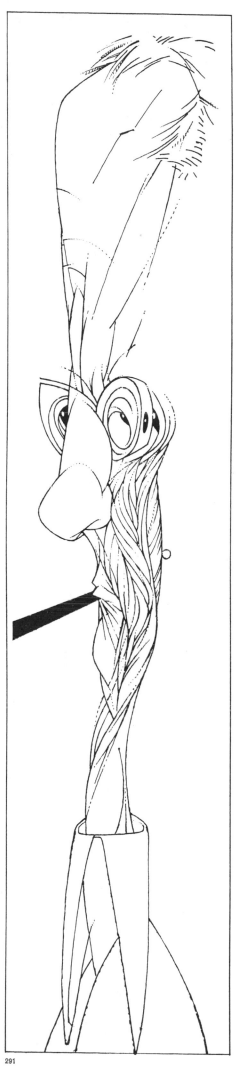

291

292

293

294

295

ARTIST / KÜNSTLER / ARTISTE:

292–299 Eugene Mihaesco

DESIGNER / GESTALTER:

292, 293 Irene Ramp
294, 295 Dietmar Meyer/
Ekkhart Blunck
296–299 Tom Bentkovsky

ART DIRECTOR:

292, 293, 296–299 Rudolph Hoglund
294, 295 Heidi Neugebauer

PUBLISHER / VERLEGER / EDITEUR:

292, 293, 296–299 Time, Inc.
294, 295 Gruner & Jahr AG & Co.

Magazine Illustrations
Zeitschriften-Illustrationen
Illustrations de périodiques

292, 293 Full-colour illustrations from *Time* magazine for a report about arms control and the US "defensive umbrella" policy. (USA)
294, 295 Polychrome illustrations for the German *View* magazine about the problems for the individual in any close personal relationship. (GER)
296–299 Illustrations in black and white to accompany a cover story in *Time* magazine concerning the life and writings of the *Nineteen Eighty-Four* author George Orwell, relating to the countries he lived in (England, France, Spain). (USA)

292, 293 Mehrfarbige Illustrationen aus dem Magazin *Time* für einen Bericht über Rüstungskontrolle und die «defensive Regenschirmpolitik» der USA. (USA)
294, 295 Farbillustrationen für die deutsche Zeitschrift *View*, mit einem Beitrag über Probleme des Einzelnen in engen menschlichen Beziehungen. (GER)
296–299 Schwarzweiss-Illustrationen zu einer Titelgeschichte in der Zeitschrift *Time* über Leben und Werk des Autors des Buches *1984*, George Orwell, die sich auf die Länder beziehen, in denen er gelebt hat (England, Frankreich, Spanien). (USA)

292, 293 Illustrations polychromes pour un article du magazine *Time* sur le contrôle des armements et le «parapluie défensif» des Américains. (USA)
294, 295 Illustrations en couleur pour le magazine allemand *View*: les problèmes de l'individu au sein d'une relation interpersonnelle étroite. (GER)
296–299 Illustrations en noir et blanc pour l'article en couverture d'un numéro du magazine *Time* consacré à la vie et à l'œuvre de l'auteur du *1984*, George Orwell, se référant aux pays où il a vécu (Angleterre, France, Espagne). (USA)

296

297

298

299

127

300

301

300–302 Complete pages as examples from the various full-colour introductory pages for the food section in the *Minneapolis Star and Tribune*. Fig. 300: Building in blue tones, vegetables in green and orange, costumes and lemon in yellow; Fig. 301: blue picture in polychrome frame; Fig. 302 shows the traditional loaf of bread and cookies left out on Christmas Eve as a snack for Santa Claus in gratitude for filling the childrens' stockings with presents. (USA)

300–302 Beispiele verschiedener, mehrfarbiger Titelseiten für den Essens-Sektor des *Minneapolis Star and Tribune* zu den Themen «Super-Nahrung», «Die Kost des Hmong-Volkes» und «Weihnachtsbäckerei», wobei der in Abb. 302 gezeigte Brotlaib und die Plätzchen nach alter Tradition für den Weihnachtsmann bereit gestellt sind, der seinerseits die Strümpfe mit Geschenken füllt. Abb. 300 ist eine Montage mit alten Stichen. (USA)

300–302 Exemples de pages de titres polychromes pour la section alimentation du *Minneapolis Star and Tribune*. Les sujets: «Super-alimentation», «L'alimentation du peuple Hmong», «Biscuits de Noël». La fig. 300 constitue un montage de vieilles estampes. Dans la fig. 302, la miche de pain et les gâteaux secs traditionnels ont été préparés pour le Père Noël qui, à son tour, remplira les bas de cadeaux. (USA)

ARTIST/KÜNSTLER/ARTISTE:

300, 301 Nancy Entwistle
302 Bruce Bjerva

PUBLISHER/VERLEGER/EDITEUR:

300–302 Minneapolis Star and Tribune

Newspaper Illustrations
Zeitungs-Illustrationen
Illustrations de journaux

303

304

305

ARTIST / KÜNSTLER / ARTISTE:
303–306 Guy Billout

DESIGNER / GESTALTER / MAQUETTISTE:
303–306 Judy Garlan

ART DIRECTOR / DIRECTEUR ARTISTIQUE:
303–306 Judy Garlan

PUBLISHER / VERLEGER / EDITEUR:
303–306 The Atlantic Monthly

303–306 Visual puns in the illustrations by artist Guy Billout, for a regular feature in the magazine *The Atlantic Monthly*. The artist has total freedom for the design of this page. The titles are, respectively: Drought; Seasons; Afternoon and Persistence. (USA)

303–306 «Visuelle Wortspiele» des Künstlers Guy Billout, der in der Gestaltung dieser regelmässig in der Zeitschrift *The Atlantic Monthly* erscheinenden Seite völlig freie Hand hat. Die Titel sind «Dürre», «Jahreszeiten», «Nachmittag» und «Fortdauer». (USA)

303–306 «Jeux de mots visuels» de l'artiste Guy Billout, qui a reçu carte blanche pour réaliser cette page périodique dans le magazine *The Atlantic Monthly*. Les titres: «Sécheresse»; «Saisons»; «Après-midi»; «Persistance». (USA)

306

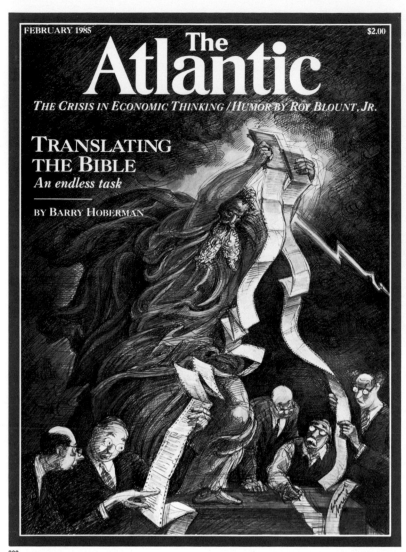

308

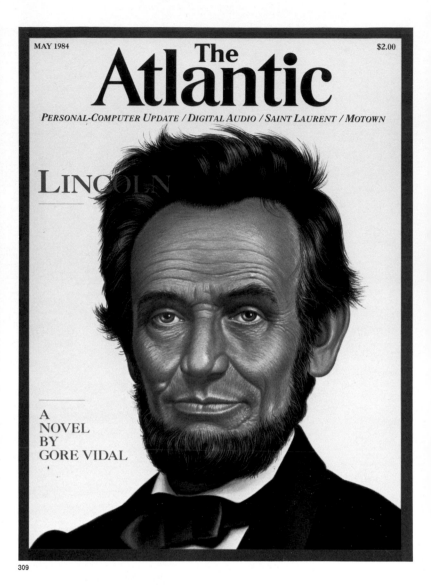

309

307

Magazine Illustrations
Zeitschriften-Illustrationen
Illustrations de périodiques

307 Illustration of Sarah Bernhardt and Thomas Edison for a regular feature appearing in *The Atlantic Monthly* magazine entitled "First Encounters". (USA)
308 Complete cover of *The Atlantic Monthly* in sombre tones; frame purple and white, text and title in white. (USA)
309–312 Cover and three double spreads illustrating an excerpt from Gore Vidal's novel *Lincoln,* appearing in *The Atlantic Monthly*. Cover with dark grey and red frame, black and red text; spreads with black-and-white clothing and dark red-brown masonry. (USA)

307 Illustration für eine regelmässig unter dem Titel «Erste Begegnungen» in *The Atlantic Monthly* erscheinende Seite, hier Sarah Bernhardt und Thomas A. Edison. (USA)
308 Umschlag in dunklen Frabtönen für eine Ausgabe von *The Atlantic Monthly*, die einen Beitrag über die Übersetzung der Bibel enthält. (USA)
309–312 Umschlag einer Ausgabe der Zeitschrift *The Atlantic Monthly* und drei mehrfarbige Doppelseiten daraus, die einen Auszug aus einem Buch über Abraham Lincoln illustrieren. (USA)

307 Illustration pour une page périodique de l'*Atlantic Monthly* intitulée «Premières Rencontres», ici celle entre Sarah Bernhardt et Thomas A. Edison. (USA)
308 Couvertures aux tons sombres pour un numéro de l'*Atlantic Monthly* contenant un article sur les traductions de la Bible. (USA)
309–312 Couverture et trois doubles pages polychromes d'un numéro de l'*Atlantic Monthly* illustrant l'extrait d'un ouvrage consacré à Abraham Lincoln. (USA)

310

ARTIST / KÜNSTLER / ARTISTE:

307, 308 Edward Sorel
309 312 Eraldo Carugati

DESIGNER / GESTALTER / MAQUETTISTE:

307–312 Judy Garlan

ART DIRECTOR / DIRECTEUR ARTISTIQUE:

307–312 Judy Garlan

PUBLISHER / VERLEGER / EDITEUR:

307 312 The Atlantic Monthly

311

312

313

Magazine Illustrations
Zeitschriften-Illustrationen
Illustrations de périodiques

314   315

ARTIST / KÜNSTLER / ARTISTE:

313 André François
314, 315 Tom Lulevitch
316 Brad Holland

DESIGNER / GESTALTER / MAQUETTISTE:

313–316 Judy Garlan

ART DIRECTOR / DIRECTEUR ARTISTIQUE:

313–316 Judy Garlan

PUBLISHER / VERLEGER / EDITEUR:

313–316 The Atlantic Monthly

313 "Eclipse"; double-spread illustration for a short story in *The Atlantic Monthly*. (USA)
314, 315 Illustrations in blue, red, green and yellow for an article in *The Atlantic Monthly* which recounts the life of the scientist Sheldon Glashow. (USA)
316 Illustration for a short story entitled "The Small Things that Save Us" in *The Atlantic Monthly*. A breed of very small cows is one of the "small things" in the story. (USA)

313 «Eklipse»; doppelseitige Illustration für eine Kurzgeschichte in *The Atlantic Monthly*. (USA)
314, 315 Illustrationen in Blau, Rot, Grün und Gelb für einen Beitrag in *The Atlantic Monthly*, in dem über das Leben des Wissenschaftlers Sheldon Glashow berichtet wird. (USA)
316 Illustration für eine Kurzgeschichte mit dem Titel «Die kleinen Dinge, die uns retten», in *The Atlantic Monthly*. In der Geschichte geht es unter anderem um Kühe. (USA)

313 «Eclipse»: illustration sur deux pages pour un récit paru dans l'*Atlantic Monthly*. (USA)
314, 315 Illustrations bleu, rouge, vert et jaune pour un article de l'*Atlantic Monthly* où il est question de la vie du chercheur Sheldon Glashow. (USA)
316 Illustration d'une nouvelle intitulée «Les Petites Choses qui nous sauvent», publiée dans l'*Atlantic Monthly*. Il y est entre autres question de vaches. (USA)

316

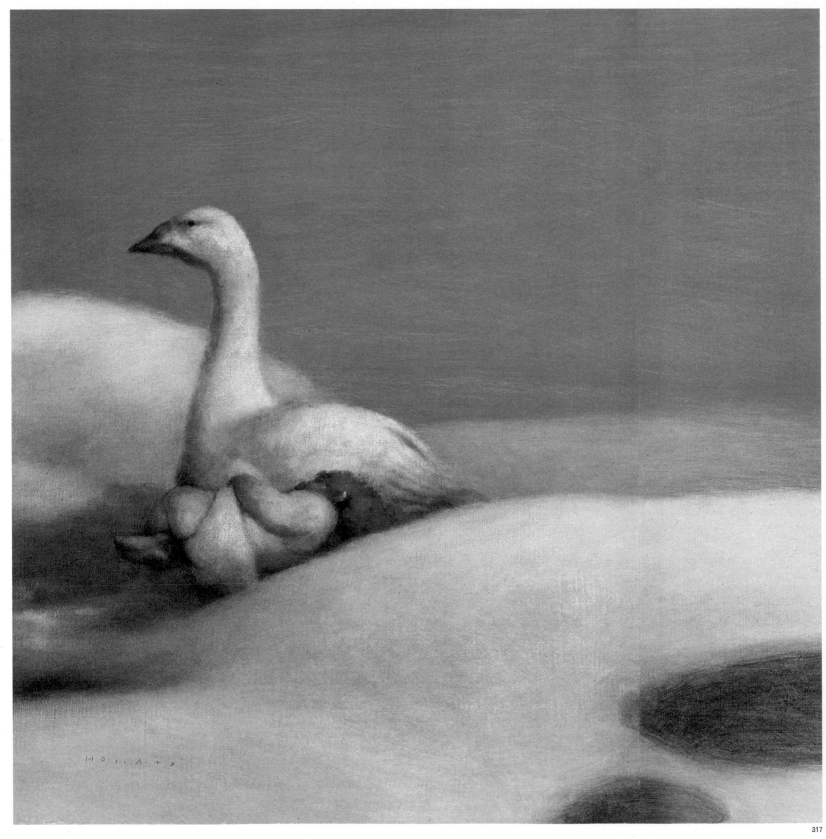

317

319

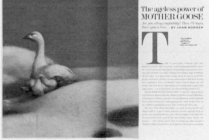

318

ARTIST / KÜNSTLER / ARTISTE:

317–319 Brad Holland

ART DIRECTOR:

317, 318 Art Niemi
319 Barbara Solowan/
Bernadette Gillen

PUBLISHER / VERLEGER / ÉDITEUR:

317–319 Comac Communications

317, 318 Illustration and the double spread shown complete from an article about the book of nursery rhymes *Mother Goose's Melodies* (published 1833), in *Quest* magazine. (CAN)
319 Picture entitled "In a Room" used as illustration for an article about childbirth with the title "Pregnant Thoughts" published in the magazine *City Woman*. (USA)

317, 318 Illustration und vollständige Doppelseite für einen Beitrag in der Zeitschrift *Quest* über *Mother Goose* (Mutter Gans), einen Klassiker der englischsprachigen Kinderliteratur. (CAN)
319 Als Illustration für einen Artikel über die Geburt («Gedanken einer Schwangeren») verwendetes Bild mit dem Titel «In einem Raum», erschienen in *City Woman*. (USA)

317, 318 Illustration et double page complète d'un article du magazine *Quest* consacré au classique de la littérature enfantine anglaise, *Mother Goose* (La mère l'oie). (CAN)
319 Peinture intitulée «Dans une chambre», utilisée pour l'illustration d'un article de *City Woman* au sujet de l'accouchement («Pensées de grossesse»). (USA)

320

321

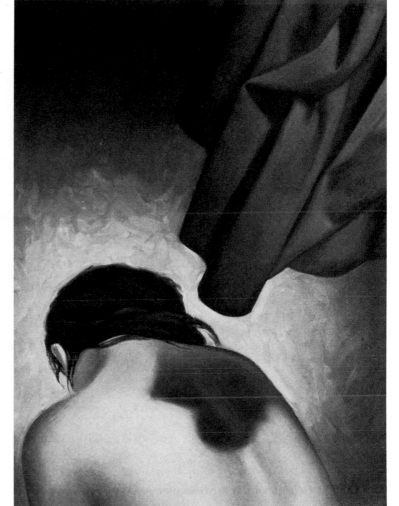

322

Magazine Illustrations
Zeitschriften-Illustrationen
Illustrations de périodiques

ARTIST / KÜNSTLER / ARTISTE:

320, 323 Brad Holland
321 Jeffrey Smith
322 Victoria Faust

DESIGNER / GESTALTER / MAQUETTISTE:

322 Judy Garlan

ART DIRECTOR / DIRECTEUR ARTISTIQUE:

330 Louise Kollenbaum
321 Doug May
322 Judy Garlan
323 Tony Iannotta Petrella

AGENCY / AGENTUR / AGENCE – STUDIO:

321 Cuisine Magazine

PUBLISHER / VERLEGER / EDITEUR:

320 Mother Jones
321 CBS Inc.
322 The Atlantic Monthly
323 Working Woman

320 "Equatorial Zone." The theme of this full-page illustration (also used as poster) is the Americans as policemen of the world; published in the magazine *Mother Jones*. (USA)
321 Full-colour illustration from the magazine *Cuisine* for an article on roasting one's own coffee. (USA)
322 Illustration for a short story entitled "Saint Marie" in *The Atlantic Monthly* magazine. (USA)
323 Illustration in soft brown tones (picture in lilac tones with red) for *Working Woman*. (USA)

320 «Die Amerikaner als Polizei der Welt» ist das Thema dieser ganzseitigen Illustration (die auch als Plakat verwendet wurde) für die Zeitschrift *Mother Jones*. (USA)
321 «Röste Deinen Kaffee selbst.» Mehrfarbige Illustration aus der Zeitschrift *Cuisine*. (USA)
322 Illustration für eine Kurzgeschichte mit dem Titel «Heilige Maria», in *The Atlantic Monthly*. (USA)
323 Illustration in sanften Brauntönen (Bild in Blautönen mit Rot) für das Magazin *Working Woman*. (USA)

320 «Les Américains policiers du monde entier», tel est le sujet de cette illustration pleine page (utilisée aussi comme affiche) pour le magazine *Mother Jones*. (USA)
321 «Torréfiez votre café vous-même.» Illustration polychrome pour le magazine *Cuisine*. (USA)
322 Pour une nouvelle intitulée «Sainte Marie», reproduite dans *The Atlantic Monthly*. (USA)
323 Illustration aux teintes brunes délicates pour le magazine *Working Woman*. Tableau bleu, rouge. (USA)

323

327

328

ARTIST / KÜNSTLER / ARTISTE:

327–329 Wilson McLean
330 Jeffrey Dever
331 Ray-Mel Cornelius
332 Steven Guarnaccia

DESIGNER / GESTALTER / MAQUETTISTE:

327–329 Kerig Pope
330 Jeffrey Dever

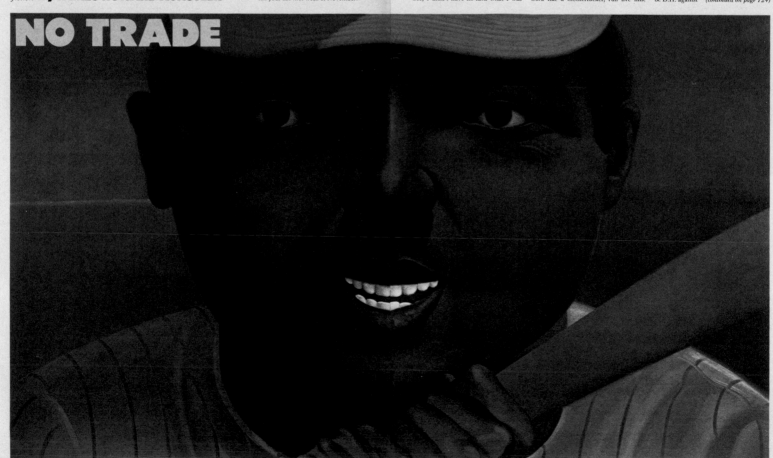

the owner of this outfit, he be the biggest asshole in baseball. i be coming off a good year and he wants to ship me to texas—but i ain't going nowheres

fiction **By JAMES HOWARD KUNSTLER**

NO TRADE

I HAVE WENT through some changes in life. Vietnam put me in the hospital, but the American League pennant race almost park me six foot under. My road roomy, Kid, say, "Roland, why you don't just forget the man, play out your option and sell your ass first week of November?"

See, I didn't have no idea what I was

Kid, he remind me of my own self when I come up: quick and brash and dumb as a box of rocks. Where I would go, anyway? Thirty-eight-year-old with a bad attitude. Troublemaker, too. "Cleveland," Kid say. Bum-fuck Egypt be more like it.

in for when I show up in St. Pete last spring. I be coming off a year anybody be glad to have: .279 with 24 home run and 90 R.B.I.s, 108 run score. Lead the league in walk. Not bad. *Sport Magazine* Comeback of the Year! Off season, I work like a motherfucker, run five mile

every day, pump Nautilus, eat like a damn parakeet. My ex, Rayette, she say I look like one of them Nubian in the gladiator flick. Thirty-eight-year-old. Hot stuff. Not bad. I show up at camp, ain't even hardly unpack at the Ramada Inn when I hear I be D.H. against *(continued on page 124)*

ILLUSTRATION BY WILSON MC LEAN

329

(continued on page 124)

330

331

ART DIRECTOR / DIRECTEUR ARTISTIQUE:

327–329 Tom Staebler
330 Jeffrey Dever/Harry Knox
331 Joseph P. Connolly
332 Will Hopkins

AGENCY / AGENTUR / AGENCE – STUDIO:

330 Harry Knox & Assoc.

PUBLISHER / VERLEGER / EDITEUR:

327–329 Playboy Enterprises, Inc.
330 Liberty Magazine
331 Boys' Life Magazine
332 American Health

327, 328 Illustration folded to page format and complete illustration folded out for a story in *Playboy* by *Godfather* author Mario Puzo, entitled "The Sicilian". Mainly green and brown, with red. (USA)
329 Double spread for a story about baseball, in *Playboy*. Illustration in green and blue tones, face dark brown. (USA)
330 Full-page illustration for a story in *Liberty*. (USA)
331 Double spread from *Boys' Life*. Blue and green on red. (USA)
332 Illustration for an article in *American Health*, on the dangers of food colouring for children. (USA)

327, 328 Auf das Format einer Seite zusammengefaltete und vollständige Illustration für eine Geschichte in *Playboy* mit dem Titel «Der Sizilianer». Grün- und Brauntöne, rote Tomaten. (USA)
329 Doppelseite für eine Geschichte über Baseball in *Playboy*. Illustration in Grün- und Blautönen, Gesicht dunkelbraun. (USA)
330 Ganzseitige Illustration für eine Geschichte in *Liberty*. (USA)
331 Doppelseite aus *Boys' Life* mit einem Beitrag über Roboter. Vorwiegend Blau- und Grüntöne, Hintergrund in warmem Rot. (USA)
332 Illustration für einen Beitrag in *American Health*, über die Gefährlichkeit von Lebensmittelfarbstoffen für Kinder. (USA)

327, 328 Illustration pliée au format d'une page, également montrée dépliée. Elle accompagne un récit publié dans *Playboy* et intitulé «Le Sicilien». Verts et bruns, tomates rouges. (USA)
329 Double page d'un récit de *Playboy* axé sur le base-ball. Illustration en divers bleus et verts, visage brun foncé. (USA)
330 Illustration sur page entière pour le périodique *Liberty*. (USA)
331 Double page de *Boys' Life*, pour un article consacré aux robots. Tons verts et bleus prédominants sur fond rouge chaud. (USA)
332 Pour un article dans l'*American Health*, traitant du danger que représente les colorants alimentaires pour les enfants. (USA)

332

ARTIST / KÜNSTLER / ARTISTE:

333, 334 Anita Kunz
335, 336 Michael Foreman
337 Mark Hess

DESIGNER / GESTALTER / MAQUETTISTE:

333 Mary Opper
334 Ursula Kaiser
335, 336 Jerry Alten

ART DIRECTOR / DIRECTEUR ARTISTIQUE:

333 Arthur Niemi
334 Ursula Kaiser
335, 336 Jerry Alten
337 Margery Peters

PUBLISHER / VERLEGER / EDITEUR:

333 Comac Communications
334 Madame au Foyer
335, 336 Triangle Publications, Inc.
337 Fortune Magazine

Magazine Illustrations
Zeitschriften-Illustrationen
Illustrations de périodiques

333

334

335

336

337

333 Illustration for an article in *Quest* about poetry written on sports—and the lack of such poetry today. (CAN)
334 Illustration for an article about artificial insemination published in the magazine *Madame au Foyer*. (CAN)
335, 336 Illustration and one complete page from the *TV Guide*. Fig. 335 concerns a TV cultural channel (ARTS) and Fig. 336 refers to the way the US image is presented to West European television viewers. (USA)
337 "Living in the shadow of industry." Illustration for an article in the business magazine *Fortune*. In green tones, with blue sky. (USA)

333 Illustration für einen Beitrag in *Quest*, in dem es um Gedichte über Bereiche des Sports geht. (CAN)
334 Illustration für einen Artikel über künstliche Befruchtung, erschienen in der Zeitschrift *Madame au Foyer*. (CAN)
335, 336 Detail einer Seite und vollständige Seite aus *TV Guide*. In Abb. 335 geht es um einen kulturell orientierten Fernsehsender, in Abb. 336 um das Bild des Amerikaners im westeuropäischen Fernsehen. (USA)
337 «Im Schatten der Industrie leben.» Illustration für einen Artikel in dem Wirtschaftsmagazin *Fortune*, in Grüntönen, mit blauem Himmel. (USA)

333 Illustration d'un article de *Quest* qui fait le tour des créations poétiques sur le sujet du sport. (CAN)
334 Illustration pour un article que le magazine *Madame au Foyer* consacre aux problèmes de l'insémination artificielle. (CAN)
335, 336 Détail d'une page et page complète de *TV Guide*. La fig. 335 se rapporte à une chaîne TV aux ambitions culturelles, la fig. 336 à l'image des Américains à travers les programmes TV ouest-européens. (USA)
337 «Vivre à l'ombre de l'industrie.» Illustration d'un article du magazine économique *Fortune*. Divers tons verts, ciel bleu. (USA)

338

ARTIST/KÜNSTLER/ARTISTE:

338 Frank Hammond
339, 340 Tullio Pericoli
341 Paola Piglia
342, 343 Blair Drawson

338 "The Art of the Conductor." Illustration in the *Radio Guide*. (CAN)
339, 340 Complete double spread and illustration for an article in *L'Espresso* dealing with the writing of diaries. (ITA)
341 Illustration in actual size for a comments page on money in *Life* magazine. (USA)
342 Full-page illustration in full colour for an article in *Saturday Night*. The subject is a family empire built on whisky. (CAN)
343 Full-page colour illustration for *Quest* relating to an ex-patriot's return. (CAN)

338 Für einen Artikel über die Kunst des Dirigierens, in *Radio Guide*. (CAN)
339, 340 Vollständige Doppelseite und Illustration für einen Beitrag in *L'Espresso*, der sich mit dem Schreiben von Tagebüchern befasst. (ITA)
341 Illustration in Originalgrösse für Kommentare über Geld, im Magazin *Life*. (USA)
342 Ganzseitige, mehrfarbige Illustration für einen Beitrag in *Saturday Night*. Das Thema ist ein auf Whisky aufgebautes Familienimperium. (CAN)
343 Für einen Beitrag in *Quest*, in dem es um Emigration und Rückkehr geht. (CAN)

338 Pour un article de *Radio Guide* sur l'art du chef d'orchestre. (CAN)
339, 340 Double page complète et illustration qui y figure. L'article en question, paru dans *L'Espresso*, traite des journaux intimes. (ITA)
341 Illustration du magazine *Life* (format original) sur le sujet de l'argent. (USA)
342 Illustration polychrome sur page entière pour un article de *Saturday Night*. On y présente une famille qui a construit un empire sur le commerce du whisky. (CAN)
343 Pour un article de *Quest* sur l'émigration et le retour au pays. (CAN)

339

340

341

DESIGNER / GESTALTER / MAQUETTISTE:

338 B. J. Galbraith
341 Nora Sheehan
342 Joel Cuyler
343 Mary Opper

ART DIRECTOR / DIRECTEUR ARTISTIQUE:

338 B. J. Galbraith
341 Bob Ciano
342 Louis Fishauf
343 Arthur Niemi

PUBLISHER / VERLEGER / EDITEUR:

338, 342 Saturday Night Publishing
339, 340 L'Espresso
341 Time, Inc.
343 Comac Communications

342

343

BEST & WORST

Here it is again: our annual exercise in sheer effrontery. Some of you are going to get mad. Some of you are going to write angry letters. Worst of all, some of you are going to telephone and demand to speak to The Jerk Who Wrote Best and Worst.

The truth is, there is no such Jerk. The judgments expressed here are hammered out in a series of committees that make the Bloody Assizes look like a New England town meeting. In the end, a tyrannous majority prevails, and proclaims the beatification or perdition of a baked potato or a public figure.

Sure, we're hiding behind the anonymity of an institution. But our decisions are, as Ned Sherrin says on "We Interrupt This Week," arbitrary, prejudiced, and final.

So don't call us. It's the Other Guy who impugned your favorite politician's honor, assaulted your favorite restaurant, lampooned your favorite law firm. But don't get us wrong. We welcome your thoughts; we value your opinions. Honest. To prove it, we've provided a coupon on page 83. Whereby you can retaliate with your own Best and Worsts. Those with merit may find their way into print in these pages.

344

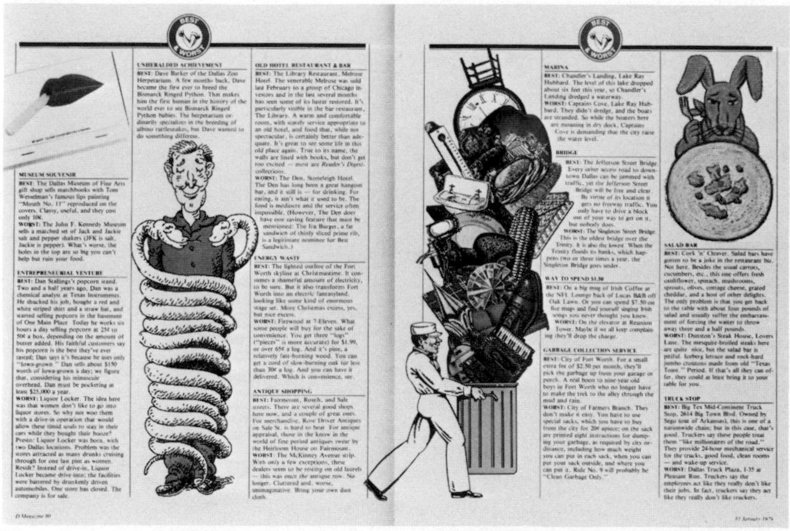

MUSEUM SOUVENIR

BEST: The Dallas Museum of Fine Arts gift shop sells matchbooks with Tom Wesselman's famous lips painting "Mouth No. 11" reproduced on the covers. Classy, useful, and they cost only 10¢.
WORST: The John F. Kennedy Museum sells a matched set of Jack and Jackie salt and pepper shakers (JFK is salt, Jackie is pepper). What's worse, the holes in the top are so big you can't help but ruin your food.

ENTREPRENEURIAL VENTURE

BEST: Dan Stallings's popcorn stand. Two and a half years ago, Dan was a chemical analyst at Texas Instruments. He shucked his job, bought a red and white striped shirt and a straw hat, and started selling popcorn in the basement of One Main Place. Today he works six hours a day selling popcorn at 25¢ to 50¢ a box, depending on the amount of butter added. His faithful customers say his popcorn is the best they've ever tasted; Dan says it's because he uses only "Iowa-grown." Dan sells about $150 worth of Iowa-grown a day; we figure that, considering his minuscule overhead, Dan must be pocketing at least $25,000 a year.
WORST: Liquor Locker. The idea here was that women don't like to go into liquor stores. So why not woo them with a drive-in operation that would allow these timid souls to stay in their cars while they bought their booze? Presto: Liquor Locker was born, with two Dallas locations. Problem was the stores attracted as many drunks cruising through for one last pint as women. Result? Instead of drive-in, Liquor Locker became drive-into; the facilities were battered by drunkenly driven automobiles. One store has closed. The company is for sale.

UNHERALDED ACHIEVEMENT

BEST: Dave Barker of the Dallas Zoo Herpetarium. A few months back, Dave became the first ever to breed the Bismarck Ringed Python. That makes him the first human in the history of the world ever to see Bismarck Ringed Python babies. The herpetarium ordinarily specializes in the breeding of albino rattlesnakes, but Dave wanted to do something different.

OLD HOTEL RESTAURANT & BAR

BEST: The Library Restaurant, Melrose Hotel. The venerable Melrose was sold last February to a group of Chicago investors and in the last several months has seen some of its luster restored. It's particularly visible in the bar-restaurant, The Library. A warm and comfortable room, with stately service appropriate to an old hotel, and food that, while not spectacular, is certainly better than adequate. It's great to see some life in this old place again. True to its name, the walls are lined with books, but don't get too excited — most are *Reader's Digest* collections.
WORST: The Den, Stoneleigh Hotel. The Den has long been a great hangout bar, and it still is — for drinking. For eating, it ain't what it used to be. The food is mediocre and the service often impossible. (However, The Den does have one saving feature that must be mentioned: The Ira Burger, a fat sandwich of thinly sliced prime rib, is a legitimate nominee for Best Sandwich.)

ENERGY WASTE

BEST: The lighted outline of the Fort Worth skyline at Christmastime. It consumes a shameful amount of electricity, to be sure. But it also transforms Fort Worth into an electric fantasyland, looking like some kind of enormous stage set. More Christmas excess, yes, but nice excess.
WORST: Firewood at 7-Eleven. What some people will buy for the sake of convenience. You get three "logs" ("pieces" is more accurate) for $1.99, or over 65¢ a log. And it's pine, a relatively fast-burning wood. You can get a cord of slow-burning oak for less than 30¢ a log. And you can have it delivered. Which is convenience, see.

ANTIQUE SHOPPING

BEST: Fairmount, Routh, and Sale streets. There are several good shops here now, and a couple of great ones. For merchandise, Rose Driver Antiques on Sale St. is hard to beat. For antique appraisal, those in the know in the world of fine period antiques swear by the Heirloom House on Fairmount.
WORST: The McKinney Avenue strip. With only a few exceptions, these dealers seem to be resting on old laurels — this was once *the* antique row. No longer. Cluttered and, worse, unimaginative. Bring your own dust cloth.

MARINA

BEST: Chandler's Landing, Lake Ray Hubbard. The level of this lake dropped about six feet this year, so Chandler's Landing dredged a waterway.
WORST: Captains Cove, Lake Ray Hubbard. They didn't dredge, and the boats are stranded. So while the boaters here are moaning in dry dock, Captains Cove is demanding that the city raise the water level.

BRIDGE

BEST: The Jefferson Street Bridge. Every other access road to downtown Dallas can be jammed with traffic, yet the Jefferson Street Bridge will be free and clear. By virtue of its location it gets no freeway traffic. You only have to drive a block out of your way to get on it, but nobody does.
WORST: The Singleton Street Bridge. This is the oldest bridge over the Trinity. It is also the lowest. When the Trinity floods its banks, which happens two or three times a year, the Singleton Bridge goes under.

WAY TO SPEND $1.50

BEST: On a big mug of Irish Coffee at the NFL Lounge back of Lucas B&B off Oak Lawn. Or you can spend $7.50 on five mugs and find yourself singing Irish songs you never thought you knew.
WORST: On the elevator at Reunion Tower. Maybe if we all keep complaining they'll drop the charge.

GARBAGE COLLECTION SERVICE

BEST: City of Fort Worth. For a small extra fee of $2.50 per month, they'll pick the garbage up from your garage or porch. A real boon to nine-year-old boys in Fort Worth who no longer have to make the trek to the alley through the mud and rain.
WORST: City of Farmers Branch. They don't make it easy. You have to use special sacks, which you have to buy from the city for 20¢ apiece; on the sack are printed eight instructions for dumping your garbage, as required by city ordinance, including how much weight you can put in each sack, when you can put your sack outside, and where you can put it. Rule No. 9 will probably be "Clean Garbage Only."

SALAD BAR

BEST: Cork 'n' Cleaver. Salad bars have gotten to be a joke in the restaurant biz. Not here. Besides the usual carrots, cucumbers, etc., this one offers fresh cauliflower, spinach, mushrooms, sprouts, olives, cottage cheese, grated cheddar, and a host of other delights. The only problem is that you get back to the table with about four pounds of salad and usually suffer the embarrassment of forcing the waiter to throw away three and a half pounds.
WORST: Dunston's Steak House, Lovers Lane. The mesquite-broiled steaks here are quite nice, but the salad bar is pitiful. Iceberg lettuce and rock-hard jumbo croutons made from old "Texas Toast." Period. If that's all they can offer, they could at least bring it to your table for you.

TRUCK STOP

BEST: Big Tex Mid-Continent Truck Stop, 2614 Big Town Blvd. Owned by Sego (out of Arkansas), this is one of a nationwide chain; but in this case, that's good. Truckers say these people treat them "like millionaires of the road." They provide 24-hour mechanical service for the trucks, good food, clean rooms — and wake-up service.
WORST: Dallas Truck Plaza, I-35 at Pleasant Run. Truckers say the employees act like they really don't like their jobs. In fact, truckers say they act like they really don't like truckers.

345

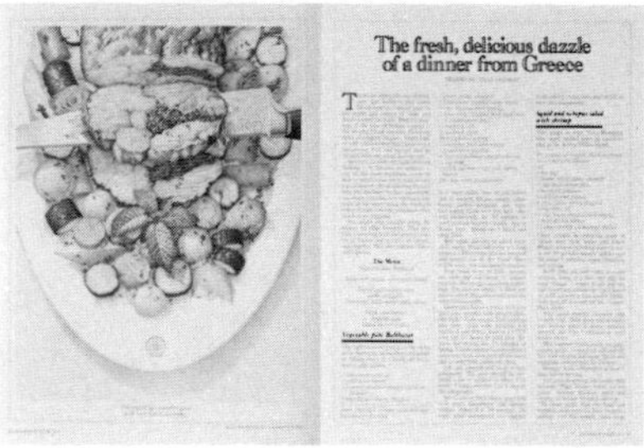

The fresh, delicious dazzle of a dinner from Greece

346

347

Magazine Illustrations
Zeitschriften-Illustrationen
Illustrations de périodiques

348

ARTIST / KÜNSTLER / ARTISTE:

344, 345 Jerry Jeanmard
346, 347 James Tughan
348 Carolyn Gowdy
349, 350 Hisashi Saito

DESIGNER / GESTALTER / MAQUETTISTE:

344, 345 Woody Pirtle/Carol Burke
346, 347 James Tughan
348 Frank Jagarelli
349, 350 Kyoji Nakatani

ART DIRECTOR / DIRECTEUR ARTISTIQUE:

344, 345 Woody Pirtle
346, 347 Gillian Tsintzras
348 Frank Jagarelli
349, 350 Kyoji Nakatani

AGENCY / AGENTUR / AGENCE – STUDIO:

344, 345 Pirtle Design
349, 350 Kyoji Nakatani Design Office

PUBLISHER / VERLEGER / EDITEUR:

344, 345 Wick Allison
346, 347 Good Life Magazine
348 Knapp Communications Corp.
349, 350 Kodansha Ltd.

349

350

344, 345 Title page and double spread from an article in a magazine listing the best and the worst in various categories: zoological achievement, garbage collection and salad bars, among others. (USA)
346, 347 Complete page and illustration of a Greek dish of roast lamb and vegetables from *Good Life*. (CAN)
348 For an article in *Geo*. Scientists believe that caterpillars and other herbivores need to eat more CO_2-enriched plants, thereby endangering the world's vegetation. (USA)
349, 350 Full-colour double spreads with table of contents for a Japanese publication with recipes. (JPN)

344, 345 Seite und Doppelseite aus einem Artikel in einem Konsumentenmagazin, in dem das Beste und das Schlechteste aus verschiedenen Sparten (zoologische Erfolge, Müllabfuhr, Salat-Buffets) gegenübergestellt wird. (USA)
346, 347 Vollständige Seite und Illustration eines griechischen Gerichts aus der Zeitschrift *Good Life*. (CAN)
348 Illustration für einen Artikel in der amerikanischen Ausgabe von *Geo*: Insekten fressen die Vegetation der Erde auf, eine Möglichkeit, die auf den steigenden Kohlendioxydgehalt der Luft zurückgeführt wird. (USA)
349, 350 Doppelseiten mit Inhaltsverzeichnissen für eine japanische Publikation mit Kochrezepten. (JPN)

344, 345 Première et double pages d'un article paru dans un magazine de consommateurs: on y présente le meilleur et le pire dans diverses branches (performances zoologiques, ramassage des ordures, bars à salades). (USA)
346, 347 Page complète et illustration d'un plat grec (gigot d'agneau) pour le magazine *Good Life*. (CAN)
348 Pour un article de *Geo*: les insectes dévorant la végétation terrestre – un scénario rendu possible par la teneur accrue de CO_2 dans l'atmosphère. (USA)
349, 350 Doubles pages d'une publication culinaire japonaise: tables des matières. En polychromie. (JPN)

351

351 Black-and-white illustration for an article in the magazine *Saturday Night*. (CAN)
352, 353 Linocuts for Nikolai Gogol's *Taras Bulba and Other Tales*. Black and white. (USA)
354, 355 Linocuts from the magazine *The Progressive*. Fig. 354 refers to the non-separation of church and state and free speech; Fig. 355 to the censorship of school newspapers. (USA)
356 Collage of various linocuts on coloured paper as illustration for an article entitled "Are you an egomaniac?" appearing in the magazine *Success*. (USA)
357 Linocut for *The Progressive*; the US government's invasion of citizens' privacy. (USA)

351 Schwarzweiss-Illustration für einen Beitrag in der Zeitschrift *Saturday Night*. (CAN)
352, 353 Linolschnitte für Nikolaj Gogols *Taras Bulba und andere Geschichten*. Schwarzweiss. (USA)
354, 355 Linolschnitte aus der Zeitschrift *The Progressive*. In Abb. 354 geht es um Kirche, Staat und freie Meinungsäusserung, in Abb. 355 um die Zensur von Schülerzeitungen. (USA)
356 Collage aus verschiedenen Linolschnitten auf farbigem Papier als Illustration für einen Artikel mit dem Titel «Sind Sie Egozentriker?», erschienen in der Zeitschrift *Success*. (USA)
357 Linolschnitt für *The Progressive*: Die Verletzung der Privatsphäre durch die US-Regierung. (USA)

351 Illustration noir-blanc pour un article publié dans *Saturday Night*. (CAN)
352, 353 Linogravures pour la *Taras Boulba* de Nicolaï Gogol, en noir et blanc. (USA)
354, 355 Linogravures pour le magazine *The Progressive*. Fig. 354: les Eglises, l'Etat et la libre expression des opinions individuelles; fig. 355: la censure des revues estudiantines. (USA)
356 Collage de diverses linogravures sur papier couleur illustrant un article du magazine *Success* intitulé «Etes-vous un égocentrique forcené?» (USA)
357 Linogravure pour *The Progressive*: le gouvernement violant l'intimité des citoyens. (USA)

352

353

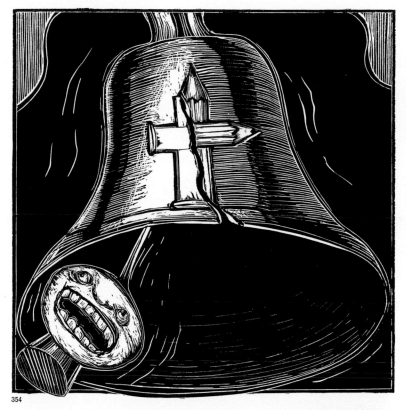

354

355

356

357

ART DIRECTOR / DIRECTEUR ARTISTIQUE:

351 Louis Fishauf
352, 353 Michael Mendelsohn
354, 355, 357 Patrick Flynn
356 Peggy Robertson

ARTIST / KÜNSTLER / ARTISTE:

351 Barbara Klunder
352–355 Frances Jetter
356, 357 Randall Enos

DESIGNER / GESTALTER / MAQUETTISTE:

351 Joel Cuyler

PUBLISHER / VERLEGER / EDITEUR:

351 Saturday Night Publishing
352, 353 The Franklin Library
354, 355, 357 The Progressive
356 Success Magazine

358

Magazine Illustrations
Zeitschriften-Illustrationen
Illustrations de périodiques

ARTIST / KÜNSTLER / ARTISTE:

358, 359 Ralph Giguere
360 David Street
361 Marshall Arisman

DESIGNER / GESTALTER / MAQUETTISTE:

358, 359 Judy Garlan
360 Paula Jaworski

ART DIRECTOR / DIRECTEUR ARTISTIQUE:

358, 359 Judy Garlan
360 Paula Jaworski
361 Richard Bleiweiss

PUBLISHER / VERLEGER / EDITEUR:

358, 359 The Atlantic Monthly
360 Baltimore Magazine
361 Penthouse International Ltd.

359

360

358, 359 Black-and-white illustration for a short story in *The Atlantic Monthly* and complete page. (USA)
360 Polychrome illustration in the *Baltimore Magazine* for an article entitled "Darling but Deadly" on the danger of the rabid raccoons which raid the garbage in Baltimore. (USA)
361 Illustration in actual size for a report in *Penthouse* on ruthless murderers who kill for no apparent motive. (USA)

358, 359 Schwarzweiss-Illustration für eine Kurzgeschichte in *The Atlantic Monthly* und vollständige Seite. (USA)
360 Mehrfarbige Illustration in *Baltimore Magazine* für einen Beitrag über die Gefahr tollwütiger Waschbären. (USA)
361 Illustration in Originalgrösse zu einem Bericht im Magazin *Penthouse* über Mörder, die kein Motiv für ihre Tat haben, und die ein völlig unauffälliges Leben führen. (USA)

358, 359 Illustration en noir et blanc pour un récit paru dans *l'Atlantic Monthly*, et page où elle figure. (USA)
360 Illustration polychrome du *Baltimore Magazine* pour un article sur les ratons laveurs, victimes de la rage. (USA)
361 Illustration au format original pour une étude, parue dans le magazine *Penthouse*, des assassins que rien ne signale à l'attention et qui frappent au hasard. (USA)

361

362

ARTIST / KÜNSTLER / ARTISTE:

362 Fred Otnes
363, 364 Alice Brickner

DESIGNER / GESTALTER / MAQUETTISTE:

363, 364 Elizabeth Van Itallie

ART DIRECTOR / DIRECTEUR ARTISTIQUE:

362 Richard Bleiweiss
363, 364 Ron Albrecht

PUBLISHER / VERLEGER / EDITEUR:

362 Penthouse International Ltd.
363, 364 Condé Nast Publication

Magazine Illustrations

362 Illustration for a report in *Penthouse* entitled "The Barbie Whitewash" concerning the US cover-up of its thirty-year involvement with the Nazi war criminal Klaus Barbie. (USA)
363, 364 Illustration in actual size and complete double spread from the magazine *Self* entitled "Anxiety Aches" dealing with the physical reactions caused by emotional stress. (USA)

362 Illustration für einen Bericht im Magazin *Penthouse*, der von langjährigen amerikanischen Vertuschungstaktiken im Falle des Nazikriegsverbrechers Klaus Barbie handelt. (USA)
363, 364 Illustration in Originalgrösse und vollständige Doppelseite aus dem Magazin *Self* über Körperreaktionen, die durch Emotionen und Stress hormonell ausgelöst werden. (USA)

362 Illustration pour un article du magazine *Penthouse* sur les manœuvres dilatoires qui, en Amérique, ont réussi à masquer longtemps les agissements du criminel de guerre Klaus Barbie. (USA)
363, 364 Illustration au format original et page double complète du magazine *Self* au sujet des réactions induites par les émotions et le stress frappant le système endocrinien. (USA)

363

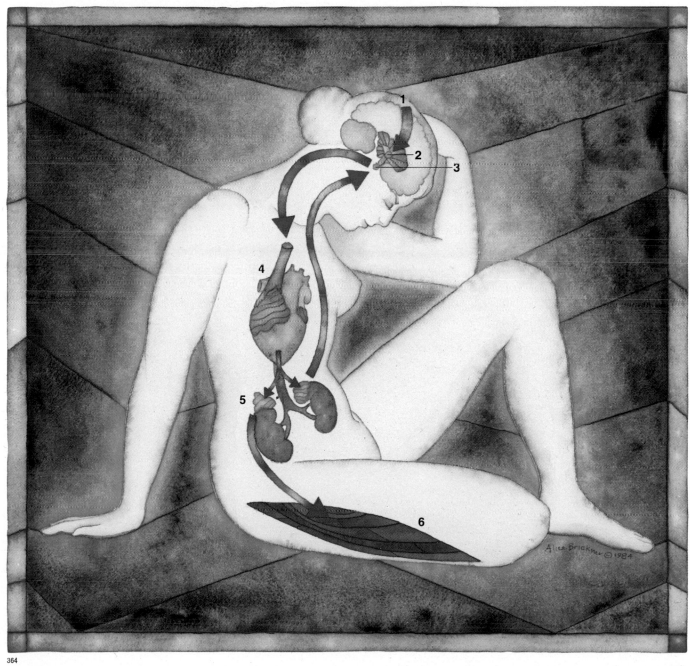

364

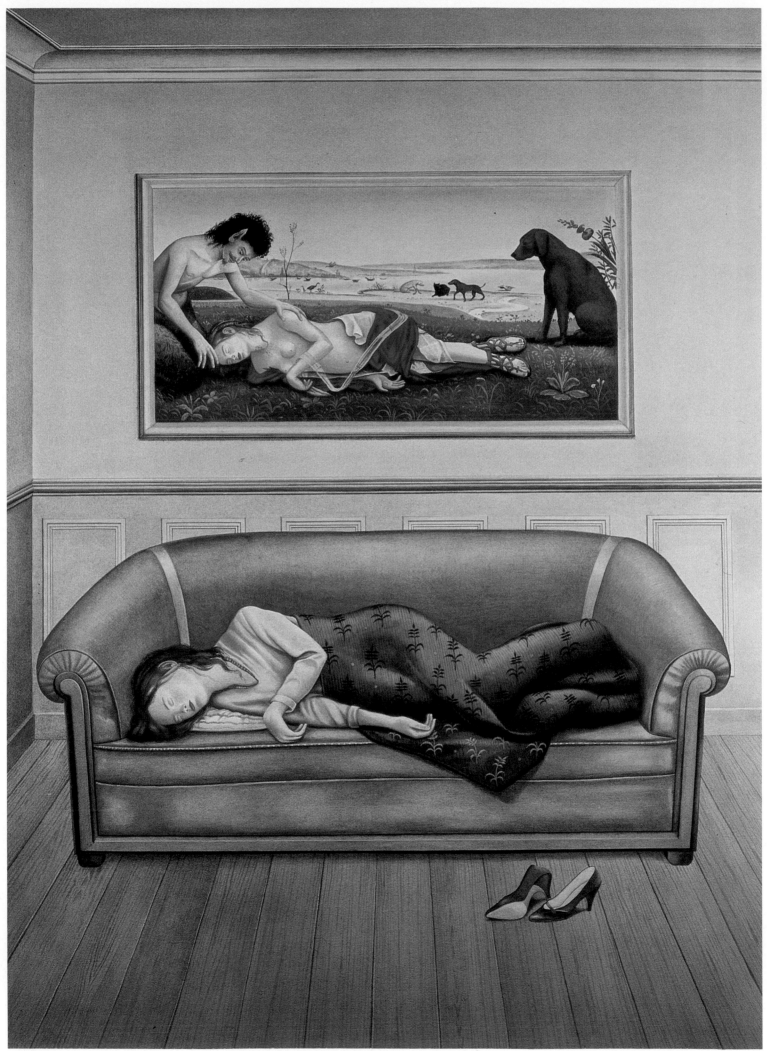

ARTIST / KÜNSTLER / ARTISTE:

365 Wasyl Bagdaschwili
366 Tullio Pericoli
367 Randall Enos
368 Dagmar Frinta

DESIGNER / GESTALTER:

365 Wasyl Bagdaschwili
368 Hans Teesma

ART DIRECTOR:

365 Manfred Neussl
367 Elliott Negin
368 Hans Teesma

PUBLISHER / VERLEGER / EDITEUR:

365 Burda Verlag
366 L'Espresso
367 Public Citizen Magazine
368 New England Magazine

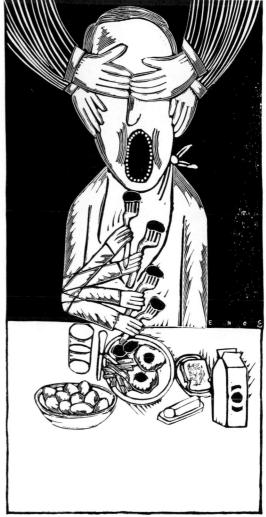

367

366

Magazine Illustrations
Zeitschriften-Illustrationen
Illustrations de périodiques

368

365 Illustration for a short story entitled "A Mythical Theme", in the magazine *Freundin*. (GER)
366 Illustration in brown and beige tones, with red tongues and yellow beaks, to accompany an article in *L'Espresso* concerning the continuous talking on television. (ITA)
367 Black-and-white linocut illustrating an article dealing with the government's lack of information given to the consumer on food, dietary programmes etc. (USA)
368 Illustration in muted tones for a feature in the monthly magazine *New England*. (USA)

365 Illustration für eine Kurzgeschichte mit dem Titel «Ein mythologisches Thema», in der Zeitschrift *Freundin*. (GER)
366 Illustration in Braun- und Beigetönen, mit roten Zungen und gelben Schnäbeln für einen Artikel in *L'Espresso*, der vom fast pausenlosen Sprechen am Fernsehen handelt. (ITA)
367 Schwarzweiss-Linolschnitt für einen Artikel, der die zurückhaltende Politik in der Inhaltsdeklaration von Nahrungsmitteln und Medikamenten zum Thema hat. (USA)
368 Illustration in gedämpften Farben für einen Artikel im Monatsmagazin *New England*. (USA)

365 Illustration d'un récit publié dans le magazine *Freundin* sous le titre de «Un Thème mythologique». (GER)
366 Illustration aux tons brun et beige (langues rouges, becs jaunes) pour un article de *L'Espresso* critiquant les «téléraseurs» emplissant de leurs bavardages l'étrange lucarne. (ITA)
367 Linogravure en noir et blanc pour un article stigmatisant la politique consistant à ne pas livrer toute l'information requise sur les produits alimentaires et les médicaments. (USA)
368 Illustration aux tons adoucis pour un article publié dans le magazine mensuel *New England*. (USA)

369

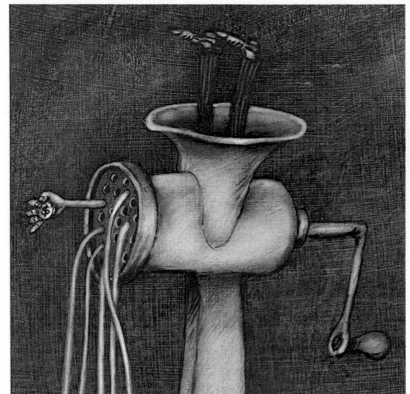

370

371

372

ARTIST / KÜNSTLER / ARTISTE:

369 Jean Tuttle
370 Jerzy Kolacz
371 Bob Hambly
372 Steven Guarnaccia
373 Marshall Arisman

DESIGNER / GESTALTER / MAQUETTISTE:

369 Joel Cuyler
370, 371 Mary Opper

ART DIRECTOR / DIRECTEUR ARTISTIQUE:

369 Louis Fishauf
370, 371 Arthur Niemi
372 Bill Butt
373 Richard Bleiweiss

PUBLISHER / VERLEGER / EDITEUR:

369 Saturday Night Publishing
370, 371 Comac Communications
372 Médecine et Enfance
373 Penthouse International Ltd.

373

369 Black-and-white illustration (with grey) for an article in *Saturday Night* about possible long-term damaging effects on athletes who take steroids. (CAN)
370 Illustration in *Quest* for an article in which the author describes his experience with the Inland Revenue auditors in Canada. (CAN)
371 Black-and-white chessboard and coloured pawns symbolize the divorced parents (each with two children) who form a new union, in this feature on a stepfamily in the *Quest* magazine (CAN)
372 Full-colour illustration for an article in the magazine *Médecine et Enfance*, entitled "The Myth of a Jewish Mother". (FRA)
373 Illustration for a report in *Penthouse* about a small-time dealer who became a financial manipulator involved in narcotics deals. (USA)

369 Schwarzweiss-Illustration (mit Grau) für einen Artikel in *Saturday Night* über mögliche Langzeit-schäden bei Athleten, die künstlich hergestellte männ-liche Hormone einnehmen. «Starke Medizin.» (CAN)
370 Illustration in *Quest* über Erfahrungen des Autors mit den staatlichen Steuerprüfern. (CAN)
371 Illustration mit Schachbrettfussboden in der Zeit-schrift *Quest*. Die Figuren symbolisieren geschiedene Eltern, deren Kinder und ihre Konstellation gegenüber dem neuen Ehepartner und dessen Kindern. (CAN)
372 Mehrfarbige Illustration für einen Artikel in der Zeitschrift *Médecine et Enfance*. (FRA)
373 Illustration für einen *Penthouse-Bericht* über einen ehemaligen Strichjungen, der im internationalen Drogenhandel eine zentrale Rolle spielte. (USA)

369 Illustration noir-blanc (avec du gris) pour un article de *Saturday Night* qui pose le problème des fortes doses d'androgènes synthétiques données aux athlètes et de leurs effets à long terme. (CAN)
370 Illustration de *Quest*: les effets des contrôles fiscaux subis par l'auteur. (CAN)
371 Illustration au sol en damier, pour le magazine *Quest*. Les figurines symbolisent les parents divorcés, leurs enfants et leur situation face aux nouveaux parte-naires et à leurs enfants. (CAN)
372 Illustration polychrome d'un article paru dans *Médecine et Enfance*. (FRA)
373 Illustration du magazine *Penthouse*. Elle repré-sente un ancien garçon de passe devenu une vedette du trafic international de la drogue. (USA)

Magazine Illustrations
Zeitschriften-Illustrationen
Illustrations de périodiques

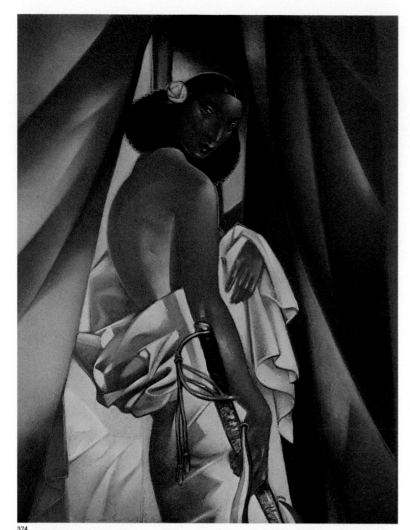

374

374 Full-page illustration in *Texas Monthly* entitled "The Yellow Rose of Texas". (USA)
375 Full-page polychrome illustration in the *North Western Mutual Life* magazine on creating the entrepreneurial spirit within the corporation. (USA)
376 "Blacks and Jews: How wide the rift?" is the title of the article to which this full-page illustration belongs. In black-and-white with soft-toned background. (USA)
377 Illustration in almost actual size to a report in *Texas Monthly*. (USA)

374 Ganzseitige Illustration in *Texas Monthly*. Titel: «Gelbe Rose von Texas.» (USA)
375 Illustration im Magazin *North Western Mutual Life* für einen Artikel über die Förderung des unternehmerischen Geistes innerhalb einer Firma. (USA)
376 Ganzseitige Illustration über die Diskriminierung von Schwarzen und Juden und deren Verhältnis untereinander. Schwarzweiss, mit Hintergrund in zarten Farben. (USA)
377 Illustration (ungefähr Originalgrösse) zu einem Beitrag in *Texas Monthly*. (USA)

374 Illustration pleine page pour le *Texas Monthly*: «Rose jaune du Texas.» (USA)
375 Illustration du magazine *North Western Mutual Life* accompagnant un article sur le développement de l'esprit d'entreprise parmi les salariés. (USA)
376 Illustration pleine page interprétant la discrimination dont sont victimes les Juifs et les Noirs, et leurs relations mutuelles. Noir-blanc sur fond de couleurs douces. (USA)
377 Illustration approximativement au format original pour le *Texas Monthly*. (USA)

375

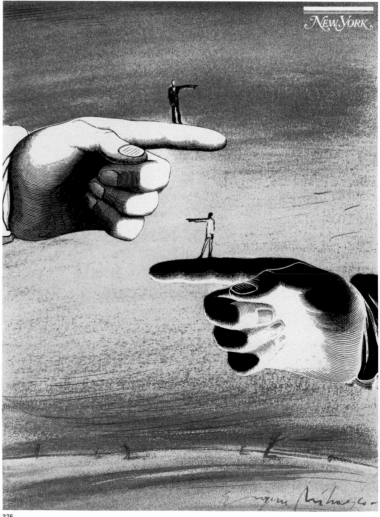

376

JIMMY DEAN

378

ARTIST / KÜNSTLER / ARTISTE:

378 Sidney Fischer
379 Alexa Grace
380–382 Peter Sis
383 Jerzy Kolacz
384 Jorge Zurroza
385 Wayne Anderson

DESIGNER / GESTALTER / MAQUETTISTE:

378 Rita Baker
379 Drew Hodges/Terry Koppel
380, 381 Judy Garlan
384 Félix Beltrán
385 Dale Pollekoff

ART DIRECTOR / DIRECTEUR ARTISTIQUE:

378 David Miller
379 Terry Koppel
380, 381 Judy Garlan
382 Cynthia Friedman
383 Ursula Kaiser
384 Félix Beltrán
385 Dale Pollekoff

AGENCY / AGENTUR / AGENCE – STUDIO:

379 Mantel, Koppel & Scher
383 Reactor Art & Design

PUBLISHER / VERLEGER / EDITEUR:

378 The Denver Post
379 Vision Magazine
380, 381 The Atlantic Monthly
382 Diversions Magazine
383 Comac Communications
384 Punto S.A.
385 Time-Life, Inc.

379

378 Illustration in actual size from the *Denver Post* magazine entitled "New weapons in the health war". (USA)
379 For an article in *Vision* about stress. In full colour. (USA)
380, 381 Portrait of the US poet Allan Ginsberg for a book review, and illustration from a feature on Stephen Sondheim and his musical, entitled *Company*, in *The Atlantic Monthly*. (USA)
382 "Life's Great Questions." From *Diversions* magazine. (USA)
383 "Everything for the Criminal" (e.g., defence counsel at the taxpayers' expense). From *Homemaker's Magazine*. (CAN)
384 For a feature on the artist Pedro Coronel. (MEX)
385 From a "Dragon Guide" in *Time-Life*. Green tones. (USA)

378 Illustration in Originalgrösse aus dem Magazin der *Denver Post*: «Neue Waffen im Krieg für die Gesundheit.» (USA)
379 Für einen Beitrag über «Stress» in *Vision*. In Farbe. (USA)
380, 381 Porträt Allan Ginsbergs für eine Buchbesprechung und Illustration aus einem Beitrag über Stephen Sondheim und dessen Musical *Company* (Gesellschaft) in *The Atlantic Monthly*. (USA)
382 «Die grossen Fragen des Lebens.» Aus *Diversions*. (USA)
383 «Alles für den Verbrecher.» Aus *Homemaker's Magazine*. (CAN)
384 Für einen Artikel über den Künstler Pedro Coronel. (MEX)
385 Aus einem «Drachen-Führer» von *Time-Life*. Grüntöne. (USA)

378 Illustration grandeur nature pour le magazine du *Denver Post*: «De nouvelles armes de guerre pour la santé.» (USA)
379 Pour un article sur le stress dans *Vision*. Polychromie. (USA)
380, 381 Portrait d'Allan Ginsberg pour un compte rendu de livre, et illustration d'un article consacré à Stephen Sondheim et à sa Musical *Company*, dans l'*Atlantic Monthly*. (USA)
382 «Les grandes questions de la vie», dans *Diversions*. (USA)
383 «Tout pour le criminel» (par exemple, un défenseur aux frais de l'Etat). Dans *Homemaker's Magazine*. (CAN)
384 Pour un article sur l'artiste Pedro Coronel. (MEX)
385 «Guide des dragons» de *Time-Life*. Tons verts. (USA)

380

381

382

VILLAIN TAKES ALL

The offender has all the professionals looking after him — at taxpayers' expense. What about the victim?
By Jerry Amernic

Most people, at some time in their lives, are victims of crime. Relatively few are victims of violent crime, but for those affected — the victims, if they survive, and their families — nothing will ever be the same again. To

383

384

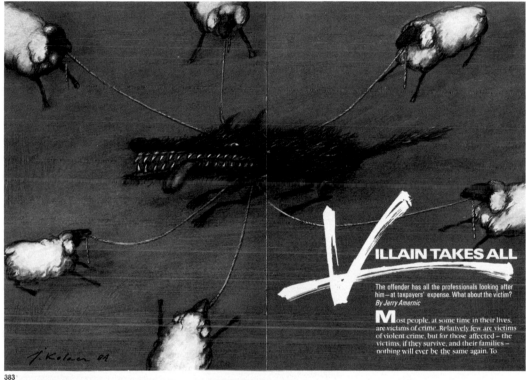

A FIELD GUIDE TO DRAGONS

Few human beings cared to discover more about dragons than how to avoid them or — failing that — kill them. Yet humankind was always curious, and dragons became a subject for scholars. Studying them was a daunting task, for the nature of dragons was confusing. The creatures seemed to defy sensible cataloguing, as though each dragon were a separate species.

Some were in fact unique. For example, hundred-headed Typhon, with his earthquake-tread, was a monstrous rebuke to the idea that nature had organization. But later, lesser dragons were somewhat more consistent in behavior and appearance, and there arose schemes for classifying them. In the West, dragons were described by body type (*overleaf*) and defined by habitat (*pages 34-37*). In China, however, they were classified according to their purposes and functions (*pages 38-39*).

385

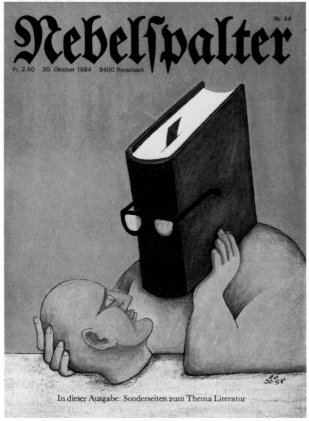

386

387

389

390

386–392 Covers for the satirical weekly magazine *Nebelspalter*. Fig. 386: for an issue with special pages devoted to literature—skin-coloured head, green-bound book on grey body, bright yellow background; Fig. 387: a comment on the topic of photography, in water-colours; Fig. 388: punk dressed in black, with green hair, on a green lawn; Fig. 389: for a March issue—a girl with yellow hair, blue flowers and red dress, on a green background; Fig. 390: at the start of the Olympics, a green Statue of Liberty with red flaming torch; Fig. 391: the first Swiss lady to become a Federal Councillor—Elisabeth Kopp—pictured in soft brown shades, with dress, shoes and saw in blue; Fig. 392: "Like son, like father"—a parody on the proverb. (SWI)

386–392 Umschläge für die humoristisch-satirische Wochenzeitschrift *Nebelspalter*. Abb. 386: für eine Ausgabe mit Sonderseiten zum Thema Literatur – hautfarbener Kopf, grün eingebundenes Buch auf grauem Körper vor leuchtend gelbem Hintergrund; Abb. 387: ein Kommentar zum Thema Photographie – in Aquarellfarben; Abb. 388: schwarz gekleideter Punk mit grünem Haar auf grünem Rasen; Abb. 389: für die März-Ausgabe – Mädchen mit gelbem Haar, blauen Blumen, rotem Kleid, vor grünem Hintergrund; Abb. 390: zum Beginn der Olympiade – grüne Freiheitsstatue mit feuerroter Fackel; Abb. 391: die erste Schweizer Bundesrätin Elisabeth Kopp – in sanften Brauntönen, Kleid, Schuhe und Säge in Blau; Abb. 392: «Wie der Sohn, so der Vater». (SWI)

388

391

ARTIST / KÜNSTLER / ARTISTE:

386, 390 Jürg Spahr
387 Fernando Puig Rosado
388, 389, 392 Wolf Barth
391 Fredy Sigg

ART DIRECTOR / DIRECTEUR ARTISTIQUE:

386, 391, 392 Werner Meier
387–390 Franz Mächler

PUBLISHER / VERLEGER / EDITEUR:

386–392 Nebelspalter-Verlag

386–392 Couvertures de l'hebdomadaire satirique *Nebelspalter*. Fig. 386: pour un numéro comportant des pages littéraires spéciales – tête chair, reliure verte sur corps gris, fond jaune lumineux; fig. 387: commentaire sur la photographie, teintes d'aquarelle; fig. 388: punk vêtu de noir, aux cheveux verts, sur un gazon vert; fig. 389. pour le numéro de mars: jeune fille aux cheveux paille, fleurs bleues, robe rouge, sur fond vert; fig. 390: au début des Jeux Olympiques de Los Angeles: statue de la Liberté verte, torche rouge feu; fig. 391: la première conseillère fédérale (ministre) suisse Elisabeth Kopp: teintes brunes adoucies prédominants, robe, chaussures et scie en bleu; fig. 392: «Tel fils, tel père» – une parodie du proverbe. (SWI)

392

July 2, 1984   THE NEW YORKER   Price $1.50

393

Magazine Covers/Zeitschriftenumschläge
Couvertures de périodiques

ARTIST/KÜNSTLER/ARTISTE:

393 R.O.Blechman
394, 396 Jean-Jacques Sempé
395 André François

ART DIRECTOR/DIRECTEUR ARTISTIQUE:

393–396 Lee Lorenz

PUBLISHER/VERLEGER/EDITEUR:

393–396 The New Yorker

393–396 Covers for the magazine *The New Yorker*. Fig. 393 commemorates the US national holiday on July 4th; cover-drawing by Blechman; © 1984 The New Yorker Magazine, Inc.; Fig. 394: a cartoon for Valentine's Day with the knave of hearts and the chess queen, in colour; cover-drawing by Sempé; © 1983 The New Yorker Magazine, Inc.; Fig. 395: in muted green and blue tones; cover-drawing by André François; © 1983 The New Yorker Magazine, Inc.; Fig. 396: a racing cyclist "at the pits"; cover-drawing by Sempé; © 1983 The New Yorker Magazine, Inc. (USA)

393–396 Umschläge für die Zeitschrift *The New Yorker*. Abb. 393: zum Nationalfeiertag der USA am 4. Juli; Abb. 394: ein Kommentar zum Valentinstag mit «Herzbube» und «Schachdame», in Farbe; Abb. 395: in sanften Grün- und Blautönen; Abb. 396: ein Radrennfahrer «an den Boxern». (USA)

393–396 Couvertures du magazine *The New Yorker*. La fig. 393 se réfère à la fête nationale des Etats-Unis le 4e juillet; fig. 394: commentaire de la Saint-Valentin, avec «valet de cœur» et «dame» d'un jeu d'échecs, en couleur; fig. 395: divers bleus et verts adoucis; fig. 396: un cycliste au «poste de ravitaillement». (USA)

394

395

396

397

398

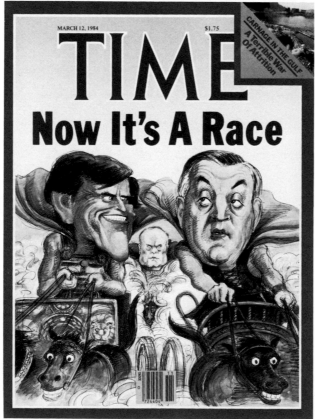

399

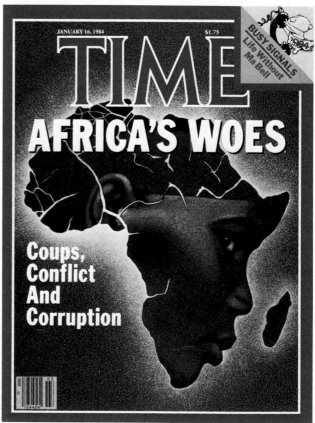

400

397–400 Full-colour covers for the weekly magazine *Time*. Fig. 397 portrays Jackson, one of the democratic candidates for the presidency; Fig. 398: the democratic mascot "kicks off" for the political game in San Francisco; Fig. 399: democrat Gary Hart's sudden appearance made things tougher for candidate Walter Mondale in the presidential primaries; Fig. 400: the cover story in this issue is devoted to Africa's struggles. (USA)
401, 402 Polychrome covers of the *Victorian Arts Center Magazine*. (AUS)
403 Cover of the *TV Guide* on the topic of the American presidential election. Brown and white eagle, blue and white star banner, red text. (USA)
404 Cover of the magazine *Classical Music*, in restrained brown tones with light blue and light green. The corresponding article deals with programmes which offer something for everybody. (GBR)

397–400 Mehrfarbige Umschläge für das Wochenmagazin *Time*. Abb. 397 zeigt Jackson, einen der demokratischen Bewerber um die Präsidentschaftskandidatur: «Schwarzer Stolz, weisse Belange»; Abb. 398: «Ausschlagen der Demokraten – Krieg oder Frieden in San Francisco?»; Abb. 399: «Jetzt ist es ein Wettrennen» (das Auftauchen Gary Harts als Mitbewerber Mondales um die Präsidentschaftskandidatur); Abb. 400: «Afrikas Leid». (USA)
401, 402 Mehrfarbige Umschläge des *Victorian Arts Center Magazine*. (AUS)
403 Umschlag für *TV Guide* zum Thema der amerikanischen Präsidentschaftswahl. Braun-weisser Adler, blau-weisses Sternenbanner, rote Schrift. (USA)
404 Umschlag der Zeitschrift *Classical Music*, in sanften Brauntönen mit Hellblau und Hellgrün. In dem dazugehörigen Artikel geht es um Programme, die für jeden etwas bieten. (GBR)

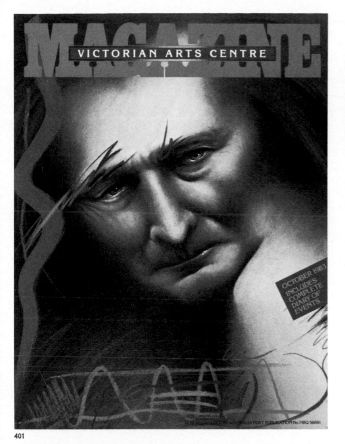

401

ARTIST / KÜNSTLER / ARTISTE:

397, 398 Mark Hess
399 Edward Sorel
400 Alex Gnidziejko
401 Lena Gan
402 Faye Plamka
403 Braldt Bralds
404 Carolyn Gowdy

DESIGNER / GESTALTER / MAQUETTISTE:

401, 402 Ken Cato
403 Jerry Alten
404 Joanne Barber

ART DIRECTOR / DIRECTEUR ARTISTIQUE:

397–400 Rudolph Hoglund
401, 402 Ken Cato
403 Jerry Alten
404 Joanne Barber

AGENCY / AGENTUR / AGENCE – STUDIO:

401, 402 Ken Cato Design Co Pty Ltd

PUBLISHER / VERLEGER / EDITEUR:

397–400 Time, Inc.
401, 402 Victorian Arts Centre
403 Triangle Publications, Inc.
404 Classical Music Magazine

403

402

404

397–400 Couvertures polychromes pour le magazine hebdomadaire *Time*. La fig. 397 montre Jackson, un des candidats démocrates potentiels à la présidence des Etats-Unis: «fierté noire, problèmes blancs»; fig. 398: «Ruade des Démocrates – la guerre ou la paix à San Francisco?»; fig. 399: «Et maintenant la course» (entre Gary Hart et Walter Mondale, candidats démocrates potentiels à la présidence); fig. 400: «Détresse de l'Afrique». (USA)
401, 402 Couvertures polychromes du *Victorian Arts Center Magazine*. (AUS)
403 Couverture de *TV Guide* sur le thème des présidentielles américaines. Aigle brun blanc, bannière étoilée bleu blanc, texte en rouge. (USA)
404 Couverture du magazine *Classical Music*; divers bruns adoucis, avec du bleu clair et du vert clair. L'article en question traite de programmes où chacun trouve son compte. (GBR)

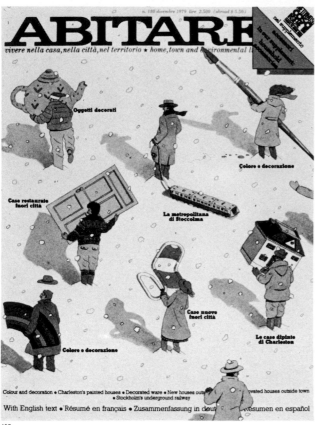

405

406

407

408

ARTIST / KÜNSTLER / ARTISTE:

405 Steven Guarnaccia
406 Gerd Huss/Monika Zucht
407 Wendy Wortsman
408 Adolf Born
409, 410 Michael Mathias Prechtl

DESIGNER / GESTALTER:

406, 409, 410 Rainer Wörtmann
407 B.J. Galbraith

Magazine Covers
Zeitschriftenumschläge
Couvertures de périodiques

405 Full-colour cover for the magazine *Abitare* (Living). (ITA)
406 Cover for *Der Spiegel*. "The Woman at 40." Black, white, blue and red. (GER)
407 Cover for *Saturday Night* about the reforms in Ottawa's public service. (CAN)
408 Cover in pale green shades with blue and red for *A Propos*, a Bulgarian publication for humour and satire. (BUL)
409, 410 Complete cover and illustration from *Der Spiegel*—"Doubting Freud". The water-colour illustration is entitled "Cupid & Psyche examine Freud". (GER)

405 Mehrfarbiger Umschlag für die Zeitschrift *Abitare* (Wohnen). (ITA)
406 Umschlag für den *Spiegel*. In Schwarzweiss, Blau und Rot. (GER)
407 *Saturday-Night*-Umschlag über die Regierungsausgaben für Ottawa. (CAN)
408 Umschlag in hellen Grüntönen mit Blau und Rot für *A Propos*, eine bulgarische Publikation für Humor und Satire. (BUL)
409, 410 Vollständiger Umschlag und Illustration für den *Spiegel*. Das Aquarell trägt den Titel «Amor & Psyche untersuchen Freud». (GER)

405 Couverture polychrome pour le magazine *Abitare* (L'Habitat). (ITA)
406 Couverture du *Spiegel*. Noir et blanc, bleu et rouge. (GER)
407 Pour *Saturday Night*: Les dépenses du Gouvernement pour Ottawa. (CAN)
408 Couverture aux tons vert clair, avec du bleu et du rouge, pour *A Propos*, publication satirique bulgare. (BUL)
409, 410 Couverture complète et illustration pour *Der Spiegel*. L'aquarelle est intitulée «Eros & Psyché en examinant Freud». (GER)

ART DIRECTOR / DIRECTEUR ARTISTIQUE:

405 Italo Lupi
406, 409, 410 Rainer Wörtmann
407 B. J. Galbraith
408 Georgi Dimitrov Chaoushov

PUBLISHER / VERLEGER / EDITEUR:

405 Abitare
406, 409, 410 Spiegel-Verlag
407 Saturday Night Publishing
408 Apropos

409

410

JUNE/JULY/AUGUST 1984

QUEST

CANADA'S URBAN MAGAZINE

TRUDEAU AND THE WAY WE WERE
OLYMPIC MARATHON MEMORIES • NEW STOCK EXCHANGE
GAMES • WINNIPEG'S DANGEROUS WAR ON MOSQUITOES

411

$5

AMERICA'S GRAPHIC DESIGN MAGAZINE
MAY-JUNE 1984
PRINT XXXVIII:III

Print

412

gap
ITALIA

gruppo anteprima
per le
selezioni moda

gennaio 1983

81

lire 3000

MENSILE/ SPED. ABB. POST. GR. III/70

STILISTI UOMO PITTI UOMO
PITTI CASUAL MAGLIERIA

413

TRANS ✕ ATLANTIK

Februar 2/1984   Acht Mark   B 5183 E

Dieter Kampe zum Thema »Legaler Betrug«

... aus der Luft

Bernd Dost über Krebs ...

... Sportreporter

... Macondo

... Robert Wilson

... Kibbuzniks

... unsere Russen

Frank Chr. Nicolaus pariert: »Nichts gegen die Endzeit«

414

ARTIST / KÜNSTLER / ARTISTE:

411 Anita Kunz
412 Matt Mahurin
413 Werner
414 Dieter Wiesmüller
415, 416 Ri Kaiser

DESIGNER / GESTALTER / MAQUETTISTE:

411 Mary Opper
412 Matt Mahurin
414 Klaus Meyer
415, 416 Ri Kaiser

ART DIRECTOR / DIRECTEUR ARTISTIQUE:

411 Arthur Niemi
412 Andrew Kner
413 Werner
414 Rainer Wörtmann
415, 416 Wolfgang Behnken

PUBLISHER / VERLEGER / EDITEUR:

411 Comac Communications
412 RC Publications
413 Publimedia
414 NewMag Verlag
415, 416 Gruner & Jahr AG & Co.

411 Cover of an issue of *Quest* with a feature on Pierre Trudeau's last days as Prime Minister. In predominantly green tones. (CAN)
412 Cover of *Print*, a magazine for graphic design. (USA)
413 Collage (ink, fabric, paper) for *Gap*, a fashion magazine for men. (ITA)
414 Cover of an issue of *TransAtlantik*. Bluish-grey knight's armour, brown umbrella, brown bag, background merging from yellow to grey. (GER)
415, 416 Illustration and complete unpublished cover of the magazine *Stern*, with Rubens' three graces wearing the "aerobic look". (GER)

411 Umschlag einer Ausgabe von *Quest* mit einem Artikel über Trudeaus letzte Tage als kanadischer Premierminister. Vorwiegend in Grüntönen. (CAN)
412 Umschlag für *Print*, eine Fachzeitschrift für Graphik-Design. (USA)
413 Collage (Tusche, Stoff, Papier) für *Gap*, eine Mode-zeitschrift für Männer. (ITA)
414 Umschlag für eine Ausgabe von *TransAtlantik*. Bläuliche Ritterrüstung, brauner Schirm und braune Tasche, Hintergrund von Gelb in Grau verlaufend. (GER)
415, 416 Illustration und vollständiger, unveröffentlichter Umschlag des Magazins *Stern*, mit den drei Grazien von Rubens im «Aerobic-Look». (GER)

411 Couverture d'un numéro de *Quest* contenant un rapport sur les derniers jours du règne de P. E. Trudeau au Canada. Tons verts prédominants. (CAN)
412 Couverture de *Print*, revue spécialisée dans le design graphique. (USA)
413 Collage (encre de Chine, tissu, papier) pour *Gap*, une revue de mode masculine. (ITA)
414 Couverture d'un numéro de *TransAtlantik*. Cuirasse bleuâtre, parapluie brun, sac brun, sur fond dégradé de jaune en gris. (GER)
415, 416 Illustration et couverture inédite complète du magazine *Stern*. On y voit les trois Grâces de Rubens en tenue aérobic. (GER)

415

416

Magazine Covers
Zeitschriftenumschläge
Couvertures de périodiques

418

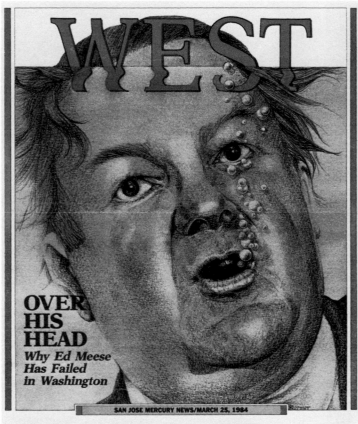

419

420

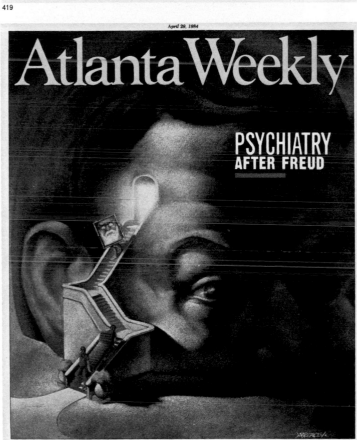

421

422

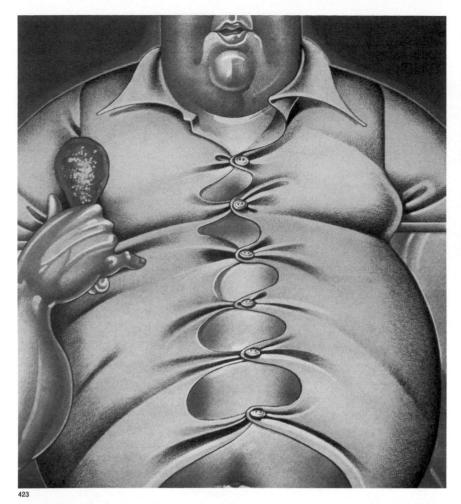

423

424

425

426

Ber Nachteil der neuen Technik. Diesen banalen Ur-Nutzen der Zeitung hat Kaspar Stieler, der „Vater der deutschen Zeitungskunde", vielleicht bedacht, aber er hat kein Wort darüber verloren in seiner umfassenden Darstellung „Zeitungs Lust und Nutz" (1695). Damals war nicht nur die Nachricht, es war auch das Material wertvoll, auf dem sie stand. Schon gar, als man noch auf Pergament schrieb. Da wurde notfalls die Schrift getilgt, um den Stoff noch einmal beschreiben zu können.

Originale zweckentfremdet zu nutzen gilt von jeher als großer Schimpf. Catull schrieb, die „Scheißannalen" des Volusius („Annales Volusii, cacata carta", sozusagen „Analen" also), diese Schriften würden in Padua zum Einwickeln von Makrelen benutzt. Ausgerechnet Makrelen! Das waren nämlich keine frischen Fische. Sie wurden von spanischen und mauretanischen Fischern beim Übergang vom Atlanticus ins Mare Ibericum gefangen. Auf den langen und heißen Handelswegen stanken sie dann, spätestens in Padua. (Man verwendete sie zu Fischlake, die mußte so-

wieso zwei Monate lang gären.) Vielleicht hatte aber der Fischhändler auf dem Markt in Padua sein großes Aha-Erlebnis, angesichts der Annalen des Volusius? Einem Snob wie Catull kam so etwas nicht in den Sinn.

In Gedichte eingewickelte Makrelen wurden zum Klischee. Martial drohte einem aufdringlichen Dichter, er solle seine Gäste nicht weiter mit selbstgemachter Poesie anöden, sonst werde er künftig allein speisen müssen. „Gib die verruchten Gedichte, darein Makrelen zu wickeln!" Auch für eigene Gedichte fürchtete Martial angeblich dieses Schicksal. Er riet ihnen darum, einen sachverständigen Gönner zu finden. Ein Topos also. Auch Thunfische galten als Schänder der Poesie. Das Motiv schleppte sich fort bis zu Grabbe, der (in „Scherz, Satire, Ironie") einen Schulmeister vermuten läßt, die

Makrelen, eingewickelt in Gedichte

„neuen Skribenten" würden leibhaftig „um einen verfaulten Hering gewickelt", nicht nur ihre Papiere. Angeblich hat der portugiesische Rechtsgelehrte Agostino Barbosa einem Fleischer Einwickelpapier abgekauft, als er gemerkt hatte, daß die Wurst in ein Manuskript „De officio Episcopi" packte. Mit dem Kommentar zu diesem Werk habe Barbosa seinen Ruhm begründet.

Bei Edmond Rostand ist dieses Motiv dramatisch geworden. In seiner Komödie um Cyrano de Bergerac versucht ein mäzenatischer Pastetenbäcker, zu Altpapier degradierte Gedichte zu retten. „Die hehre Poesie, die mich begeistert, zu schnöden Tüten für Gebäck verkleistert!"

Makulatur bildete die Basis der Gelehrsamkeit des berühmten Gotthelf Fibel, „poetisches, juristisches, chemisches Gedrucktes aus dem Gewürzladen". Freilich, meint Jean Paul (im Kapitel „Heringspapiere"), nicht für jeden Gelehrten tauge diese Art Lektüre, denn man könne sie nicht zitieren, „aus Mangel an Titelblättern, und weil sie, wie das Epos, bald mitten, bald hinten anfängt". „Man sauge sich also ‚elend voll Kenntnisse, ohne imstand zu sein, nur einen Tropfen wieder aus sich zu

42

ARTIST / KÜNSTLER / ARTISTE:

423 Dave Lafleur
424 Ed Soyka
425 Andrzej Dudzinski
426 Heinz Edelmann
427, 428 Steve Guarnaccia
429 Steve Carver

DESIGNER / GESTALTER / MAQUETTISTE:

423, 424 Greg Paul
425, 427–429 Ronn Campisi

ART DIRECTOR / DIRECTEUR ARTISTIQUE:

423, 424 Greg Paul
425, 427–429 Ronn Campisi
426 Hans-Georg Pospischil

PUBLISHER / VERLEGER / EDITEUR:

423, 424 Sunshine Magazine
425, 427–429 The Boston Globe
426 Frankfurter Allgemeine Zeitung GmbH

Weekend Supplements
Wochenendbeilagen
Suppléments dominicaux

427

428

423, 424 Full-page illustrations from the *Sunshine Magazine*. Fig. 423 (blue shirt, brown skin) relates to an article about menus "à discrétion", Fig. 424 (mainly in green tones, playing cards blue) is for an article about gamblers. (USA)
425 Illustration for an article about the fate of a mentally retarded woman, in *The Boston Globe Magazine*. Natural-coloured wicker seat, room and face in dark blue with various coloured stripes. (USA)
426 Page entitled "Mackerels wrapped up in poetry", from an article in the *Frankfurter Allgemeine Magazin*. Illustration: Dark blue, red and brown tones. (GER)
427–429 Double spread and illustrations from *The Boston Globe Magazine*. Figs. 427, 428 (in pastel shades) accompany an article about life in Washington, Fig. 429 (in brown tones) is for an article about the diminishing value of the dollar. (USA)

423, 424 Ganzseitige Illustrationen aus *Sunshine Magazine*. Abb. 423 (blaues Hemd, braune Haut) gehört zu einem Beitrag über Menus «à discrétion», Abb. 424 (vorwiegend Grüntöne, Spielkarten blau) zu einem Artikel über Spieler. (USA)
425 Illustration für einen Beitrag über das Schicksal einer geistig behinderten Frau, in *The Boston Globe Magazine*. Naturfarbener Korbsessel, Raum und Gesicht in dunklem Blau mit verschiedenen Farbstreifen. (USA)
426 Seite mit dem Titel «Makrelen, eingewickelt in Gedichte», aus einem Beitrag im *Frankfurter Allgemeine Magazin*. Illustration: Dunkelblau, Rot- und Brauntöne. (GER)
427–429 Doppelseite und Illustrationen aus *The Boston Globe Magazine*. Abb. 427, 428 (in Pastellfarben) gehören zu einem Beitrag über das Leben in Washington, Abb. 429 (in Brauntönen) zu einem Artikel über die schrumpfende Kaufkraft des Dollars. (USA)

423, 424 Illustrations pleine page du *Sunshine Magazine*. La fig. 423 (chemise bleue, peau brune) accompagne un article sur les menus à gogo, la fig. 424 (tons verts prédominants, cartes bleues) un article sur les joueurs. (USA)
425 Illustration d'une étude sur le destin d'une handicapée mentale, dans le *Boston Globe Magazine*. Fauteuil en rotin au coloris naturel, chambre et visage bleu foncé, avec diverses rayures colorées. (USA)
426 Page intitulée «Maquereaux emballés dans des poèmes». Article du *Frankfurter Allgemeine Magazin*. Illustration: tons bleu foncé, rouge, brun. (GER)
427–429 Double page et illustrations du *Boston Globe Magazine*. Les fig. 427 et 428 (teintes pastel) accompagnent un article sur la vie à Washington, la fig. 429 (divers bruns) est pour un article sur le pouvoir d'achat faiblissant du dollar. (USA)

429

430

431

430–434 Double spreads with colourful illustrations by the American artist Seymour Chwast for humorous articles in the *Frankfurter Allgemeine Magazin*. Figs. 430–432 accompany an article to mark the 300th birthday of Johann Sebastian Bach; Fig. 433 illustrates a feature entitled "Conditions as in old Rome", polychrome illustration on turquoise background; Fig. 434 shows one of the possibilities for the use of the portable personal computer: it helps its owner in the choice of suitable menus in a restaurant by taking into account diverse factors such as calories and budget. (GER)

430–434 Doppelseiten mit farbenfrohen Illustrationen des Amerikaners Seymour Chwast für humorvolle Beiträge im *Frankfurter Allgemeine Magazin*. Abb. 430–432 gehören zu einem Artikel zum 300sten Geburtstag von Johann Sebastian Bach; Abb. 433 illustriert «Zustände wie im alten Rom»; Abb. 434 zeigt eine der Möglichkeiten für den Einsatz des tragbaren Personal Computers: unter Berücksichtigung diverser Faktoren wie Kalorien und Budget hilft er seinem Besitzer bei der Wahl des geeigneten Menus im Restaurant. (GER)

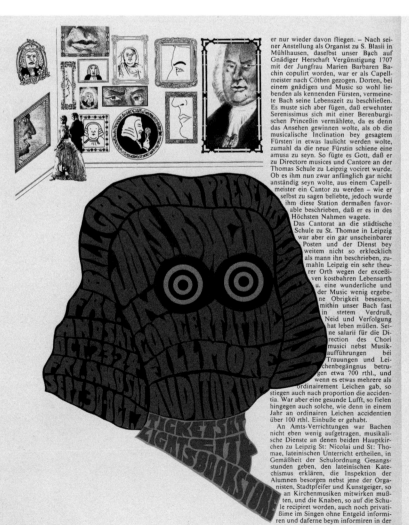

432

433

ARTIST / KÜNSTLER / ARTISTE:
430–434 Seymour Chwast

ART DIRECTOR / DIRECTEUR ARTISTIQUE:
430–434 Hans-Georg Pospischil

PUBLISHER / VERLEGER / EDITEUR:
430–434 Frankfurter Allgemeine Zeitung GmbH

430–434 Doubles pages hautes en couleur illustrées par l'Américain Seymour Chwast. Il s'agit de pages humoristiques du *Frankfurter Allgemeine Magazin*. Les fig. 430–432 font partie d'un article sur le tricentenaire de Johann Sebastian Bach; la fig. 433 illustre «des mœurs comme dans la Rome antique»; la fig. 434 montre l'une des applications d'un microprocesseur portable: calculant divers facteurs tels que la teneur en calories et le budget disponible, il permet à son heureux propriétaire de choisir au restaurant le menu le plus approprié. (GER)

434

435

Hochzeit mit einer Amerikanerin vor. Er war dazu auf dem Standesamt und sollte dort zur Identifikation seinen Führerschein vorlegen. Doch er fährt nicht Auto. Welche Urkunden sollte er also bei diesem helfenden Kategorien an Geburtsurkunde, Stammbuch, Abiturzeugnis). Doch weit gefehlt: "No problem", sagt der Beamte. "You just show us some of your major credit cards and everything will be o.k." So einfach ist das.

Allerdings hat ja die Kreditkarte in ihrem Lande auch eine sehr viel größere Verbreitung als bei uns. Jeder Amerikaner, ob Greis, ob Säugling, besitzt laut Statistik sechs Karten. Der Rekord des Kaliforniers Walter Cavanagh, der tausenddrei "plastic" sein eigen nennt, kann noch stark verbessert werden, da ja nicht nur die Banken ihre diversen Zahl-Karten (Visa, American Express, Diners, Master Charge) auf dem Markt haben, sondern auch Flug- und Hotelgesellschaften, Tankstellen, Supermärkte und Spielcasinos – nach couragierten Schätzungen gibt es rund zehntausend amerikanische Kartensysteme.

Eigentlich dürfe die Karte nicht Kreditkarte, sondern müßte Kreditwürdigkeitskarte heißen", lerne ich bei den American-Express-Leuten, "schließlich ist sie nicht für Leute, die den Kredit brauchen, sondern für solche, die ihn haben!" Der semantisch unglückliche Zungenschlag hat nach Meinung der Frankfurter Branchenführer dazu beigetragen, daß Deutschland bis heute im Plastikverbrauch für den Zahlungsverkehr als hoffnungslos hinterhumpelndes Entwicklungsland gilt. Die Zahl der Kreditkarten in deutschen Brieftaschen ist gerade die Millionengrenze geschafft, verglichen mit den fünf Millionen in England, geschweige denn den fünfhundert Millionen in den Vereinigten Staaten, wirkt die Bundesrepublik tatsächlich wie ein fortschrittsresistentes Operettenherzogtum.

Das zu ändern, haben die großen Karten-Häuser gerade jetzt in die Taschen gegriffen und sich schicke, vierfarbige Werbekampagnen entwerfen lassen. Denen begegne ich, wann immer ich in eine der großen Zeitungen

R sich nicht: Den Plünderern wird in der Grabkammer die kalte Schulter gezeigt – und die altägyptische Kreditkarte

436

KREDITKARTEN
Von Horst-Dieter Ebert
Illustrationen Christoph Blumrich

Bis vor ein paar Monaten war ich der womöglich letzte auch außer Landes herumreisende deutsche Journalist, der keine einzige Kreditkarte besaß. Dann gab eine neue New-York-Reise den Ausschlag, daß ich meine Zahlungsmittel nun nicht länger bar in der Geldscheinklammer mit mir trage, sondern reduziert auf jenes Stück Plastik, das in der Hemdtasche kaum aufträgt und doch mehr wert ist: Ich wollte in Manhattan nicht zum wiederholten Mal als kauziger Sonderling auftreten, der alles „cash" aus der Tasche nestelt und deswegen auch schon gelegentlich in besseren Hotels wie der Prototyp des Zechprellers angeguckt und barsch um die Hinterlegung eines größeren Dollarbetrages angegangen worden ist.

Die Karte kommt am Abend vor dem Abflug. Es bleibt keine Zeit mehr, mit ihr ein bißchen zu üben. So reise ich also mit dem noch jungfräulichen Stück Plastik los. Schon während des Fluges ertappe ich mich bei dem Gedanken, daß, falls ich heute abstürzen sollte, meine Versicherungssumme nun um eine halbe Million höher ist, als wenn mir das vorgestern – noch ohne Karte – passiert wäre (bis ich später beim Studium des Kleingedruckten herausfinde, daß dies natürlich nur zutrifft, wenn das Flugticket mit der Karte gekauft worden ist). Im New Yorker Hotel Parker Meridien, wo alle Angestellten um einen französischen Akzent bemüht sind, zücke ich auf die übliche Frage, wie ich denn meine Rechnung zu begleichen gedächte, erstmals das kleine Kunststoffkärtchen: „Akzeptieren Sie das?" – „Mais certainement, Monsieur!" strahlt die jugendliche Blonde an der Rezeption, schiebt es einmal flink durch den Kreditkartenhobel, und schon gelte ich in diesem Haus als zulänglich zahlungsfähiger Gast.

Wie sehr das kapitalistische Sein und Haben das Bewußtsein bestimmen, dafür liefert mir am nächsten Tag der deutsche Resident Manager des Meridien ein anschauliches Beispiel. Er bereite, so erzählt er in dem schwerblütigen Deutsch dessen, der seit zwanzig Jahren in New York lebt, seine

D as wiegt manchen Geldstapel auf: Zwar sind die Plastikkärtchen am Ohr Leichtgewichte – doch an der Kasse zählen sie

17

437

Weekend Supplements
Wochenendbeilagen
Suppléments dominicaux

ARTIST / KÜNSTLER / ARTISTE:

435 Serge Cohen / Christoph Blumrich / Marion Nickig
436, 437 Christoph Blumrich
438–440 Peter Krämer

ART DIRECTOR / DIRECTEUR ARTISTIQUE:

435–440 Hans-Georg Pospischil

PUBLISHER / VERLEGER / EDITEUR:

435–440 Frankfurter Allgemeine Zeitung GmbH

438

439

435–440 Cover and double spreads from the *Frankfurter Allgemeine Magazin*. Fig. 435 informs on the contents of the issue; Figs. 436 and 437 (in gold-yellow with blue, red and brown tones) accompany an article about credit cards; Fig. 438, with polychrome illustration, introduces an article about the Frankfurter sausage; Figs. 439 and 440, with polychrome illustrations, are double spreads from an article about electrical current. (GER)

435–440 Umschlag und Doppelseiten aus dem *Frankfurter Allgemeine Magazin*. Abb. 435 informiert über den Inhalt der betreffenden Ausgabe; Abb. 436 und 437 (in Goldgelb mit Blau-, Rot- und Brauntönen) gehören zu einem Artikel über Kreditkarten; Abb. 438, mit mehrfarbiger Illustration, leitet einen Beitrag über Frankfurter Würstchen ein; Abb. 439 und 440, mit mehrfarbigen Illustrationen, sind Doppelseiten aus einem Beitrag über Strom. (GER)

435–440 Couverture et doubles pages du *Frankfurter Allgemeine Magazin*. La fig. 435 renseigne sur le sommaire du numéro en question; les fig. 436 et 437 (jaune or, avec du bleu, du rouge et du brun) accompagnent une étude sur les cartes de crédit; la fig. 438, en polychromie, introduit un article sur les saucisses de Francfort; les fig. 439 et 440 sont des doubles pages d'un article sur le courant électrique, illustrée en polychromie. (GER)

440

441

442

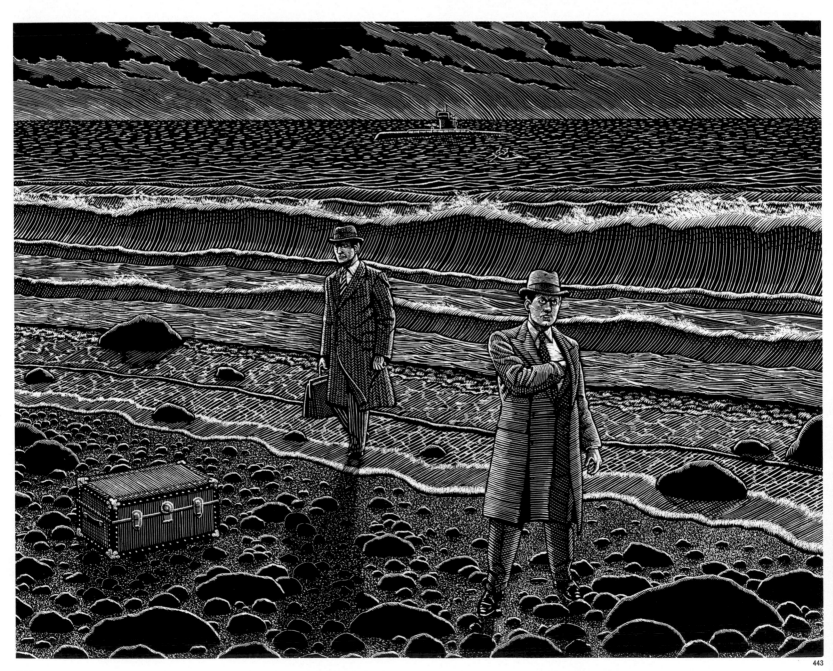

443

Weekend Supplements

444

441 Portrait of the country singer Kenny Rogers in the *Dallas Times Herald*. Red and brown. (USA)
442 For the short story "My Walk" in the *Tages Anzeiger Magazin*. Light brown, light green. (SWI)
443 "The spies who came in from the coast." Illustration in scratchboard technique for a story in *Boston Globe Magazine*. (USA)
444 Illustration for an article on the mud-flats, in the magazine of *Hamburger Abendblatt*. (GER)

441 Porträt des Country-Sängers Kenny Rogers im *Dallas Times Herald*. Rot- und Brauntöne. (USA)
442 Für die Kurzgeschichte «Mein Spaziergang» im *Tages Anzeiger Magazin*. Hellbraun, hellgrün. (SWI)
443 «Die Spione, die von der Küste kamen.» Für eine Geschichte im *Boston Globe Magazine*. (USA)
444 Illustration für einen Artikel über das Wattenmeer im Magazin des *Hamburger Abendblatt*. (GER)

441 Portrait du chanteur de country Kenny Rogers, dans *Dallas Times Herald*. Rouge, brun. (USA)
442 Pour le récit «Ma Promenade», dans *Tages Anzeiger Magazin*. Brun clair, vert clair. (SWI)
443 «Les espions venus de la côte.» Récit publié dans le *Boston Globe Magazine*. (USA)
444 Pour un article sur les vasières littorales du N-O. Magazine du *Hamburger Abendblatt*. (GER)

Nr. 44   28. Oktober 1983

ZEIT*magazin*

EIN MANN,
EIN ZIEL
Das Selbstporträt
des Kanadiers Alex
Colville meint
nicht Mord oder
Aggression: Über
Kimme und Korn
visiert der Maler
die Realität an
(Seite 38)

445

445, 446 Cover of *Zeitmagazin* with a self-portrait of the Canadian artist Alex Colville and a double spread with two of his pictures, from an article to mark the occasion of a retrospective of his work at the Berlin Kunsthalle. (GER)
447 Illustration for the section "Freizeit" (Leisure) in the supplement *Züri-Tip* of the *Tages Anzeiger*. The corresponding article is about Indonesian cooking—with its many spices. (SWI)
448, 449 Double spreads with illustrations in soft colours from *Zeitmagazin*. They relate to a series of articles which analyze both halves of the human brain. (GER)

445, 446 Umschlag des *Zeitmagazin* mit einem Selbstporträt des kanadischen Künstlers Alex Colville und eine Doppelseite mit zwei Bildern des Künstlers, aus einem Artikel, der anlässlich einer Retrospektive seines Werkes in der Berliner Kunsthalle erschien. (GER)
447 Illustration für die Rubrik «Freizeit» in der *Züri-Tip*-Beilage des *Tages Anzeiger*. Hier geht es um die Gewürzvielfalt der indonesischen Küche. (SWI)
448, 449 Doppelseiten mit Illustrationen in sanften Farben aus dem *Zeitmagazin*. Sie gehören zu einer Beitragsreihe, die sich mit den beiden Hälften des menschlichen Gehirns auseinandersetzt. (GER)

445, 446 Couverture du *Zeitmagazin* avec un autoportrait de l'artiste canadien Alex Colville, et une double page illustrée de deux de ses tableaux. L'article qui lui est consacré se réfère à la rétrospective de ses œuvres organisée à la Kunsthalle de Berlin. (GER)
447 Illustration pour la section «Loisirs» du *Züri-Tip*, supplément du *Tages Anzeiger*. Il s'agit ici de la grande variété des épices caractéristiques de la cuisine indonésienne. (SWI)
448, 449 Doubles pages du *Zeitmagazin* illustrées en couleurs douces. Elles font partie d'une série d'articles consacrés à la latéralisation du cerveau humain. (GER)

447

ARTIST / KÜNSTLER / ARTISTE:

445, 446 Alex Colville
447 Dora Wespi
448, 449 Ute Osterwalder

DESIGNER / GESTALTER / MAQUETTISTE:

445, 446 Ingo Goetsche

ART DIRECTOR / DIRECTEUR ARTISTIQUE:

445, 446, 448, 449 Christian Diener
447 Peter Stöckli

PUBLISHER / VERLEGER / EDITEUR:

445, 446, 448, 449 Zeitverlag Gerd Bucerius
447 Tages-Anzeiger AG

Mehr als zehn Jahre liegen zwischen diesen beiden Bildern (»Laser«, 1976, oben und »To Prince Edward Island«, 1965). Aber etwas für Colville sehr Charakteristisches verbindet sie: Das Gesicht der Seglerin ist halb verdeckt, die Frau auf dem Dampfer verbirgt ihr Gesicht hinter dem Fernglas. Das Gesicht, hat Colville einmal gesagt, würde vom Eigentlichen des Bildes ablenken, und so findet sich in seinem Œuvre nur ein Bild, auf dem sich ein Gesicht dem Betrachter unverhüllt aussetzt: sein Selbstporträt (siehe Titelbild)

446

Warum sind die meisten Menschen Rechtshänder? Das muß – würden wohl die meisten antworten – eins dieser unausrottbaren Vorurteile sein. Irgendwann haben sich die Menschen angewöhnt, ihre linken Hände »links liegen zu lassen«, und das schleppt nun die Erziehung von einer Generation in die nächste. Diese Theorie aber ist falsch

DIE UND DIE SCHLIMME EDLE RECHTE LINKE

448

ZWEI GEISTER WOHNEN, ACH! IN MEINEM KOPF

Daß die beiden Seiten des Gehirns unterschiedliche Arbeitsstile haben, hat Spekulanten aller Art angezogen: Jeder glaubte, in diesen Unterschieden eine Bestätigung für seinen eigenen Lieblingsgegensatz zu finden. So wurde die Hemisphärenforschung immer wieder zu einer Tummelwiese für obskure Heilslehren

449

ARTIST / KÜNSTLER / ARTISTE:

450 Randall Enos
451, 452 Eduard Prüssen

ART DIRECTOR / DIRECTEUR ARTISTIQUE:

450 Bett McLean

PUBLISHER / VERLEGER / EDITEUR:

450, 13–30 Corporation
451, 452 BPA

451

452

450 Collage made from various linocuts which were printed on coloured paper, as illustration to an article about employee performance, in the magazine for the veterinary community, *Veterinary Practice Management*. (USA)
451, 452 Linocuts in black and white for the professional magazine *Der praktische Arzt* (The General Practitioner). Fig. 451: for an article about the superfluity of medical students. (A detail of the illustration was also used for the cover.) Fig. 452: cover illustration on the topic of family planning. (GER)

450 Collage aus verschiedenen Linolschnitten, die auf farbiges Papier gedruckt wurden, als Illustration zu einem Beitrag über die Leistung der Angestellten in der Tierarztpraxis, erschienen in der Fachzeitschrift für Tierärzte, *Veterinary Practice Management*. (USA)
451, 452 Linolschnitte in Schwarzweiss für die Fachzeitschrift *Der praktische Arzt*. Abb. 451, von der ein Detail auch für den Umschlag verwendet wurde, gehört zu einem Artikel, der sich mit dem Übermass an Zulassungen zum Medizinstudium befasst. Abb. 452 ist eine Umschlagillustration zum Thema Familienplanung. (GER)

450 Collage de diverses linogravures imprimées sur papier couleur. Illustration d'un article sur les prestations des assistants des vétérinaires, publié dans la revue spécialisée *Veterinary Practice Management*. (USA)
451, 452 Linogravures en noir et blanc pour la revue professionnelle *Der praktische Arzt* (le généraliste). La fig. 451, dont un détail figure en couverture, accompagne un article critique sur le libre accès des bacheliers à la Faculté de médecine. La fig. 452 est une illustration de couverture sur le thème du planning familial. (GER)

Trade Magazines
Fachzeitschriften
Revues professionnelles

CURRENT CONCEPTS IN INFECTIOUS DISEASES
今日の感染症

453 Cover of an issue of the medical magazine *Current Concepts in Infectious Diseases*. (JPN)
454 Full-page illustration in grey and beige tones, thermometers with red scale, for an article entitled "On managing the febrile child", in *Emergency Medicine*. (USA)
455 A New Year's resolution to cut down on smoking is the theme of this illustration in *American Health Magazine*. Light violet background, white border. (USA)
456 Illustration in green, grey and brown tones for an article in *Emergency Medicine* entitled "Overlooked anatomy—examining a boy's genitals". (USA)
457–459 Illustrations to articles on a symposium on sports medicine at high schools and the University of Wisconsin, in the magazine *The Physician and Sportsmedicine*. (USA)

453 Umschlag für eine Ausgabe der medizinischen Fachzeitschrift *Current Concepts in Infectious Diseases*, die sich mit infektiösen Krankheiten befasst. (JPN)
454 Ganzseitige Illustration in Grau- und Beigetönen, Fiebermesser mit roter Skala, für einen Beitrag über die Behandlung von Kindern mit Fieber, in *Emergency Medicine*. (USA)
455 Das Abgewöhnen des Rauchens als guter Vorsatz zum neuen Jahr ist Thema dieser Illustration in *American Health Magazine*, einem Gesundheitsmagazin. (USA)
456 Illustration in Grün-, Grau- und Brauntönen für einen Artikel in *Emergency Medicine*: «Die Untersuchung der Genitalien eines Jungen». (USA)
457–459 Illustrationen zu Beiträgen über verschiedene Themen der Sportmedizin in der Fachzeitschrift *The Physician and Sportsmedicine*. (USA)

453 Couverture d'un numéro de la revue médicale *Current Concepts in Infectious Diseases* où il est question des maladies infectieuses. (JPN)
454 Illustration pleine page, tons gris et beige, thermomètres à graduation rouge, pour un article sur les soins aux enfants fiévreux, dans *Emergency Medicine*. (USA)
455 La décision de renoncer à la cigarette en début d'année est le sujet de cette illustration de l'*American Health Magazine*, un magazine de santé. (USA)
456 Illustration vert, gris, brun pour un article paru dans *Emergency Medicine*: «L'Examen des organes génitaux chez le garçon». (USA)
457–459 Illustrations pour divers articles de la revue spécialisée *The Physician and Sportsmedicine* consacrés à trois aspects de la médecine sportive. (USA)

453

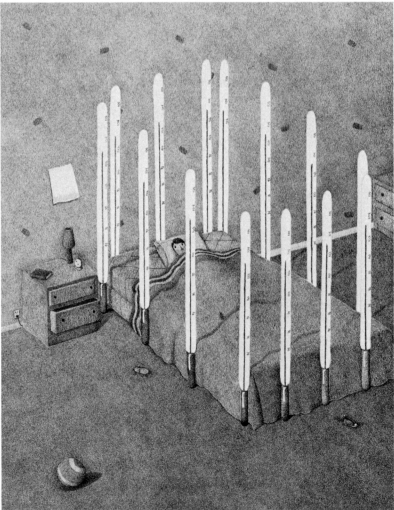

454

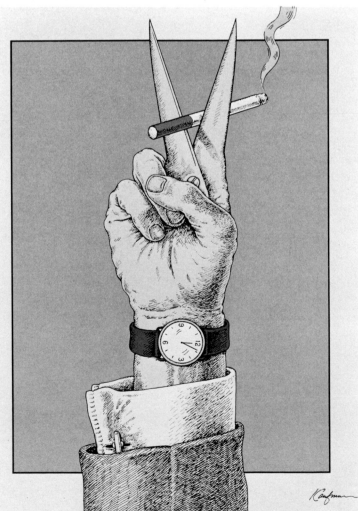

455

456

ARTIST / KÜNSTLER / ARTISTE:

453 Theresa Grygorcewicz
454 Paul Yalowitz
455 Robert J. Kaufman
456 Peter DeSeve
457–459 Mary Grandpre

DESIGNER / GESTALTER / MAQUETTISTE:

453 Bruno Ruegg
454, 456 James T. Walsh

ART DIRECTOR / DIRECTEUR ARTISTIQUE:

453 Bruno Ruegg
454, 456 James T. Walsh
455 Will Hopkins
457–459 Tina Adamek

PUBLISHER / VERLEGER / EDITEUR:

453 Sieber & McIntyre
454, 456 Fischer Medical Publications
455 American Health
457–459 McGraw Hill Publishing Co.

457

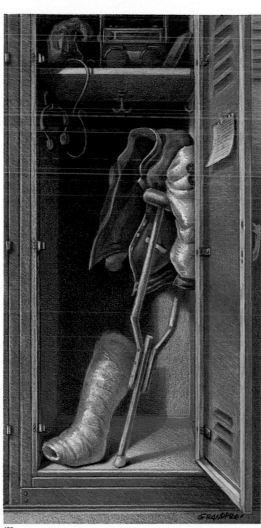

458

459

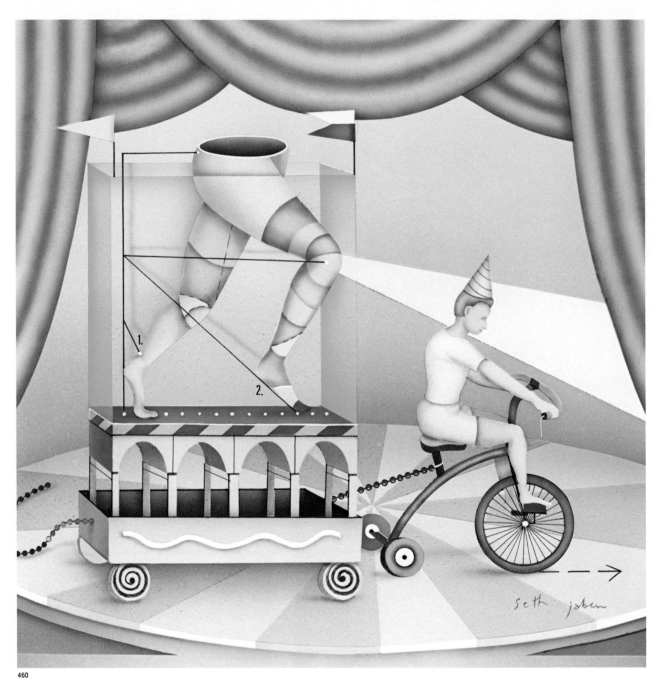

460

461

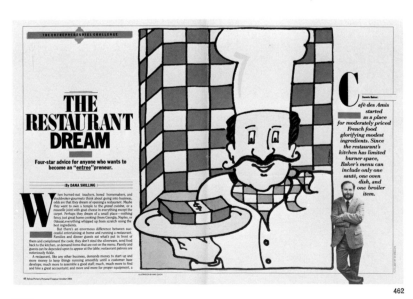

462

463

ARTIST / KÜNSTLER / ARTISTE:

460, 461 Seth Jaben
462, 463 Mike Quon
465 Michael David Brown
466 Alan Wallerstein

DESIGNER / GESTALTER / MAQUETTISTE:

462, 463 Ralph Rubino
464 Peter Grundy/Oswaldo Miranda
465 Michael David Brown
466 Kerin Quigley

A DICTIONARY BY
PETER GRUNDY

X(ĕKs).

464

460, 461 Illustration and double spread from an article dealing with gait problems in children in *Postgraduate Medicine*. (USA)
462, 463 Double spreads from *Sylvia Porter's Personal Finance* for the regular section entitled "The Entrepreneurial Challenge", here, with advice on opening a restaurant and tax-planning. (USA)
464 Double spread from the trade magazine *Gráfica* with an "X" dictionary ("X" for xplosion, xaggerate, etc.) Red, black, grey. (BRA)
465 Double spread in full colour with black background for an article on retarded physical effects. In *Science*. (USA)
466 Double spread from *Emergency Medicine* relating to eye drops and the danger of their entering the circulation. (USA)

460, 461 Illustration und Doppelseite aus *Postgraduate Medicine*. Thema: Rotations- und Gehprobleme bei Kindern. (USA)
462, 463 Doppelseiten aus *Sylvia Porter's Personal Finance* für die Rubrik «Die unternehmerische Herausforderung». (USA)
464 Doppelseite aus der Fachzeitschrift *Gráfica* mit Variationen zum Buchstaben «X». Rot, Schwarz, Grau auf Weiss. (BRA)
465 Mehrfarbige Doppelseite (Hintergrund in Schwarz) für einen Artikel über körperliche Spätreaktionen. In *Science*. (USA)
466 Doppelseite aus *Emergency Medicine*. Thema des Artikels: Eindringen von Augentropfen in den Blutkreislauf. (USA)

460, 461 Illustration et double page de *Postgraduate Medicine*. Sujet: l'équilibration et la marche chez les enfants. (USA)
462, 463 Doubles pages de *Sylvia Porter's Personal Finance*, pour la section «Le Défi à l'esprit d'entreprise». (USA)
464 Double page de la revue professionnelle *Gráfica*: variations sur la lettre «X». Rouge, noir, gris sur blanc. (BRA)
465 Double page polychrome (sur fond noir) pour un article sur les réactions de contre-choc paru dans *Science*. (USA)
466 Double page d'*Emergency Medicine*, sur le problème de la pénétration des collyres dans le torrent circulatoire. (USA)

You thought
it was over
four years ago.
It wasn't.

THE RISE
AND
(MAYBE NOT THE)
FALL OF
TOXIC SHOCK
SYNDROME
BY PETER RADETSKY

465

Trade Magazines
Fachzeitschriften
Revues professionnelles

ART DIRECTOR / DIRECTEUR ARTISTIQUE:

460, 461 Tina Adamek
462, 463 Ralph Rubino
464 Oswaldo Miranda
465 John Isley
466 James T. Walsh

AGENCY / AGENTUR / AGENCE – STUDIO:

465 Michael David Brown, Inc.

PUBLISHER / VERLEGER / EDITEUR:

460, 461 McGraw Hill Publishing Co.
462, 463 Sylvia Porter's Personal Finance
464 Gráfica
465 American Association for the Advancement of Science
466 Fischer Medical Publications

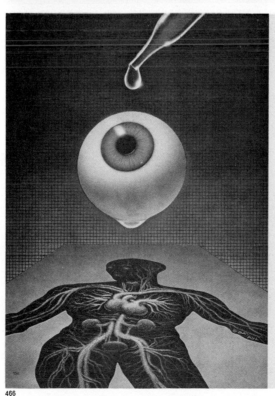

466

Ophthalmic
agents applied locally
don't necessarily
remain local in their
effect, which
may account for
some odd
symptoms

DRUGS
IN
THE EYE—
AND
BEYOND

Eye drops are
intended to exert an effect on
or within the eye—usually
either dilation or contraction
of the pupil or paralysis of
accommodation. To most
patients and perhaps many
nonophthalmologic physi-
cians, that's as far as it goes.
But that's a mistake, Dr. Be-
atrice L. Selvin, clinical profes-
sor of anesthesiology at the
University of Maryland Medical Systems and Hospital in
Baltimore, told EM. "Eye drops
frequently enter the systemic
circulation with /continued

EMERGENCY MEDICINE/NOVEMBER 15, 1984   157

467

468

ARTIST / KÜNSTLER / ARTISTE:

467 Geoffrey Moss
468 Rubem Campos Grilo
469, 470 Jim Jacobs
471, 472 Oswaldo Miranda (Miran)

467 Illustration from *Planning Review*, a magazine for corporate planners. The topic deals with how the historical process plays a dominant role in determining a planner's strategy. (USA)
468 Woodcut in black and white for a cover of *Gráfica*. (BRA)
469, 470 Introductory double spreads for features in *Legal Assistant Today*, a magazine for the legal community. Fig. 469: ways on dealing with rejection; Fig. 470: advantages of "networking"—a new word for the "old boys' network". Black and white with red connecting sparks. (USA)
471 Introductory double spread to an article entitled "Young Queen". In *Raposa*. (BRA)
472 For a feature on Napoleon in the *City News* weekend supplement. (BRA)

467 Illustration aus *Planning Review*, einer Zeitschrift für Firmenplaner. Thema: Risiken des Unternehmensplaners und dessen Abhängigkeit von geschichtlichen Hintergründen. (USA)
468 Holzschnitt in Schwarzweiss für einen Umschlag von *Gráfica*. (BRA)
469, 470 Einleitende Doppelseiten für Beiträge in *Legal Assistant Today*, einer Fachzeitschrift für Juristen. Abb. 469: Vom positiven Umgang mit Zurückweisungen. In Schwarzweiss; Abb. 470: Funktion eines Beziehungsnetzes. Schwarz auf Weiss, mit roten «Verbindungsblitzen». (USA)
471 Einleitende Doppelseite zu einem Beitrag mit dem Titel «Junge Königin». In *Raposa*. (BRA)
472 Zu einem Artikel über Napoleon, in der Wochenendausgabe von *City News*. (BRA)

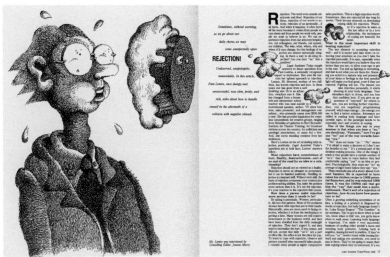

469

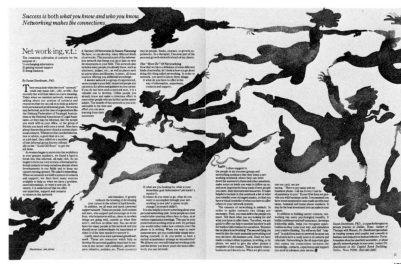

470

The queen illustration with calligraphic text, displaying the words:

A
Jovem
Rainha

eypin d'Ai-
gues. Embora
o Cristianismo
afirme que o
Redentor apareceu há dois
mil anos, um número sem-
pre maior de grupos étni-
cos (bascos, irlandeses, fla-
mengos, occitanos, bre-
tões, tiroleses, corsas, cata-
lões, etc...), considera-se
irredimido. Há, no entan-
to, diferença – reveladora

de mutação profunda, en-
tre o irredentismo do final
do século 19 e o da atuali-
dade. A irredenta italiana
Oitocentista, e as demais
que nela se inspiram, so-
bretudo a alemã, visavam
redimir nações (fragmenta-
das sob soberanias múlti-
plas) pelo estabelecimento
de Estados Nacionais que
abarcariam todos os que
falam a mesma língua.

471

467 Illustration de *Planning Review*, revue spécialisée dans la planification de l'entreprise: les risques qu'encourt le planificateur et le poids des conditions historiques de son travail. (USA)
468 Gravure sur bois, noir et blanc, pour une couverture de *Gráfica* (BRA)
469, 470 Doubles pages initiales d'articles parus dans *Legal Assistant Today*, revue professionnelle pour juristes. Fig. 469: de la manière positive de traiter les récusations; noir et blanc. Fig. 470: fonction d'un réseau de relations. Noir-blanc, «éclairs» rouges. (USA)
471 Double page initiale d'un article de *Raposa* intitulé «Jeune Reine». (BRA)
472 Pour un article sur Napoléon 1er publié dans l'édition dominicale de *City News*. (BRA)

Trade Magazines
Fachzeitschriften
Revues professionnelles

472

DESIGNER / GESTALTER / MAQUETTISTE:

467 Ner Beck
468, 471, 472 Oswaldo Miranda (Miran)
469 Vikki Foster
470 Jim Jacobs

ART DIRECTOR / DIRECTEUR ARTISTIQUE:

467 Ner Beck
468, 471, 472 Oswaldo Miranda
469, 470 Jim Jacobs

AGENCY / AGENTUR / AGENCE – STUDIO:

467 Beck Graphics
468, 471, 472 Miran Studio
469, 470 Jim Jacobs' Studio

PUBLISHER / VERLEGER / EDITEUR:

467 Robert J. Allio & Assoc.
468 Gráfica Magazine
469, 470 Legal Assistant Today
471 Raposa Magazine
472 City News

ARTIST / KÜNSTLER / ARTISTE:

473 Tom Leonard
474 Cheryl Gries Bach/Stan Martucci
475 Barry Root
476 Greg Couch
477 Ed Soyka
478, 479 Teresa Fasolino

DESIGNER / GESTALTER / MAQUETTISTE:

473, 478, 479 Rosalyn Migdal
474, 476 Anita Genco
475 Gerard Kunkel
477 Mary Zisk

ART DIRECTOR / DIRECTEUR ARTISTIQUE:

473–476, 478, 479 Mitch Shostak/Mary Zisk
477 Mitch Shostak

PUBLISHER / VERLEGER / EDITEUR:

473–479 Ziff-Davis Publishing Co.

COVER STORY/BARBARA KRASNOFF

The Many Faces Of dBASE II

As a programming language, dBASE II has been showing up in all the best places, from restaurants to golf courses, from schools to racetracks.

473

SOFTWARE/RICHARD N. AARONS

To CP/M And Back

Xeno-Copy and Systran bring us closer to a perfect future when all diskettes will run on all machines.

474

473–479 Introductory double spreads and full-page illustration (Fig. 476) in full colour, from the computer magazine *PC Magazine*. Fig. 473 shows some of the many users who benefit from a new programming language; Fig. 474 relates to inconsistency problems with the profusion of disk formats; Fig. 475 refers to a new piece of integrated software allowing two-way communication between a personal computer and a lap computer; Fig. 476 refers to the use of personal computers in laundries; Fig. 477 illustrates an article on an executive software package to aid better communications processing; Figs. 478, 479 illustrate a feature on computer dietary and exercise analyses. (USA)

473–479 Einleitende Doppelseiten und ganzseitige Illustration (Abb. 476) aus der Computer-Fachzeitschrift *PC Magazine*. Abb. 473 bezieht sich auf die vielen «Gesichter», die unkomplizierte Software verwenden; Abb. 474 illustriert das Problem unterschiedlicher Formate von Disketten; Abb. 475: «Die Wüste der Kompatibilität mit Fernsteuerung durchqueren»; Abb. 476 gehört zu einem Artikel über den Gebrauch von Personal Computers in Reinigungsbetrieben; Abb. 477 illustriert einen Artikel über Software, die vielbeschäftigten Managern den Zugriff zu den Zahlen erleichtern soll; Abb. 478, 479: «Programme für die Gesundheit». (USA)

473–479 Doubles pages initiales et illustration pleine page (fig. 476) de la revue d'informatique *PC Magazine*. La fig. 473 se réfère aux nombreux «visages» qui utilisent des logiciels peu compliqués; la fig. 474 illustre le problème des dimensions hétérogènes des disquettes; fig. 475: «Traverser le désert de la comptabilité à l'aide d'une télécommande»; la fig. 476 accompagne un article sur l'ordinateur au service des entreprises de nettoyage; la fig. 477 montre comment les cadres supérieurs surmenés peuvent accéder sans délai à toute donnée chiffrée grâce à l'ordinateur; fig. 478, 479: «Programmes de santé». (USA)

SOFTWARE ▲ HARVEY BERGER

Crossing the Compatibility Desert with Remote Control

The word processing, communications, and remote access software offered by Kensington Microware, Ltd. enables the PC to talk to two popular lap computers, the NEC PC-8201A and the Model 100.

PC MAGAZINE • OCTOBER 2, 1984   PC MAGAZINE • OCTOBER 2, 1984

475

476

477

478

479

PUBLISHER / VERLEGER / EDITEUR:

480 Open Court Publishing Company
481, 482 Rusconi Editore
483, 484 INC. Publishing Co.
485 The Producer

ARTIST / KÜNSTLER / ARTISTE:

480 Friso Henstra
481, 482 Giovanni Mulazzani
483, 484 RAG
485 Lonni Sue Johnson

DESIGNER / GESTALTER / MAQUETTISTE:

481, 482 Giovanni Mulazzani

ART DIRECTOR / DIRECTEUR ARTISTIQUE:

480 John Grandits
481, 482 Carlo Rizzi
483, 484 Paul Shaffrath
485 Peg Patterson

480

481

480 Complete cover of an issue of *Cricket,* a children's monthly magazine: "Cat Family's Story Hour." Coloured inks with background in pale blue. (USA)
481, 482 From the magazine *Arbiter.* The topic dealt with is power within a group. (ITA)
483, 484 Polychrome illustrations from the trade magazine *Inc.,* for an article on the importance of software and services for small firms for the easier access of information. (USA)
485 Illustration for an article in the magazine *The Producer* relating to a special insurance scheme for musical instruments which the manufacturing company offers its customers. (USA)

482

483

484

480 Vollständiger Umschlag für eine Ausgabe von *Cricket*, ein monatlich erscheinendes Kindermagazin: «Lesestunde bei Familie Katze.» Farbige Tusche, Hintergrund in Hellblau. (USA)
481, 482 Aus der Zeitschrift *Arbiter*, zum Thema Macht innerhalb einer Gruppe. (ITA)
483, 484 Mehrfarbige Illustrationen aus der Fachzeitschrift *Inc.*, für einen Artikel, in dem es um die Wichtigkeit von Software für kleine Firmen und den neuesten Informationsstand geht. (USA)
485 Illustration für einen Artikel in der Zeitschrift *The Producer*. Thema: Spezialversicherung für Musikinstrumente, die von den Verkaufsgeschäften ausgeliehen werden. (USA)

480 Couverture complète d'un numéro de *Cricket*, un magazine mensuel pour enfants: «Séance de lecture chez les Chats.» Encre de Chine de couleur sur fond bleu clair. (USA)
481, 482 Double page et illustration pour la revue *Arbiter*: le pouvoir au sein d'un groupe. (ITA)
483, 484 Illustrations polychromes pour la revue professionnelle *Inc.* L'article en question expose l'utilité des bons logiciels pour les petites entreprises et l'intérêt des nouveautés. (USA)
485 Illustration d'un article du magazine *The Producer*. Le sujet: une assurance tous risques pour les instruments de musique faisant l'objet d'un contrat de location-vente. (USA)

485

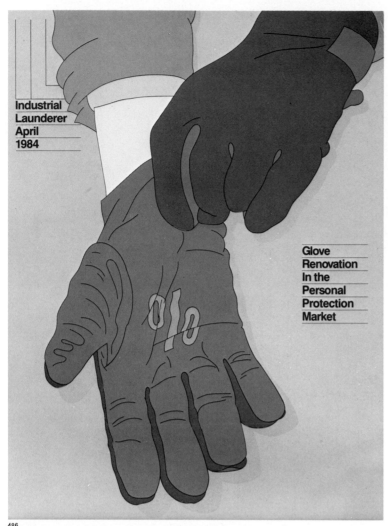

486

487

488

489

490

486 Cover of the trade magazine *Industrial Launderer*.
Background in strong blue, gloves in orange and magenta,
green and yellow cuffs. (USA)
487 Full-page illustration for an article in *Meetings and
Conventions* about the increasing popularity of downtown hotels as meeting venues. (USA)
488 Cover of *Print* magazine. Philadelphia City Centre is
visualized as a Maya temple circa 1050. (USA)
489 Full-page illustration in *New Perspectives* issued by
the U.S. Commission on Civil Rights. Collage in olive, grey,
red, white and black. (USA)
490 Cover of the large-format bi-monthly magazine *Clue*,
in which interviews with famous personalities are presented. Shown here is the architect Philip Johnson. (USA)

486 Umschlag der Fachzeitschrift *Industrial Launderer*.
Hintergrund in kräftigem Blau, Schutzhandschuhe in
Orange und Magenta, Ärmelaufschlag in Grün. (USA)
487 Ganzseitige Illustration für einen Artikel in *Meetings
and Conventions*, bei dem es um die Wiederentdeckung von
Hotels in der City als Treffpunkt geht. (USA)
488 Umschlag für *Print*, auf dem die Innenstadt Philadel-
phias als Maya-Tempel um 1050 dargestellt ist. (USA)
489 Ganzseitige Illustration in *New Perspectives*, herausgegeben von der U.S. Kommission für Zivilrechte. Collage
in Olive, Grau, Rot, Weiss und Schwarz. (USA)
490 Umschlag der grossformatigen Zweimonatszeitschrift
Clue, die in Interviews bekannte Persönlichkeiten vorstellt.
Hier der Architekt Philip Johnson. (USA)

486 Couverture de la revue professionnelle *Industrial
Launderer*. Fond bleu vif, gants de protection orange et
magenta, revers de manche vert et jaune. (USA)
487 Illustration pleine page pour un article de *Meetings and
Conventions*, qui remet à l'honneur les hôtels des centres
villes pour les séminaires et conférences. (USA)
488 Couverture de *Print*. On y voit le centre de Philadelphie
sous forme de temple maya de l'an 1050. (USA)
489 Illustration pleine page pour *New Perspectives*, la
revue de la commission américaine des droits de l'homme.
Collage olive, gris, rouge, noir, blanc. (USA)
490 Couverture de la revue bimestrielle *Clue* au grand
format, qui dresse le portrait de personnalités célèbres. Ici
l'architecte Philip Johnson. (USA)

Trade Magazines
Fachzeitschriften
Revues professionnelles

491

493

492

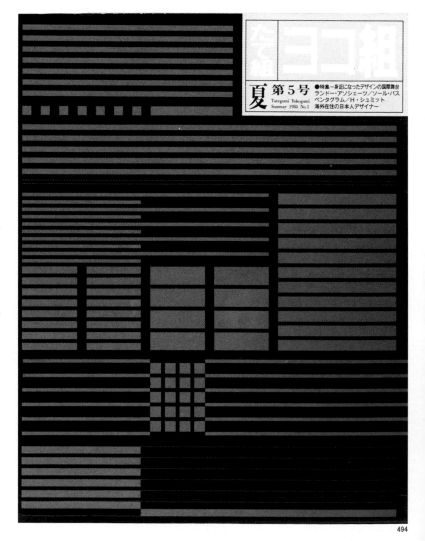

494

Trade Magazines
Fachzeitschriften
Revues professionnelles

495

491, 492 Full-page illustrations to features in the *AT&T Magazine*. Fig. 491, mainly white with blue tones, relates to new ways for measuring a company's success; Fig. 492, blue, white, green and grey on orange-yellow, illustrates an article about a new complex computer system. (USA)
493 Cover of an issue of *Ambassador*, the in-flight magazine of TWA. Red title, green block, black text, polychrome illustrations, on white. (USA)
494 Cover of a magazine for clients of a Japanese photo type-setter. Grey on black, block at top right in turquoise. (JPN)
495, 496 Complete double spread and illustration in grey for an article about stress in *Legal Assistant Today*. (USA)
497 Detail of an illustration for an article about finishing agents and detergents, in *Industrial Launderer*. (USA)

491, 492 Ganzseitige Illustrationen zu Beiträgen im *AT&T Magazine*. Abb. 491, vorwiegend weiss mit Blautönen, gehört zu einem Beitrag über Geschäftspolitik und Erfolg; Abb. 492, blau, weiss, grün und grau auf Orangegelb, illustriert einen Artikel über ein Computer-System. (USA)
493 «Wie man die Telekommunikations-Revolution überlebt.» Umschlag für eine Ausgabe von *Ambassador*, Kundenzeitschrift der TWA. (USA)
494 Umschlag der Kundenzeitschrift eines japanischen Photosatz-Herstellers. Grau auf Schwarz, oberes rechtes Feld türkis. (JPN)
495, 496 Doppelseite und Illustration in Grau für einen Beitrag über Stress in *Legal Assistant Today* (Juristen-Fachorgan). (USA)
497 Detail einer Illustration für einen Beitrag über Waschmittelingredienzen, in *Industrial Launderer*, Magazin für gewerbliche Wäschereien. (USA)

491, 492 Illustrations pleine page pour des articles de l'*AT&T Magazine*. La fig. 491, en blanc avec du bleu, illustre un sujet de stratégie et succès en affaires, la fig. 492, bleu, blanc, vert et gris sur orange, un article sur un système informatique. (USA)
493 «Comment survivre à la révolution des télécommunications.» Couverture d'un numéro d'*Ambassador*, revue des passagers de TWA. (USA)
494 Couverture du magazine clients d'un atelier de photocomposition japonais. Gris sur noir, section en haut à droite turquoise. (JPN)
495, 496 Double page complète et illustration en gris pour un article sur le stress dans la revue juridique *Legal Assistant Today*. (USA)
497 Détail d'une illustration pour un article sur le blanchissage industriel, dans la revue spécialisée *Industrial Launderer*. (USA)

496

497

201

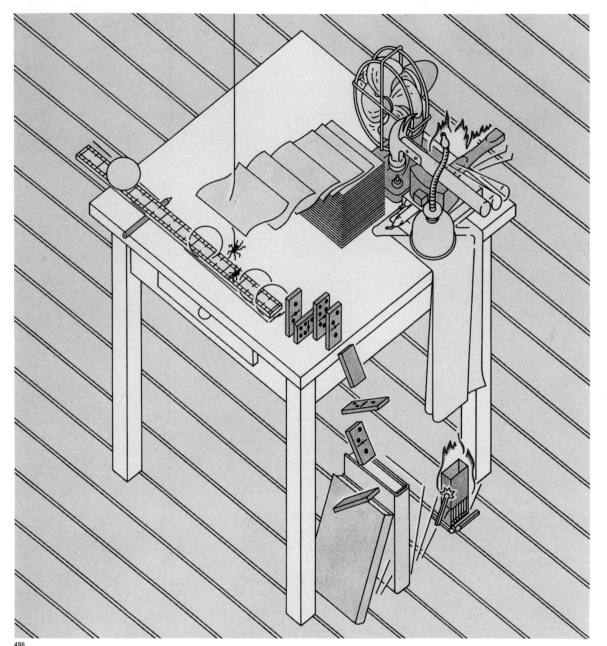

498

House Organs
Hauszeitschriften
Journaux d'entreprise

ARTIST / KÜNSTLER / ARTISTE:

498 George Hardie
499 Dan Fern
500 Darigo
501 Stanislas Bouvier
502 Fred Otnes

DESIGNER / GESTALTER / MAQUETTISTE:

498, 499 David Hillman/Sarah Pyne
500, 501 Any Dubois
502 Paul Langmuir

ART DIRECTOR / DIRECTEUR ARTISTIQUE:

498, 499 David Hillman
500, 501 Jacques Tribondeau
502 Paul Langmuir

AGENCY / AGENTUR / AGENCE – STUDIO:

498, 499 Pentagram

PUBLISHER / VERLEGER / EDITEUR:

498, 499 Ericsson Information Systems
500, 501 Essa SAF

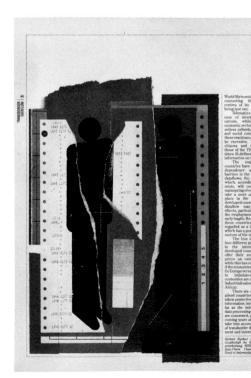
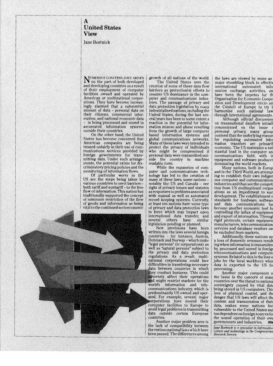

499

498, 499 Illustration and a double spread from articles in *Information Resource Management*. Fig. 498: "Potential hazards of electronic funds transfer"; Fig. 499: "Transborder Data Flow". (USA)
500, 501 Polychrome covers for *Pétrole Progrès*, the customer magazine of the French *Esso*. (FRA)
502 Cover with front flap from the annual report 1984 of *Arrow Automotive Industries*. The illustration refers to *Arrow's* role in the car-service business and shows some of its products. (USA)

498, 499 Illustration und eine Doppelseite aus Beiträgen in *Information Resource Management*. Abb. 498: «Potentielle Gefahren beim elektronischen Bankverkehr»; Abb. 499: «Grenzüberschreitender Datenverkehr». (USA)
500, 501 Mehrfarbige Umschläge für *Pétrole Progrès*, Kundenzeitschrift der französischen *Esso*. (FRA)
502 Umschlag mit vorderer Klappe für den Jahresbericht 1984 der *Arrow Automotive Industries*. Die Illustration bezieht sich auf *Arrows* Rolle im Auto-Service-Geschäft und zeigt einige Produkte. (USA)

498, 499 Illustration et page double d'articles parus dans la revue d'informatique *Information Resource Management*. Fig. 498: «Dangers potentiels du transfert de fonds électronique»; fig. 499: «Transfert de données sans frontières». Couleur. (USA)
500, 501 Couvertures polychromes de *Pétrole Progrès*, la revue clients d'*Esso*-France. (FRA)
502 Couverture (y compris le rabat de première page) du rapport annuel pour 1984 d'*Arrow Automotive Industries*. L'illustration interprète le rôle d'*Arrow* dans les services automobiles et présente certains de ses produits. (USA)

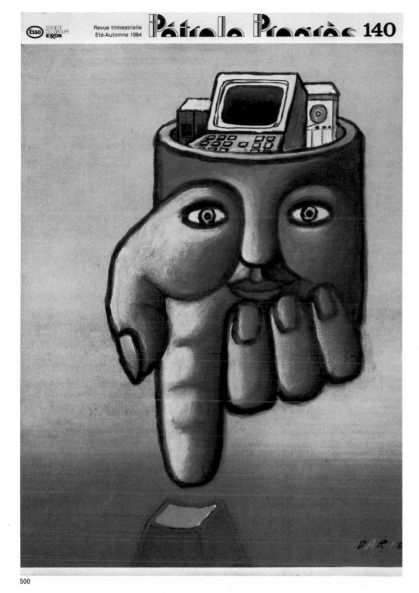

500

501

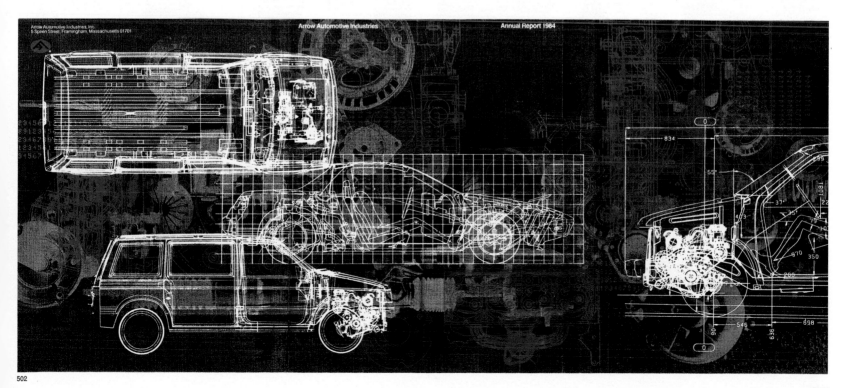

502

Annual Reports
Jahresberichte
Rapports annuels

ARTIST / KÜNSTLER / ARTISTE:

503–505 Tom Hennesy
506, 507 Alan Colvin
508 Alan E. Cober

DESIGNER / GESTALTER / MAQUETTISTE:

503–505 Bob Ankers/Dan Doherty
506, 507 Alan Colvin
508 John Waters

503–505 Cover and illustrations from the *Edgewood Children's Center* annual report. The window-pane, child and various groups of persons who aid the child have been separately die-cut to form a composite picture over six pages. In Fig. 505 the pages have been turned over to reveal the backs of the last group and the illustration hidden in Fig. 504. In black and white. (USA)
506, 507 Full-page illustrations from an annual report for the *Boy Scouts of America*. (USA)
508 Double spread with full-page illustration (pale head on blue background) from an annual report for *Curtiss Wright*, an industrial corporation engaged in aerospace, flow control etc. (USA)

503–505 Umschlag mit ausgestanztem Fensterausschnitt und Ansichten aus dem Inhalt eines Jahresberichtes für *Edgewood*, eine Fürsorgestelle für Kinder. In Abb. 504 werden ausser dem Kind einzelne, ausgestanzte Personengruppen sichtbar, die für das Kind da sind; Abb. 505 zeigt die Rückseite der Gruppen und die in Abb. 504 verdeckte Illustration. In Schwarzweiss. (USA)
506, 507 Ganzseitige Illustrationen aus einem Jahresbericht für die *Boy Scouts of America*. (USA)
508 Doppelseite mit ganzseitiger Illustration (heller Kopf vor blauem Hintergrund) aus einem Jahresbericht für *Curtiss Wright*, Hersteller von Sicherheitsventilen. (USA)

503–505 Couverture (fenêtre découpée) et diverses illustrations d'un rapport annuel du centre d'aide à l'enfance *Edgewood*. La fig. 504 montre, outre l'enfant, divers groupes de personnes en découpe, censés s'occuper des enfants; ces groupes sont vus de dos dans la fig. 505, qui révèle l'illustration masquée dans la fig. 504. Noir et blanc. (USA)
506, 507 Illustrations pleine page pour un rapport annuel de *Boy Scouts of America*. (USA)
508 Page double avec illustration pleine page (tête claire sur fond bleu) d'un rapport annuel de *Curtiss Wright*, fabricant de soupapes de sûreté de haute précision. (USA)

Edgewood Has Come To The Aid Of Troubled Children For Generations. Annual Report 1983–84

503

506

507

The Child
This child is not alone—unlike many suffering from abuse, neglect and severe learning disabilities. He is enveloped in a network of caring adults all working to heal his emotional scars and encourage his growth.

504

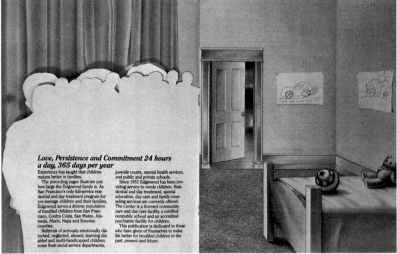

Love, Persistence and Commitment 24 hours a day, 365 days per year
Experience has taught that children mature better in families.

The preceding pages illustrate just how large the Edgewood family is. As San Francisco's only full-service residential and day treatment program for pre-teenage children and their families, Edgewood serves a diverse population of troubled children from San Francisco, Contra Costa, San Mateo, Alameda, Marin, Napa and Sonoma counties.

Referrals of seriously emotionally disturbed, neglected, abused, learning disabled and multi-handicapped children come from social service departments, juvenile courts, mental health services, and public and private schools.

Since 1851 Edgewood has been providing service to needy children. Residential and day treatment, special education, day care and family counseling services are currently offered. The Center is a licensed community care and day care facility, a certified nonpublic school and an accredited psychiatric facility for children.

This publication is dedicated to those who have given of themselves to make life better for troubled children in the past, present and future.

505

ART DIRECTOR / DIRECTEUR ARTISTIQUE:

503–505 David Gauger
506, 507 Alan Colvin/Woody Pirtle
508 John Waters

AGENCY / AGENTUR / AGENCE – STUDIO:

503–505 Gauger Sparks Silva, Inc.
506, 507 Pirtle Design
508 John Waters Associates

For controlling water and steam in nuclear reactors, Target Rock Corporation manufactures a variety of high quality safety relief valves. For the shipbuilding and chemical industries, the Buffalo Facility produces extruded seamless tubing and structural shapes.

I

n a recently applied for patent, Metal Improvement Company has disclosed the capability of electronic measurement and microprocessor control of the flow rate of metallic shot.

Curtiss-Wright Flight Systems is a supplier of flight control and actuation components and systems to the commercial and military aerospace markets, as well as to the NASA Space Shuttle Program.

In many other industries, statistical quality control methods are employed to determine if a component is acceptable or a final product is okay to ship. In this manner, a small number of units in a lot is sampled and checked, and the entire lot is statistically assumed to be acceptable if the sample is acceptable.

The people of Flight Systems are compelled to go many steps further in their quest for quality.

Because the materials, tools and production machines are of necessity very expensive, mistakes that are caught before they are shipped to the customer are still very costly. To succeed as a business enterprise, quality has to be designed in and built in, from the start.

Over the last several years, Flight Systems has invested $3.0MM in new, Numerical Control (NC) and Computer Numerical Control (CNC) machining centers. The delicate probes on many of these machines measure the quality of each workpiece *as it is manufactured*, with an accuracy generally unavailable from "off-line" inspection devices.

Computer terminals throughout the facility now track and calculate all of the data needed to stay on top of the quality task.

In the past, component parts might go through several iterations of rework and reinspection before they could be accepted. When you are working on fixed price contracts or tight delivery schedules, doing it right the first time takes on added importance.

The Buffalo Facility, which extrudes seamless thick wall tubing and structural shapes from molten alloys and stainless steel, has seen the nature of its business changing. Customer inventories are lower, lead times are shorter and competition is worldwide. The facility, to succeed, must respond, and here again, quality is the key.

In 1982, a complete organizational change in the quality department produced better performance at lower cost.

Curtiss-Wright Flight Systems Power Hinges, like this B-70 wing tip fold actuator, save weight and space while providing high torque and rugged reliability.

Curtiss-Wright Flight Systems provides the entire flap and slat actuation system (shown above) for the Grumman F-14A Tomcat, the navy's front line fighter. The entire system is tested under simulated flight conditions.

The 60-foot long payload bay door of the Space Shuttle is operated by six door hinge actuators. Each actuator is only three inches in diameter and weighs less than six pounds!

10

11

508

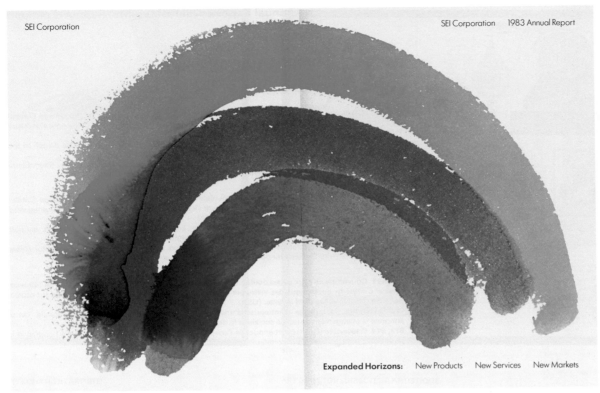

SEI Corporation

SEI Corporation   1983 Annual Report

Expanded Horizons: New Products   New Services   New Markets

515

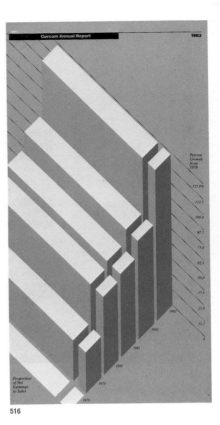

516

Annual Reports
Jahresberichte
Rapports annuels

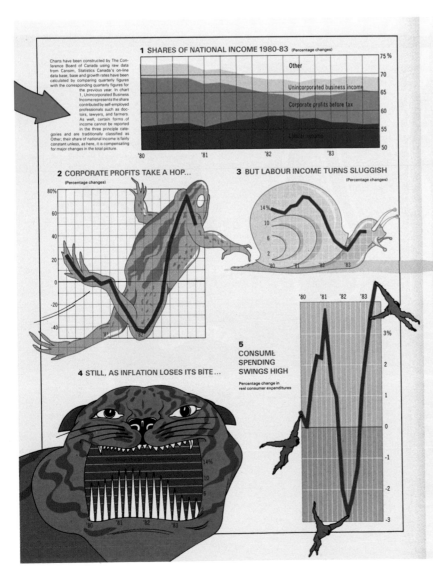

Charts have been constructed by The Conference Board of Canada using raw data from Cansim, Statistics Canada's on-line data base, base and growth rates have been calculated by comparing quarterly figures with the corresponding quarterly figures for the previous year. In chart 1, Unincorporated Business Income represents the share contributed by self-employed professionals such as doctors, lawyers, and farmers. As well, certain forms of income cannot be reported in the three principle categories and are traditionally classified as Other; their share of national income is fairly constant unless, as here, it is compensating for major changes in the total picture.

1 SHARES OF NATIONAL INCOME 1980-83 (Percentage changes)

Other
Unincorporated business income
Corporate profits before tax
Labour income

'80   '81   '82   '83

2 CORPORATE PROFITS TAKE A HOP…
(Percentage changes)

3 BUT LABOUR INCOME TURNS SLUGGISH
(Percentage changes)

4 STILL, AS INFLATION LOSES ITS BITE …

5 CONSUME SPENDING SWINGS HIGH

Percentage change in real consumer expenditures

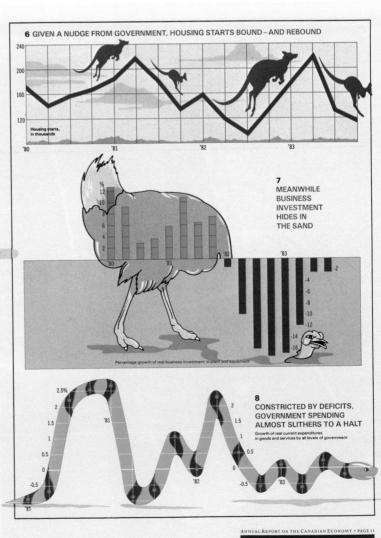

6 GIVEN A NUDGE FROM GOVERNMENT, HOUSING STARTS BOUND – AND REBOUND

Housing starts, in thousands

'80   '81   '82   '83

7 MEANWHILE BUSINESS INVESTMENT HIDES IN THE SAND

Percentage growth of real business investment in plant and equipment

8 CONSTRICTED BY DEFICITS, GOVERNMENT SPENDING ALMOST SLITHERS TO A HALT

Growth of real current expenditures in goods and services by all levels of government

ANNUAL REPORT ON THE CANADIAN ECONOMY • PAGE 11

519

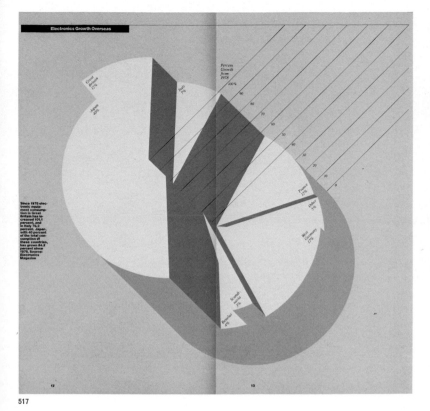

517

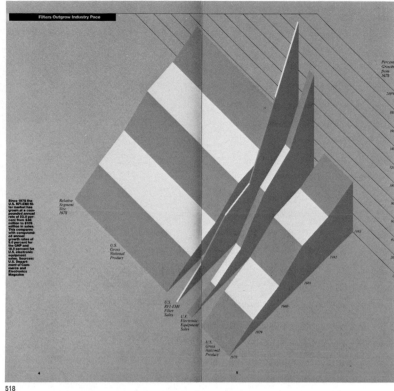

518

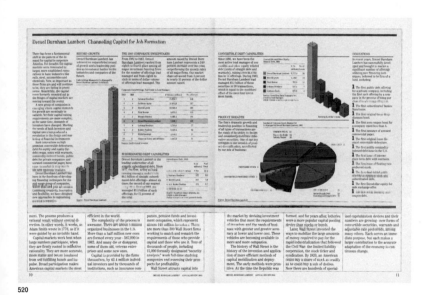

520

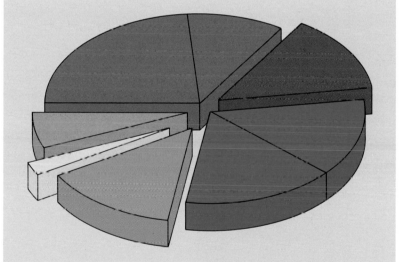

521

ARTIST / KÜNSTLER / ARTISTE:

515 George Tscherny
516 518 Wayne W Webb/Jerome W. Lenz
519 Nigel Holmes

DESIGNER / GESTALTER / MAQUETTISTE:

515 George Tscherny
516–518 Wayne W. Webb
519 Louis Fishauf
520, 521 Kaspar Schmid

ART DIRECTOR / DIRECTEUR ARTISTIQUE:

515 George Tscherny
516–518 Wayne W. Webb
519 Louis Fishauf
520, 521 Colin Forbes/Kaspar Schmid

AGENCY / AGENTUR / AGENCE – STUDIO:

515 George Tscherny, Inc.
516–518 Robertz, Webb & Co.
520, 521 Pentagram USA

515 Complete cover of the annual report of the SEI Corporation. Arcs in green, mauve, blue. (USA)
516–518 Cover and double spreads from the 1983 annual report of *Corcom*, suppliers of powerline filters to the electronics industry. All graphs in pastel shades on toning tinted paper. (USA)
519 Double spread from an "Annual report on the Canadian economy" issued by *Saturday Night* in collaboration with the Conference Board of Canada and based on data by Statistics Canada. (CAN)
520, 521 Double spread and the pie-chart from an annual report of *Drexel Burnham Lambert*. (USA)

515 «Erweiterte Horizonte – neue Produkte, neue Dienstleistungen, neue Märkte.» Vollständiger Umschlag für einen Jahresbericht der SEI Corporation. (USA)
516–518 Umschlag und Doppelseiten aus dem Jahresbericht 1983 von *Corcom*, Hersteller von Leistungsnetzfiltern für die elektronische Industrie. In Pastellfarben auf getöntem Papier. (USA)
519 Doppelseite aus einem «Jahresbericht der kanadischen Wirtschaft» mit ungewöhnlichen Diagrammen. Die jeweilige Aussage wird durch die Tiere verstärkt. (CAN)
520, 521 Doppelseite und das Diagramm aus einem Jahresbericht für *Drexel Burnham Lambert*. (USA)

515 «Horizons élargis – des produits nouveaux, des services nouveaux, des marchés nouveaux.» Couverture complète d'un rapport annuel de la SEI Corporation. (USA)
516–518 Couverture et doubles pages du rapport annuel pour 1983 de *Corcom*, fabricant de redresseurs pour l'industrie électronique. Tons pastel sur papier teinté. (USA)
519 Page double d'un «Rapport annuel de l'économie du Canada» illustré de diagrammes hors du commun. Les animaux renforcent l'effet de visualisation par graphiques. (CAN)
520, 521 Double page et diagramme circulaire. Rapport annuel de *Drexel Burnham Lambert*. (USA)

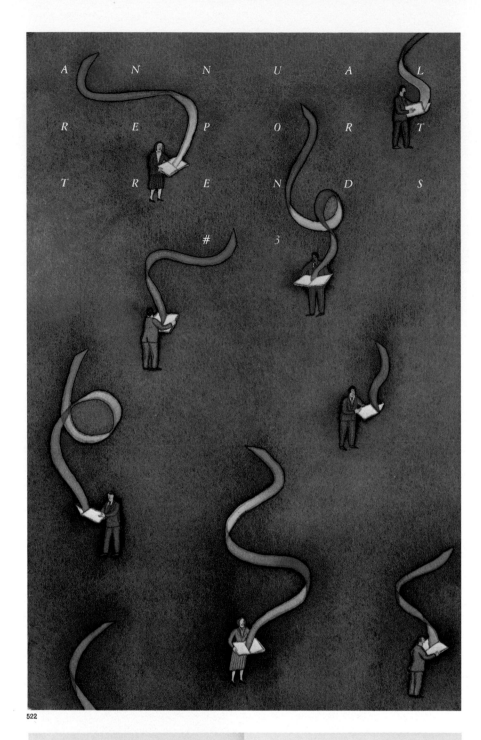

522

524

ARTIST / KÜNSTLER / ARTISTE:

522, 523 Lonni Sue Johnson
524–526 James McMullan
527 Tim Lewis/Colleen Quinn/Carol Vibbert

DESIGNER / GESTALTER / MAQUETTISTE:

522, 523 Tom Laidlaw
524–526 Karen Skelton
527 Kit Hinrichs/Lenore Bartz

ART DIRECTOR / DIRECTEUR ARTISTIQUE:

522, 523 Michael Weymouth
524–526 Milton Glaser
527 Kit Hinrichs

AGENCY / AGENTUR / AGENCE – STUDIO:

522, 523 Weymouth Design Inc.
524–526 Milton Glaser, Inc.
527 Jonson Pedersen Hinrichs & Shakery

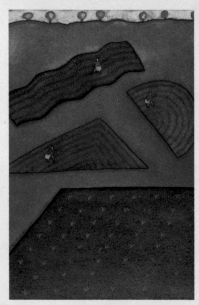

523

525

526

Annual Reports
Jahresberichte
Rapports annuels

522, 523 Cover and double spread from a brochure about the design of annual reports, issued by the paper manufacturer *Warren*. Fig. 523, with brown fields and green grass, illustrates the diversification in business of the *Chelsea Industries*. (USA)
524–526 Cover and double spreads from an annual report of *Schlumberger*. The logging of an oil well is told and illustrated in comic-strip form. All illustrations are in full colour. (USA)
527 Double spread from an article on the myths and legends associated since earliest history with certain trees, from a house organ of *Potlatch*, a paper manufacturer. (USA)

522, 523 Umschlag und Doppelseite aus einer Broschüre über die Gestaltung von Annual Reports, herausgegeben von dem Papierhersteller *Warren*. Abb. 523, mit braunen Feldern und grünem Rasen, illustriert die Diversifikation im Geschäftsbereich der *Chelsea Industries*. (USA)
524–526 Umschlag und Doppelseiten aus einem Jahresbericht von *Schlumberger*. Anhand der Bildgeschichte wird eine Ölbohrungs-Messung erläutert. Alle Illustrationen sind mehrfarbig. (USA)
527 Doppelseite aus einem Beitrag über Bäume, in der Hauszeitschrift von *Potlatch*. (USA)

522, 523 Couverture et double page d'une brochure sur la conception des rapports annuels, publiée par le papetier *Warren*. La fig. 523 – champs bruns et gazon vert – illustre la diversification intervenue dans le domaine d'activité de *Chelsea Industries*. (USA)
524–526 Couverture et doubles pages d'un rapport annuel de *Schlumberger*. La bande dessinée sert à expliquer les opérations de carottage. Toutes les illustrations sont polychromes. (USA)
527 Double page d'un article consacré aux arbres, dans la revue d'entreprise du papetier *Potlatch* Corporation. (USA)

527

528

530

Gaetano Tumiati
Roman
Suhrkamp

529

533

528 Complete cover for a book by the *Hobbit Presse*—"Dr. Lao's Great Circus". Figures and faces mainly in green and yellow shades, pink cases on wine-red ground, white title. (GER)
529 For a novel, "The Plaster Corset", in pale grey. (GER)
530–532 Covers from a series of Italian paperbacks published by *Boringhieri*. Fig. 530: "Advice to a Young Scientist", drawing in ochre; Fig. 531: a study of Freud's psychoanalysis and its influence on literature, dark brown on beige; Fig. 532: a work by six authorities on the nature of the universe. (ITA)
533, 534 Polychrome covers for books published by the *Klett-Cotta* house. Fig. 533: "To Child Maturity"—a plea for adults to maintain the child's characteristics such as a thirst for knowledge, candour, spontaneity; Fig. 534: a love story set in New York (translated from the English). (GER)
535 Cover of a book about the experiment to transform a repressive psychiatric clinic into a therapeutic community. (ITA)

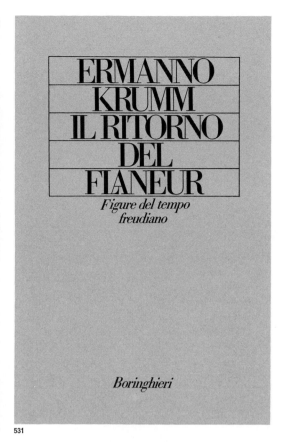

531

532

534

535

ARTIST / KÜNSTLER / ARTISTE:

528, 533, 534 Dietrich Ebert
530 Ben Shahn
535 Lidia Ferrara

DESIGNER / GESTALTER / MAQUETTISTE:

529–532 Willy Fleckhaus
535 Lidia Ferrara

ART DIRECTOR / DIRECTEUR ARTISTIQUE:

528, 533, 534 Dietrich Ebert
529–532 Willy Fleckhaus
535 Lidia Ferrara

AGENCY / AGENTUR / AGENCE – STUDIO:

528, 533, 534 D. & I. Ebert
535 Lidia Ferrara

PUBLISHER / VERLEGER / EDITEUR:

528, 533, 534 Klett-Cotta
529 Suhrkamp
530–532 Boringhieri
535 CDE Gruppo Mondadori

528 Vollständiger Umschlag für ein Buch der *Hobbit Presse*. Gestalten und Gesichter vorwiegend in Grün- und Gelbtönen, Kästen violett, Hintergrund weinrot, Titel weiss. (GER)
529 Für einen aus dem Italienischen übersetzten Roman. (GER)
530–532 Umschläge aus einer italienischen Taschenbuchreihe, herausgegeben von *Boringhieri*. Abb. 530: *Ratschläge für einen jungen Wissenschaftler*, Zeichnung in Ocker; Abb. 531: Studie über Freuds Psychoanalyse und ihren Einfluss auf die Literatur, dunkelbraun auf Beige; Abb. 532: sechs Wissenschaftler äussern sich über die Natur des Universums. (GER)
533, 534 Mehrfarbige Umschläge für Bücher des *Klett-Cotta*-Verlags. Abb. 533: hier wird für die Erhaltung kindlicher Eigenschaften wie Wissbegierde, Offenheit, Flexibilität plädiert; Abb. 534: eine Liebesgeschichte in New York. (GER)
535 Für Erfahrungsberichte über die Umwandlung einer psychiatrischen Klinik in eine therapeutische Gemeinschaft. (ITA)

528 Couverture complète d'un ouvrage publié aux Editions *Hobbit Presse*, «Le Grand Cirque du Dr Lao». Tons verts et jaunes prédominant pour les personnages et les visages, encadrements violets, fond bordeaux, titre blanc. (GER)
529 Pour le roman italien «Le Corset de plâtre». (GER)
530–532 Couvertures d'une collection de poche italienne chez *Boringhieri*. Fig. 530: *Conseils à un jeune scientifique*, dessin ocre: fig. 531: étude sur la psychanalyse et l'influence de Freud sur la littérature, brun foncé sur beige; fig. 532: six savants donnent leur version de la nature de l'univers. (ITA)
533, 534 Couvertures polychromes d'ouvrages parus aux Editions *Klett-Cotta*. Fig. 533: plaidoyer pour le maintien des vertus de l'enfant: appétit de savoir, franchise, souplesse d'esprit; fig. 534: une histoire d'amour, qui se déroule à New York. (GER)
535 «L'Institution niée»: sur la transformation d'une clinique psychiatrique en communauté thérapeutique libérée. (ITA)

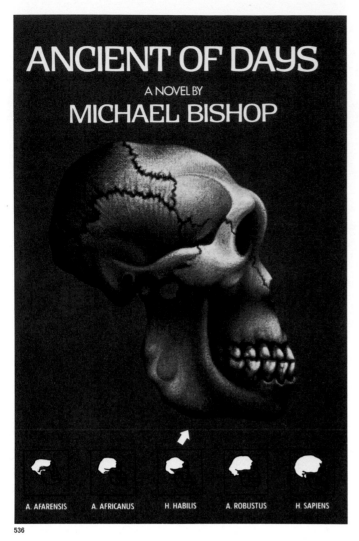

536

537

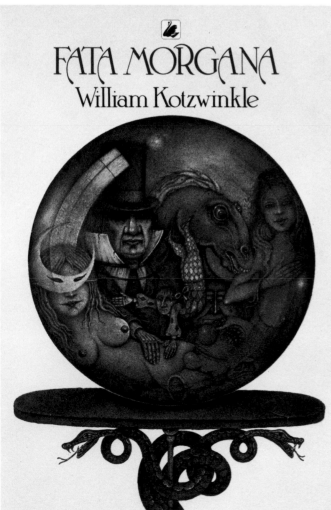

538

539

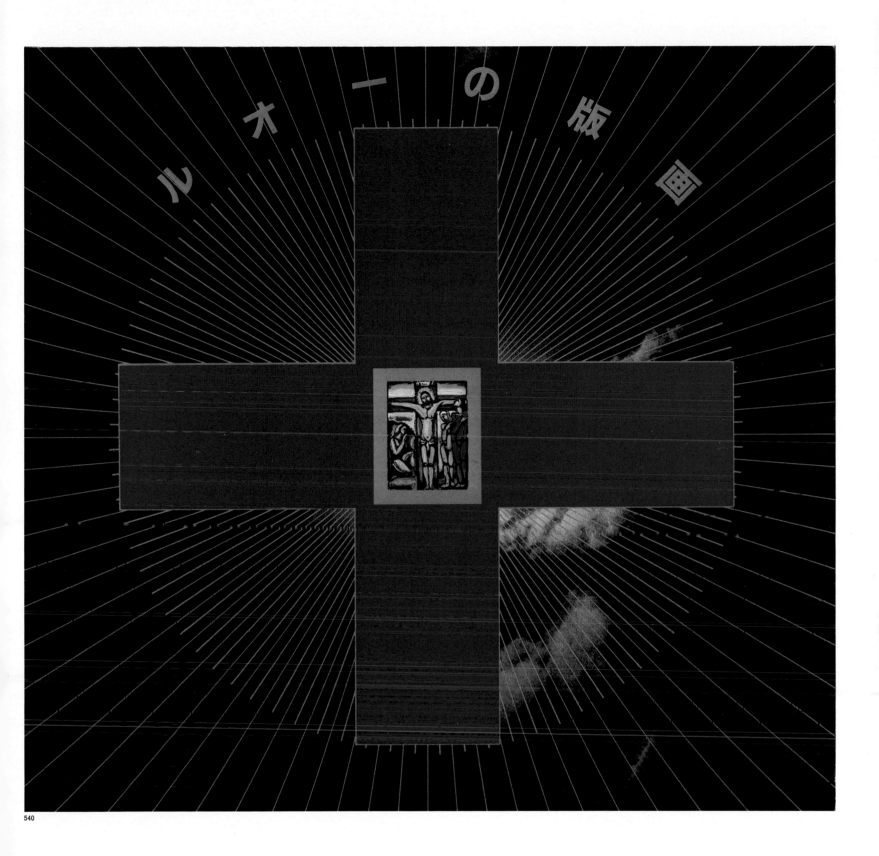

540

Book Covers / Buchumschläge
Couvertures de livres

ARTIST / KÜNSTLER / ARTISTE:

536 Christopher Zacharow
537 Mel Odom
538 Wayne Anderson
539 John Martinez
540 Kazumasa Nagai

DESIGNER / GESTALTER / MAQUETTISTE:

536, 537 Dorothy Wachtenheim
538 John Munday
539 Krystyna Skalski
540 Kazumasa Nagai

ART DIRECTOR / DIRECTEUR ARTISTIQUE:

536, 537 Dorothy Wachtenheim
538 John Munday
539 Krystyna Skalski
540 Kazumasa Nagai

AGENCY / AGENTUR / AGENCE – STUDIO:

540 Nippon Design Center

PUBLISHER / VERLEGER / EDITEUR:

536, 537 Abbor House Publishing / Hearst Books
538 Black Swan Books
539 Congdon & Wood
540 Museum of Modern Art, Toyama

536, 537 Book covers from one of a series of novels published by *Arbor House*. Fig. 536 in blue-grey, Fig. 537 polychrome. (USA)
538 Cover for "an adult fairytale" set in the year of 1861. Illustration in brown and green tones, text red and black. (GBR)
539 Cover in muted grey, green, pink, yellow, with black. (USA)
540 Cover of the catalogue for an exhibition of Rouault's prints in the Museum of Modern Art in Toyama. (JPN)

536, 537 Umschläge für eine von *Arbor House* herausgegebene Romanreihe. Abb. 536 in Blaugrau, Abb. 537 mehrfarbig. (USA)
538 Umschlag für «ein Märchen für Erwachsene» von William Kotzwinkle. Illustration in Braun- und Grüntönen. (GBR)
539 «Die Regenbogenschachtel.» In sanften Farben. (USA)
540 Umschlag für den Katalog einer Ausstellung von Rouaults graphischem Werk im Museum of Modern Art, Toyama. (JPN)

536, 537 Couvertures pour une collection de romans publiée par *Arbor House*. Fig. 536 gris bleu, 537 en polychromie. (USA)
538 Couverture d'un «conte pour adultes» de William Kotzwinkle. Illustrations en divers bruns et verts. (GBR)
539 «La Boîte arc-en-ciel.» Couleurs douces. (USA)
540 Couverture du catalogue d'une exposition de l'œuvre gravé de Rouault au Musée d'art moderne de Toyama. (JPN)

541

ARTIST / KÜNSTLER / ARTISTE:

541 Randal Pearson
542 Fred Marcellino
543 Robert Crawford
544, 545 Eleonore Schmid

DESIGNER / GESTALTER / MAQUETTISTE:

541 B. Martin Pedersen/Adrian Pulfer
542 Fred Marcellino

ART DIRECTOR / DIRECTEUR ARTISTIQUE:

541 B. Martin Pedersen/Adrian Pulfer
542 Louise Fili
543 Joseph Montebello
544, 545 Eleonore Schmid

AGENCY / AGENTUR / AGENCE – STUDIO:

541 Jonson Pedersen Hinrichs & Shakery

PUBLISHER / VERLEGER / EDITEUR:

541 Watson Guptill
542 Pentheon Books
543 Harper & Row
544, 545 Nord-Süd

541 Dust jacket for *Typography 5,* the Annual of the Type Directors Club. (USA)
542 Dust jacket for the English edition of *The Wall Jumper,* a novel by Peter Schneider. (USA)
543 A New York tube station is the setting for this illustration on the cover of a book published by *Harper & Row.* Green and brown tones, white wall tiles. (USA)
544, 545 Covers for two small-format books by the publishers *Nord-Süd.* Fig. 544: "Peeled and Cut"; Fig. 545: "Sweet, Sour, Juicy". The full-page illustrations (relating to the titles) are on tinted board, without text. (SWI)

541 Schutzumschlag für ein Jahrbuch über Typographie, herausgegeben vom Type Directors Club. (USA)
542 Schutzumschlag für die englische Ausgabe von Peter Schneiders Roman *Der Mauerspringer.* (USA)
543 «Süsse Gerechtigkeit.» Eine New Yorker U-Bahn-Station ist das Vorbild für diese Illustration eines Umschlags für einen bei *Harper & Row* erschienenen Roman. Grün- und Brauntöne, weisse Kacheln. (USA)
544, 545 Umschläge für zwei vom *Nord-Süd*-Verlag herausgegebene, kleinformatige Bücher mit Illustrationen zu den genannten Themen. (SWI)

541 Jaquette d'un annuel de l'art typographique publié par le Type Directors Club. (USA)
542 Jaquette de l'édition anglaise du roman *Le Sauteur de mur* de Peter Schneider. (USA)
543 «Douce justice.» Une station de métro newyorkais a inspiré cette illustration de couverture pour un roman publié chez *Harper & Row.* Verts et bruns, catelles blanches. (USA)
544, 545 Couvertures de deux ouvrages au petit format des Editions *Nord-Süd*: «Epluché et coupé», «Sucré, sur, juteux», avec des illustrations idoines. (SWI)

Book Covers
Buchumschläge
Couvertures de livres

542

543

544

545

546

548

547

551

546 Complete cover from Volume 1 of a continuing story of fantasy from a *Hobbit Presse* series by *Klett-Cotta* publishers. Brown stick with green string, blue nail, background in pale lilac. (GER)
547 Dust jacket for a book entitled "More Better Advertising". (JPN)
548 "Ardeshir and Stormy Wind." Cover in black on red for a volume of drawings by Ardeshir Mohassess, published by TUS, Teheran. (IRN)
549 Cover in pastel shades for a book entitled "Adulterer". (IRN)
550 Illustration in red on white for an Iranian book. (IRN)
551-553 Covers in black and white for a series published by *Odeon*, Prague, devoted to great names in cultural activities. (CSR)

549

550

ARTIST / KÜNSTLER / ARTISTE:

546 Dietrich Ebert
547 Tadanori Yokoo
548, 549 Ardeshir Mohasses
550 Parviz Shapour

DESIGNER / GESTALTER / MAQUETTISTE:

547 Tadanori Yokoo
548, 549 Ardeshir Mohasses
551–553 Jan Jiskra

ART DIRECTOR / DIRECTEUR ARTISTIQUE:

546 Dietrich Ebert
547 Tadanori Yokoo
548, 549 Ardeshir Mohasses

AGENCY / AGENTUR / AGENCE – STUDIO:

546 D. & I. Ebert

PUBLISHER / VERLEGER / EDITEUR:

546 Klett-Cotta
547 Madora Shuppan Publishing
548 TUS Publishers
549, 550 Morvareed Publishing
551–553 Odeon

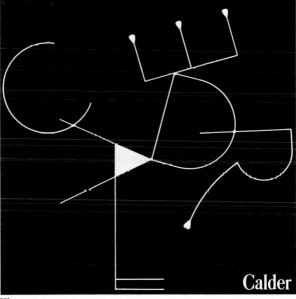

552

553

546 Vollständiger Umschlag für einen Band aus der *Hobbit-Presse*-Reihe des *Klett-Cotta*-Verlags, die anspruchsvoller Fantasy-Literatur gewidmet ist. Brauner Stock mit grüner Schnur, Hintergrund in zartem Mauve. (GER)
547 Umschlag für ein Buch mit dem Titel «Mehr bessere Werbung». (JPN)
548 «Ardeshir und stürmischer Wind.» Umschlag, schwarz auf Rot, für einen Band mit Zeichnungen von Ardeshir Mohassess, erschienen bei TUS. (IRN)
549 Umschlag in Pastellfarben für ein Buch mit dem Titel «Ehebrecher». (IRN)
550 Illustration in Rot auf Weiss, für ein iranisches Buch. (IRN)
551–553 Umschläge in Schwarzweiss für eine bei *Odeon*, Prag, erschienene Reihe, die Kulturschaffenden gewidmet ist. (CSR)

546 Couverture complète pour un volume de la collection *Hobbit Presse* des Editions *Klett-Cotta* consacrée à la fiction de haut niveau. Bâton brun, corde verte sur fond mauve délicat. (GER)
547 Jaquette de l'ouvrage «Pour une meilleure publicité». (JPN)
548 «Ardeshir et le vent de tempête.» Couverture noir sur rouge d'un album des dessins d'Ardeshir Mohassess paru chez TUS à Téhéran. (IRN)
549 Couverture aux tons pastel pour un livre intitulé «Adultère». (IRN)
550 Illustration rouge sur blanc pour un ouvrage publié en Iran. (IRN)
551–553 Couvertures noir et blanc pour trois titres d'une collection consacrée aux interprètes de la culture, chez *Odeon* à Prague. (CSR)

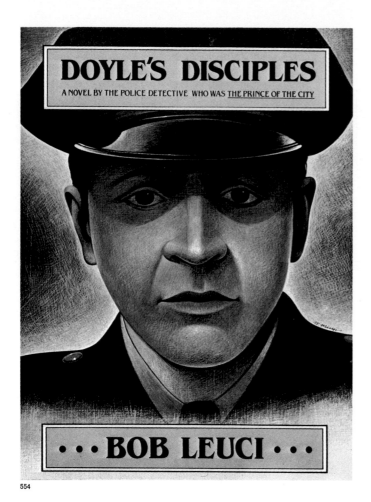

554

555

Book Covers
Buchumschläge
Couvertures de livres

554 Polychrome cover for a crime story by a former, very popular police detective. (USA)
555 For a richly-illustrated children's book which tells the story of the flower on the carpet. Carpet background blue, children and boat white. (IRN)
556 Cover design for telephone directories in the south-west of the United States. Polychrome letters on white, upper part black on yellow ground. (USA)
557 Complete cover for a novel. Illustration predominantly in brown tones. (USA)
558 For one of the novels published by *Times Books*. Woman dressed in grey, brownish meadow, white church with dark roof, blue mountains. (USA)
559 Complete cover for a paperback containing ghost stories from a competition judged by three famous authors. In brown tones, Punch dressed in red. (GBR)

554 Mehrfarbiger Umschlag für einen Kriminalroman, geschrieben von einem ehemaligen, sehr populären Kriminalkommissar. (USA)
555 Für ein reich illustriertes Kinderbuch, das von der Geschichte der Blumen des Teppichs handelt. Teppichgrund blau, Kinder und Boot weiss. (IRN)
556 Umschlaggestaltung für Telephonbücher im Südwesten der Vereinigten Staaten. Mehrfarbige Buchstaben auf Weiss, oberer Teil schwarz auf gelbem Grund. (USA)
557 Vollständiger Umschlag für einen Roman mit dem Titel «Kalter, unverschämter Baum». Illustration vorwiegend in Brauntönen. (USA)
558 Für einen bei *Times Books* erschienenen Roman. Grau gekleidete Frau in bräunlicher Wiese, weisse Kirche mit dunklem Dach vor bläulicher Landschaft. (USA)
559 Vollständiger Umschlag für eine Taschenbuchausgabe mit einer Sammlung von Gespenstergeschichten. In Brauntönen, Kaspar rot gekleidet. (GBR)

554 Couverture polychrome d'un roman policier écrit par un commissaire à la retraite jadis très populaire. (USA)
555 Pour un livre d'enfants richement illustré, qui conte l'histoire des motifs floraux des tapis. Fond de tapis bleu, barque et enfants blancs. (IRN)
556 Couverture-type des annuaires téléphoniques du Sud-Ouest des Etats-Unis: lettres polychromes sur blanc, partie supérieure noir sur fond jaune. (USA)
557 Couverture complète d'un roman intitulé «L'Arbre froid et impertinent». L'illustration est surtout exécutée en diverses teintes marron. (USA)
558 Pour un roman publié par *Times Books*. Femme vêtue de gris dans un pré marron, église blanche au toit sombre sur fond de paysage bleuâtre. (USA)
559 Couverture complète d'un livre de poche contenant un recueil d'histoires de fantômes. Divers bruns, guignol vêtu de rouge. (GBR)

556

557

558

ARTIST / KÜNSTLER / ARTISTE:

554, 557, 558 Wendell Minor
555 N. Zarrinkelk
556 Jözef Sumichrast
559 Alan Lee

DESIGNER / GESTALTER / MAQUETTISTE:

554, 557, 558 Wendell Minor
559 John Munday

ART DIRECTOR / DIRECTEUR ARTISTIQUE:

554 Ruth Kobert
555 N. Zarrinkelk
556 Tim Honnell
557 Louise Noble
558 M. Enderson

AGENCY / AGENTUR / AGENCE – STUDIO:

554, 557, 558 Wendell Minor Design
556 Tracy-Locke/BBDO

PUBLISHER / VERLEGER / EDITEUR:

554 Freundlich Books
556 Mountain Bell
557 Ticknor & Fields
558 Times Books
559 Corgi Books

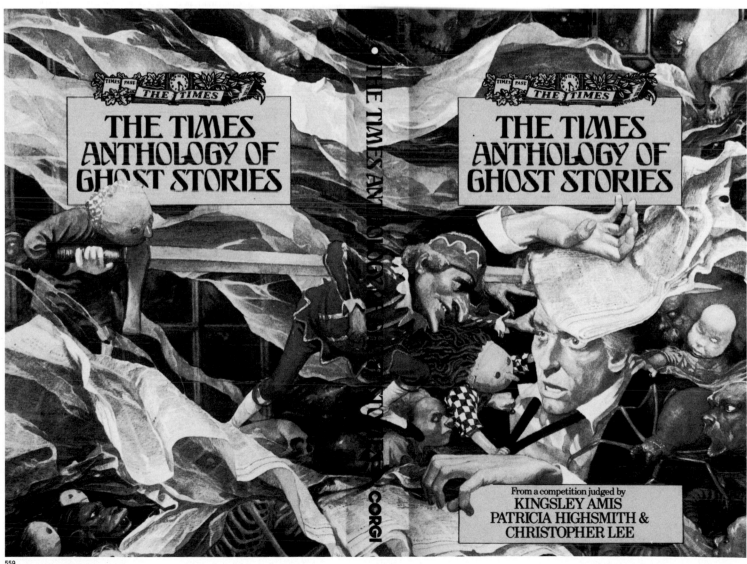

559

4

Trademarks

Letterheads

Calendars

Packaging

Record Covers

Schutzmarken

Briefköpfe

Kalender

Packungen

Schallplattenhüllen

Marques et emblèmes

En-têtes

Calendriers

Emballages

Pochettes de disques

Trademarks
Schutzmarken
Marques et emblèmes

560 Symbol and logo for the Public Broadcasting Service. Profiles in blue, white, red. (USA)
561 Symbol and logotype for the Angeles Corporation in California. (USA)
562 Symbol designed for the American Protection Industries, Inc. (USA)
563 Logo for the Central Typesetting Company. (USA)
564 Symbol for Go Tech Inc., makers of cups and plates in styrofoam and plastic. (CAN)
565 Easily recognizable logo for "Channel 39" television. (USA)
566 Symbol for the landscape planner and architect, David Baldwin. (USA)
567 Symbol for *Dacosystems*—a modular furniture manufacturing company. (USA)
568 Symbol for the Japanese bank *Mitsui*, claimed to be the oldest bank in the world. (JPN)
569 Logo for Seville's city transport (Transportes Urbano de Sevilla). (SPA)
570 Symbol for the amalgamation of two flour mills. (SWI)
571 Symbol for the LAOOC Amateur Athletic Foundation. (USA)

560 Symbol und Logo für Public Broadcasting Service. Profile in Blau, Weiss, Rot. (USA)
561 Signet für die Angeles Corporation in Kalifornien. (USA)
562 Logo für die American Protection Industries, Inc. (USA)
563 Signet für die Central Typesetting Company. (USA)
564 Symbol für Go Tech Inc., Hersteller von Tassen und Tellern aus Styropor und Plastik. (CAN)
565 Leicht erkennbares Logo für die amerikanische Fernsehstation «Channel 39». (USA)
566 Für den Landschaftsarchitekten und -Planer David Baldwin entwickeltes Signet. (USA)
567 Symbol für *Dacosystems*, einen Hersteller von Möbelelementen. (USA)
568 Symbol für die japanische *Mitsui*-Bank, die als älteste der Welt gelten soll. (JPN)
569 Logo der städtischen Verkehrsbetriebe Sevilla (Transportes Urbano de Sevilla). (SPA)
570 Für den Zusammenschluss von zwei Mühlen konzipiertes Signet. (SWI)
571 Symbol für die LAOOC-Stiftung für Amateur-Athleten. (USA)

560 Emblème et logo de Public Broadcasting Service. Profils bleu, blanc, rouge. (USA)
561 Emblème de la société californienne Angeles Corporation. (USA)
562 Emblème conçu pour American Protection Industries, Inc. (USA)
563 Logo de la Central Typesetting Company. (USA)
564 Emblème pour un fabricant de tasses et assiettes en styropore et plastique. (CAN)
565 Logo facilement reconnaissable de la chaîne de TV américaine «Channel 39». (USA)
566 Emblème créé pour l'architecte paysagiste David Baldwin. (USA)
567 Emblème de *Dacosystems*, fabricant d'éléments de mobilier. (USA)
568 Emblème de la banque japonaise *Mitsui*, considérée comme la plus vieille du monde. (JPN)
569 Logo des transports en commun de Séville (Transportes Urbano de Sevilla). (SPA)
570 Emblème conçu à l'occasion du fusionnement de deux minoteries. (SWI)
571 Emblème de la fondation LAOOC pour les athlètes amateurs. (USA)

ANGELES

561

565

560

562

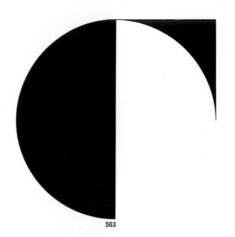

563

564

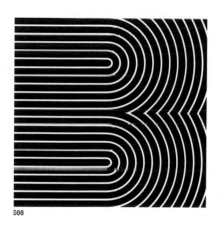

566

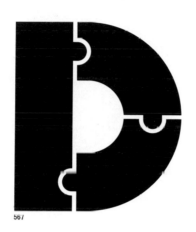

567

568

569

570

571

DESIGNER / GESTALTER / MAQUETTISTE:

560 Tom Geismar/Ivan Chermayeff
561 Paul Bice
562 Gary Hinsche
563, 567 Emmett Morava
564 Peter Adam
565 Waleo Horton
566 Alan Colvin
568 Takenobu Igarashi
569 Roberto Luna/Fernando Mendoza
570 Rosmarie Tissi
571 Ray Wood

ART DIRECTOR / DIRECTEUR ARTISTIQUE:

560 Tom Geismar/Ivan Chermayeff
561, 562 Robert Miles Runyan
563, 567 Emmet Morava/Douglas Oliver
565 Waleo Horton/Jim Frazier
566 Alan Colvin
568 Takenobu Igarashi
569 Antonio Pérez
571 Keith Bright

AGENCY / AGENTUR / AGENCE – STUDIO:

560 Chermayeff & Geismar Associates
561, 562 Robert Miles Runyan & Associates
563, 567 Morava & Oliver Design Office
564 Gottschalk & Ash International
565 Arnold Harwell McClain/Sibley Peteet Design
566 Pirtle Design
568 Takenobu Igarashi Design
569 Luna, Mendoza & Pérez
570 Odermatt & Tissi
571 Bright & Associates

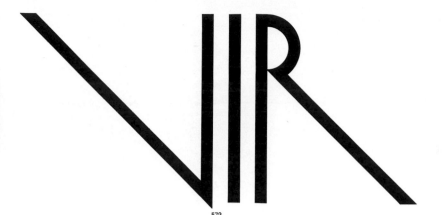

572

DESIGNER / GESTALTER / MAQUETTISTE:

572 Gianni Bortolotti
573 Alan Wood
574 Saul Bass/Art Goodman
575 Helmut Salden
576 Yukio Kanise
577 Lee Sarna
578 Kenny Garrison/Woody Pirtle
579 Jim Berte
580 Takenobu Igarashi
581 Thomas DiPaolo
582 Ken Cato
583 Rick Eiber

573

574

575

577

578

579

Trademarks / Letterheads
Schutzmarken / Briefköpfe
Marques et emblèmes / En-têtes

572 Logotype for an Italian boutique for men's fashions. (ITA)
573 Symbol for the Buckley Group. (USA)
574 Seal for the California Cheesemaking Cooperative. (USA)
575 Logo for the Stedelijk Museum in Amsterdam. (NLD)
576 Logotype for a Japanese amateur balloon club. (JPN)
577 Symbol for the Transnet Distributors Corporation. (USA)
578 Symbol for the American railroad line Railex. (USA)
579 Symbol for the Japanese publishers Obunsha. (JPN)
580 The Japanese picture-writing for "Tokyo" is presented in abstract form for this trademark for prêt-à-porter fashion. (JPN)
581 Writing paper for a graphic artist. "Di" is in red. (GER)
582 Letterhead for Dean, a firm of import consultants. (AUS)
583 For the "Type" gallery. The black-printed back of the paper allows the white letters to show through to the front. (USA)

572 Schriftzug einer italienischen Boutique für Männermode. (ITA)
573 Für die Buckley Group konzipiertes Signet. (USA)
574 Schutzmarke der kalifornischen Käse-Union. (USA)
575 Logo für das Stedelijk Museum in Amsterdam. (NLD)
576 Schriftzug für einen japanischen Amateur-Ballon-Club. (JPN)
577 Für Transnet Distributors Corp. entwickeltes Signet. (USA)
578 Signet für die amerikanische Eisenbahnlinie Railex. (USA)
579 Signet für den japanischen Verlag Obunsha. (JPN)
580 Die japanischen Schriftzeichen für «Tokyo», abstrahiert, als Markenzeichen für eine Prêt-à-Porter-Modekollektion. (JPN)
581 Briefpapier für einen Graphiker. «Di» in Rot. (GER)
582 Briefbogen für Dean, Berater der Importindustrie. (AUS)
583 Für die Galerie «Type». Von der schwarzbedruckten Rückseite des Briefpapiers scheinen die weissen Buchstaben durch. (USA)

572 Logo d'une boutique italienne de mode masculine. (ITA)
573 Emblème conçu pour le Buckley Group. (USA)
574 Le sceau de la California Cheesemaking Cooperative. (USA)
575 Logo du Stedelijk Museum d'Amsterdam. (NLD)
576 Logo d'un club des pilotes d'aérostat amateurs. (JPN)
577 Emblème créé pour Transnet Distributors Corp. (USA)
578 Emblème des chemins de fer américains Railex. (USA)
579 Emblème conçu pour l'éditeur japonais Obunsha. (JPN)
580 Marque déposée d'une collection de prêt-à-porter japonaise; créé à partir du signe calligraphique désignant «Tokyo». (JPN)
581 Papier à lettres d'un graphiste. «Di» en rouge. (GER)
582 Papier à lettres d'une firme-conseil en importation. (AUS)
583 En-tête de la galerie «Type.» Le verso imprimé en noir, les lettres blanches apparaissent en transparence. (USA)

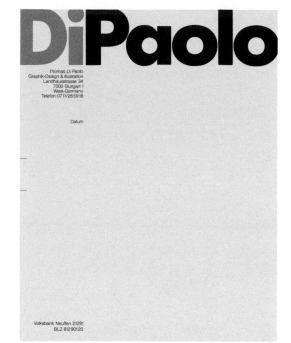

581

576

582

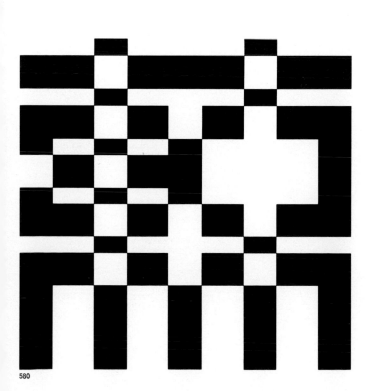

580

583

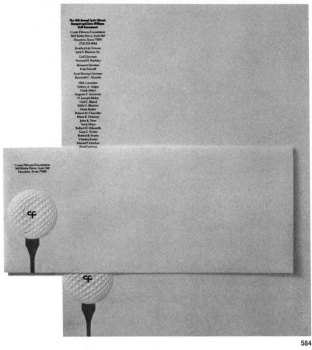

DESIGNER / GESTALTER / MAQUETTISTE:

585 Heather Cooper
588 José Costa Bello
592 Paul Bice

ARTIST / KÜNSTLER / ARTISTE:

584 Ellie Malavis
585 Heather Cooper
586 Winfried Symanzik
587 Martin Pedersen / Adrian Pulfer
588 Bjarne Norking
589 Jim Lienhart
591 Klaus Winterhager
592 Steve Sieler
594 So Man-Yee

584

585

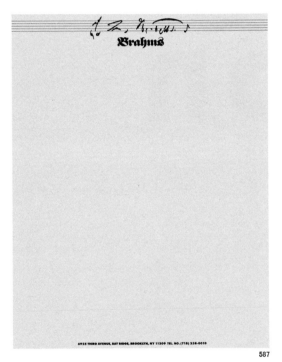

587

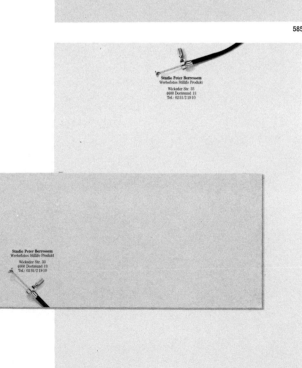

ART DIRECTOR / DIRECTEUR ARTISTIQUE:

584 Ellie Malavis
585 Heather Cooper
586 Winfried Symanzik
587 Martin Pedersen
588 Bjarne Norking / Alfredo Aquino
589 Jim Lienhart
590 Ken Cato
591 Klaus Winterhager
592 Robert Miles Runyan
594 Hon Bing-Wah

AGENCY / AGENTUR / AGENCE – STUDIO:

584 The Marschalk Co.
585 Heather Cooper Illustration & Design
586 Winfried Symanzik
587 Jonson Pedersen Hinrichs & Shakery
588 Enio, Associados Propaganda Ltda.
589 Jim Lienhart Design
590 Ken Cato Design Company Pty Ltd
592 Robert Miles Runyan & Associates
594 Kinggraphic

586

588

589

590

591

592

593

594

584 For the Cystic Fibrosis Foundation—stationery for their golf tournament, with a blind-embossed golf ball. The tee is yellow. (USA)
585 Letterhead and envelope for *Imprints*. Copper-toned and black vignette on structured paper in chamois. (CAN)
586 Letterhead and envelope for a photographic studio. Shutter release in black and white, text in magenta. (GER)
587 Letterhead in chamois with the name "Brahms" in red, grey stave. (USA)
588 Stationery for the advertising studio Enio. (BRA)
589 Red and violet on chamois; letterhead for a lithographer. (BRA)
590 Letterhead in soft colours for Lena Gan. (AUS)
591 For a federal youth culture association; black and white. (GER)
592 Letterhead for *Vuarnet-France*. Colours: blue, red and white. (FRA)
593 For the television network "Antenne 2", in blue, green, black. (FRA)
594 A three-dimensional effect is achieved with cut-outs folded and printed with Chinese characters in red on the letterhead for Man Luen Cheon. (HKG)

584 Von der Cystic-Fibrosis-Stiftung verwendetes Briefpapier und Couvert mit blindgeprägtem Golfball. Tee in kräftigem Gelb. (USA)
585 Briefpapier mit Umschlag für *Imprints*. Vignette kupferfarben und schwarz auf Chamois, strukturiertes Papier. (CAN)
586 Briefbogen und Couvert für ein Photostudio. Auslöser in Schwarzweiss, Schrift in Magenta. (GER)
587 «Brahms» in roter Frakturschrift, graue Notenlinien auf Chamois. (USA)
588 Für das Werbebüro Enio konzipiertes Briefpapier. (BRA)
589 Rot und violett auf Chamois; Briefkopf für einen Lithographen. (BRA)
590 In zarten Farben bedrucktes Briefpapier für Lena Gan. (AUS)
591 Für die Bundesvereinigung Kulturelle Jugendbildung e.V. (GER)
592 Briefkopf für *Vuarnet-France*. Farben: blau, rot und weiss. (FRA)
593 Für den Fernsehkanal «Antenne 2» konzipiertes Briefpapier. (FRA)
594 Durch vier mit chinesischen Zeichen rot bedruckte Einschnitte wird hier ein dreidimensionaler Effekt erzielt. (HKG)

584 En-tête et enveloppe utilisés par la fondation Cystic-Fibrosis. Balle de golf gaufrée à sec, tee jaune vif. (USA)
585 Papier à lettres et enveloppe pour *Imprints*. Vignette dans des tons cuivrés et noir sur chamois, papier structuré. (CAN)
586 En-tête et enveloppe d'un studio de photographie. Déclencheur en noir et blanc, texte en magenta. (GER)
587 «Brahms» en gothiques rouges, portées grises sur chamois. (USA)
588 Papier à lettres conçu pour le bureau de publicité Enio. (BRA)
589 Rouge et violet sur fond chamois; en-tête d'un lithographe. (BRA)
590 Papier à lettres aux couleurs tendres pour Lena Gan. (AUS)
591 Pour l'association culturelle de formation des jeunes. (GER)
592 En-tête de *Vuarnet-France*. Couleurs: bleu, rouge, blanc. (FRA)
593 Papier à lettres conçu pour la chaîne TV «Antenne 2». (FRA)
594 Les caractères chinois imprimés en rouge sur les incisions créent un effet tridimensionnel sur cet en-tête pour Man Luen Cheon. (HKG)

Calendars
Kalender
Calendriers

ARTIST / KÜNSTLER / ARTISTE:

595, 596 Gianfranco Ferroni
597–599 Takenobu Igarashi

DESIGNER / GESTALTER:

595, 596 Enzo Mari
597–599 Takenobu Igarashi

ART DIRECTOR:

595, 596 Giorgio Soavi
597–599 Takenobu Igarashi

AGENCY / AGENTUR / AGENCE:

597–599 Takenobu Igarashi

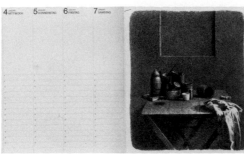

595

596

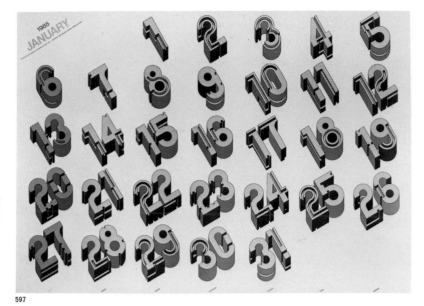

597

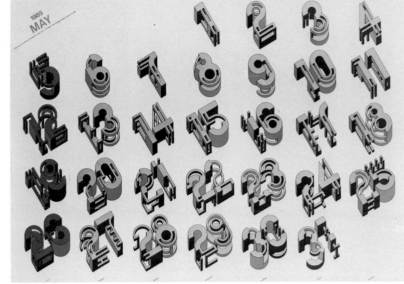

598

595, 596 Doppelseite und Illustration aus einem von *Olivetti* herausgegebenen Terminkalender, der jedes Jahr von einem anderen Künstler illustriert wird. (ITA)
597–599 Drei Monatsblätter eines Kalenders, der vom Museum of Modern Art in New York herausgegeben wurde. Jedes Blatt (alle mehrfarbig) zeigt eine andere Interpretation des Kalendariums. (USA)

595, 596 Double spread and illustration from a desk agenda issued by *Olivetti*. This company commissions a different artist every year to illustrate their agenda. (ITA)
597–599 Three monthly sheets of a calendar issued by the Museum of Modern Art in New York. Each sheet (all polychrome) shows a variation on the interpretation of the calendarium. (USA)

595, 596 Double page et illustration tirées d'un agenda édité par *Olivetti* et conçu chaque année par un artiste différent. (ITA)
597–599 Trois feuillets d'un calendrier (tout en couleurs) publié par le Musée d'Art Moderne de New York. Chacun présente une nouvelle interprétation du calendrier. (USA)

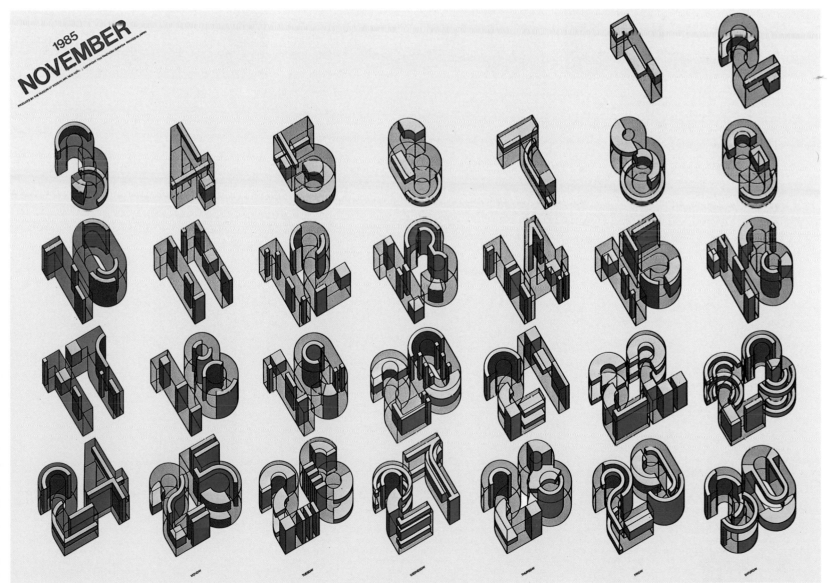

599

600

601

602

603

604

605

600–606 Six from a total of twenty-five interpretations of the Australian dollar and the complete poster-calander of the Australian Society of Accountants. The theme is: "No matter which way it is represented, the dollar has never looked better." The wide range of subjects portrayed on the calendar sheet (in airbrush technique and in photographs) refers to the wide scope of businesses the accountants assist. (AUS)

607 Poster-calendar from the paper manufacturer *Zanders Feinpapiere* to promote their products. The colours of their bookbinding materials are presented and the calendar itself is printed on their "new linen" *Efalin*. By the simple form of the calendarium (days on the left, months on the right in Roman figures) and the application of the sliders, the calender is made independent of the year. (GER)

600–606 Sechs der insgesamt fünfundzwanzig Interpretationen des Dollars (gemeint ist der australische) und vollständiger Poster-Kalender der Australian Society of Accountants (eine Vereinigung von Buchhaltern). Das Thema der sowohl in Spritztechnik als auch photographisch ausgeführten Illustrationen: «Der Dollar sah nie besser aus.» Die Vielfalt der Bereiche entspricht dem unbegrenzten Wirkungskreis der Buchhalter. (AUS)

607 Von dem Papierhersteller *Zanders Feinpapiere* als Produktwerbung versandter Poster-Kalender, der auf *Efalin*, Neuleinen, gedruckt ist und anhand dessen die Farben der Bucheinbandmaterialien vorgestellt werden. Die einfache Präsentation des Kalendariums, auf der linken Seite die Tage, auf der rechten die Monate, macht den Kalender unabhängig vom Jahr. (GER)

600–606 Six des vint-cinq variations sur le dollar (il s'agit du dollar australien) et calendrier-poster complet de l'Australian Society of Accountants (une association de comptables). Les illustrations réalisées à l'aérographe ou photographiquement ont pour thème: «Le dollar n'a jamais eu meilleure apparence.» La diversité des domaines que les illustrations évoquent correspond au champ d'action illimité des comptables. (AUS)

607 Calendrier-poster autopromotionnel distribué par l'entreprise *Zanders Feinpapiere* et imprimé sur leur papier *Efalin*, Neuleinen (nouvelle toile). Sur l'illustration, on peut voir toute la gamme de couleurs du matériel de reliure. La simplicité de la présentation, à gauche les jours, à droite les mois en chiffres romains, permet une utilisation prolongée du calendrier. (GER)

606

ARTIST / KÜNSTLER / ARTISTE:
600–606 Flett Henderson & Arnold

DESIGNER / GESTALTER / MAQUETTISTE:
600–606 Flett Henderson & Arnold
607 Klaus Winterhager

AGENCY / AGENTUR / AGENCE – STUDIO:
600–606 Flett Henderson & Arnold

607

233

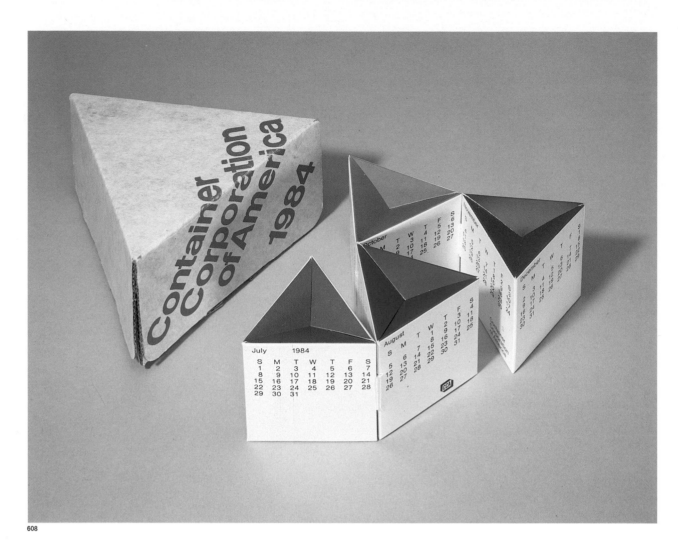

608

ARTIST / KÜNSTLER / ARTISTE:

611 Robert Van Nutt
612 Patty Dryden
613 Steve Carter
614 Niklaus Troxler

DESIGNER / GESTALTER / MAQUETTISTE:

608 Joseph Hutchcroft/Bob Swanson
609 Alan Peckolick
610 Tony DiSpigna

ART DIRECTOR:

608 Joseph Hutchcroft
611 Allen Weinberg
612 Mark Larson
613 Tony Lane/Nancy Donald
614 Niklaus Troxler

AGENCY / AGENTUR / AGENCE – STUDIO:

608 Container Corporation of America
614 Niklaus Troxler Graphik-Studio

PUBLISHER / VERLEGER / EDITEUR:

611–613 CBS Records
614 Hat Hut Records Ldt.

Calendars / Record Covers
Kalender / Schallplattenhüllen
Calendriers / Pochettes de disques

608 The *Container Corporation of America's* three-dimensional calendar and its corrugated cardboard box. The four connected triangles form a larger triangle which fits snugly into the box. (USA)
609, 610 The February sheet and the cover sheet of a calendar for PM Typography. (USA)
611 Album sleeve in blue tones on a dark backround for recordings by a Cuban saxophonist. (USA)
612 For the group The Frogs, an album cover in light and dark contrasts. (USA)
613 Album sleeve incorporating elements of earlier covers for a rock group. (USA)
614 Cover of an album with music by Erik Satie. Red, green and blue on white. (SWI)

611

612

609

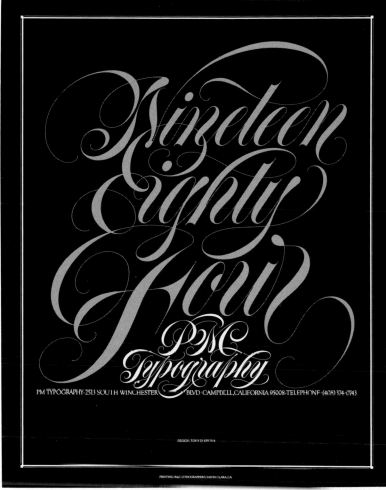

610

608 Dreidimensionaler Kalender der *Container Corporation of America*, mit Wellkarton-Verpackung. Die vier kleinen zusammenhängenden Dreiecke bilden wiederum ein grösseres Dreieck. (USA)
609, 610 Das Februar-Monatsblatt und Deckblatt eines Kalenders für PM Typography. (USA)
611 Hülle in Blautonen vor dunklem Hintergrund für Aufnahmen eines Saxophonisten. (USA)
612 Schallplattenhülle mit Hell/Dunkelkontrasten für Aufnahmen der Gruppe The Frogs. (USA)
613 Mit Elementen früherer Umschläge gestaltete Schallplattenhülle für eine Rock-Gruppe. (USA)
614 Hülle für eine Platte mit Musik von Erik Satie. Rot, grün und blau auf Weiss. (SWI)

608 Calendrier tridimensionnel de la *Container Corporation of America* avec emballage de carton ondulé. Les quatre prismes triangulaires s'emboîtent pour former un triangle. (USA)
609, 610 Page de février et feuillet de garde d'un calendrier pour PM Typography. (USA)
611 Tons bleus sur fond sombre pour la pochette de disque d'un saxophoniste cubain. (USA)
612 Pochette avec effets de clair-obscur pour un enregistrement du groupe The Frogs. (USA)
613 Des éléments d'anciennes couvertures ornent cette pochette de disque d'un groupe de rock. (USA)
614 Pochette d'un disque de musique d'Erik Satie. Rouge, vert et bleu sur fond blanc. (SWI)

613

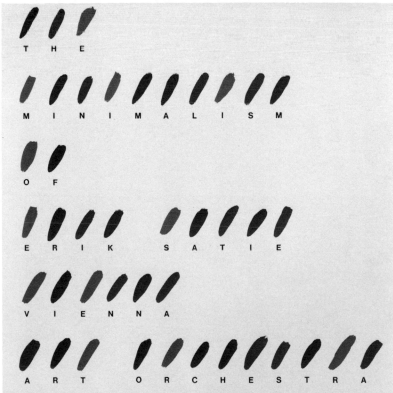

614

235

615, 616 "Origamic architecture." Three-dimensional calendar sheets, each with two toning papers. Fig. 615 is in dusty pink and wine red, Fig. 616 is in chamois and dark brown. (JPN)
617, 618 Woodcuts in various colours from a calendar for Amnesty International, referring to the Universal Declaration of Human Rights—here, the prohibition of slavery and torture. (SWI)
619 An example of the monthly sheets from the wall calendar of Herlin Press Inc. Each sheet is an interpretation by a creative designer, photographer or art director. (USA)
620–622 Redskin, clown and blonde—three of the three-dimensional faces in paper-cut technique as apt illustrations for the calendar of Face photo-typesetters. (FRA)

615, 616 «Origamische Architektur.» Aus jeweils zwei getönten Papieren gestaltete, dreidimensionale Kalenderblätter. Abb. 615 in Mauve und Weinrot, Abb. 616 in Chamois und Dunkelbraun. (JPN)
617, 618 Mehrfarbige Holzschnitte aus einem Kalender für Amnesty International, zu den Artikeln der Allgemeinen Erklärung der Menschenrechte, hier das Verbot der Sklaverei und der Folter. (SWI)
619 Eines der von verschiedenen Designern und Photographen gestalteten Monatsblätter für einen Wandkalender der Herlin Press Inc. (USA)
620–622 Indianer, Clown, Blondine – dreidimensionale Illustration (Papierschnittechnik) eines Kalenders für Face-Photosatz, dem Doppelsinn des Namens entsprechend mit Gesichtern. (FRA)

615, 616 «Architecture origamique.» Feuillets de calendrier tridimensionnels, réalisés avec deux papiers teintés. Fig. 615: mauve et lie-de-vin; fig. 616: chamois et brun foncé. (JPN)
617, 618 Gravures sur bois polychromes figurant dans un calendrier d'Amnesty International et illustrant des articles de la Déclaration générale des droits de l'homme, en l'occurrence l'interdiction de l'esclavage et de la torture. (SWI)
619 Un feuillet du calendrier d'Herlin Press Inc., illustré par divers créateurs. (USA)
620–622 Indien, clown, blonde: illustrations tridimensionnelles (découpages) d'un calendrier pour Face (photocomposition). Les visages font allusion au nom de la firme. (FRA)

615

616

617

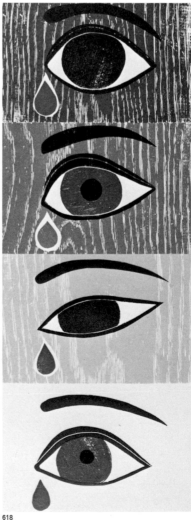

618

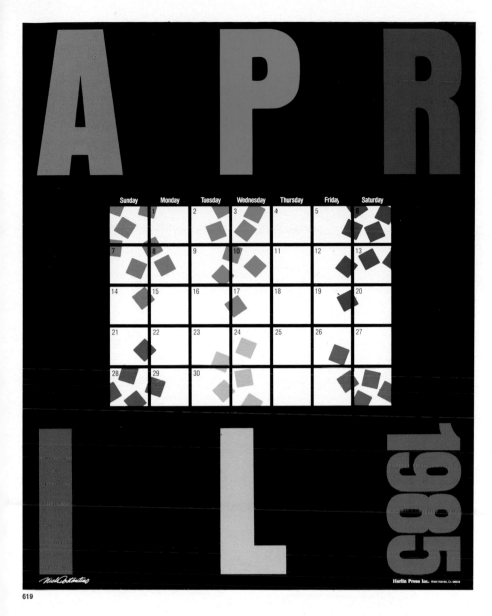

619

ARTIST / KÜNSTLER / ARTISTE:

615, 616 Masahiro Chatani
617, 618 Françoise Pochon-Emery
619 Nick Costantino

DESIGNER / GESTALTER / MAQUETTISTE:

615, 616 Yoshio Akimoto
617, 618 Ecole des Beaux-Arts, Lausanne
620–622 John McConnell/John Rushworth

ART DIRECTOR / DIRECTEUR ARTISTIQUE:

615, 616 Yoshio Akimoto
617, 618 Françoise Pochon-Emery
620–622 John McConnell

AGENCY / AGENTUR / AGENCE – STUDIO:

620–622 Pentagram

620

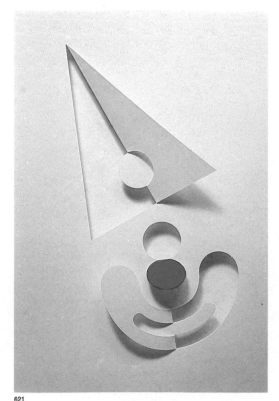

621

622

623

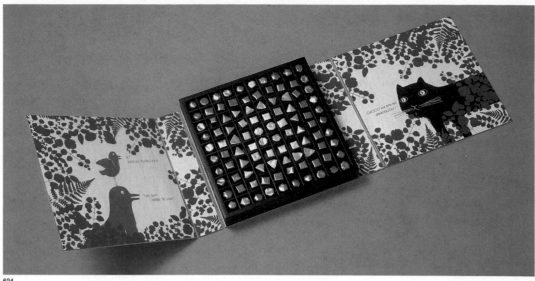

624

623, 624 Closed wooden box in dark blue with gold and a red tie, and the presentation of the contents (chocolates) in the opened box, sent as advertising by the Wood Package Committee. (JPN)
625 Cylindrical containers with plastic airtight closures for confectionery by *Seibu*. (JPN)
626, 627 Packaging design for two brands of cigarettes, shown here the boxes closed and the presentation by half opened flap. (GBR)
628 Design concept for two kinds of tea—both in loose and teabag form. Identification of the sort is by slight design variation and through the colour—one sort red, the other blue. (GBR)
629 Packaging design for Japanese specialities of the *Seibu* department store. Shown here the separate cartons, one with window aperture, and the total presentation in a box. (JPN)

623, 624 Geschlossene Holzschachtel in Dunkelblau mit Goldfarbe und rotem Band und Präsentation des Inhalts (Schokolade) bei geöffneter Schachtel, als Werbung eines japanischen Komitees für Holzverpackungen (Wood Package Committee). (JPN)
625 Zylindrische Behälter mit Plastikverschluss für Konfekt des Kaufhauses *Seibu*. (JPN)
626, 627 Packungsgestaltung für zwei Zigarettenmarken, hier die geschlossenen Schachteln und die Präsentation bei halb geöffnetem Klappdeckel. (GBR)
628 Gestaltungskonzept für zwei Teesorten, original und in Teebeuteln. Leichte Sortenidentifikation durch verschiedene Farbgebung der Kartons (blau und rot). (GBR)
629 Packungsgestaltung für japanische Spezialitäten des Kaufhauses *Seibu*. Hier die einzelnen Kartonschachteln, eine davon mit Sichtfenstern, und die Gesamtpräsentation in einer Schachtel. (JPN)

623, 624 Boîte en bois bleu foncé et or, fermée d'un lien rouge, et présentation du contenu (chocolats) une fois la boîte ouverte. Il s'agit de la publicité d'un comité japonais d'emballages en bois (Wood Package Committee). (JPN)
625 Boîtes cylindriques avec couvercle de plastique pour les friandises de *Seibu*. (JPN)
626, 627 Emballages conçus pour deux marques de cigarettes. Ici, les paquets fermés et la présentation des paquets demi-ouverts. (GBR)
628 Conception d'emballages pour deux sortes de thé, en feuilles et en sachets. La couleur du carton (bleu ou rouge) permet de les identifier immédiatement. (GBR)
629 Conditionnement des spécialités japonaises du grand magasin *Seibu*. Ici, les boîtes de carton, dont une avec fenêtres de cellophane, et la présentation d'ensemble en coffret. (JPN)

625

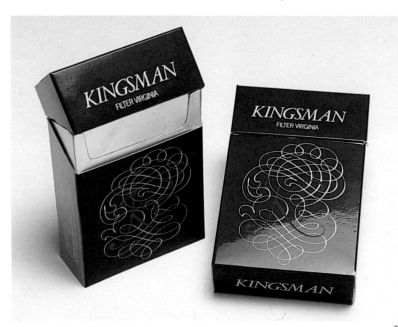

626   627

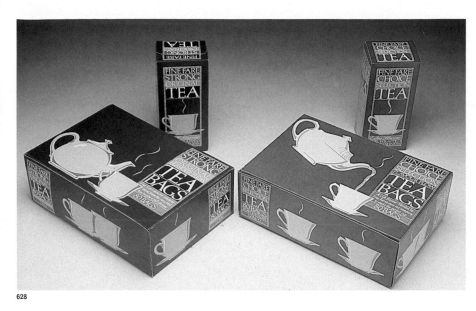

ARTIST / KÜNSTLER / ARTISTE:

623, 624 Shigeru Akizuki
625, 629 Kenji Maezawa
628 Kim Lane

DESIGNER / GESTALTER / MAQUETTISTE:

623, 624 Shigeru Akizuki
625, 629 Kenji Maezawa
626 David Hillman/Nancy Slonims
627 David Hillman/Sarah Pyne
628 Tony Burton/Gail Sharp

ART DIRECTOR / DIRECTEUR ARTISTIQUE:

623, 624 Shigeru Akizuki
625, 629 Kenji Maezawa
626, 627 David Hillman
628 Gail Sharp

AGENCY / AGENTUR / AGENCE – STUDIO:

626, 627 Pentagram
628 Michael Peters & Partners

628

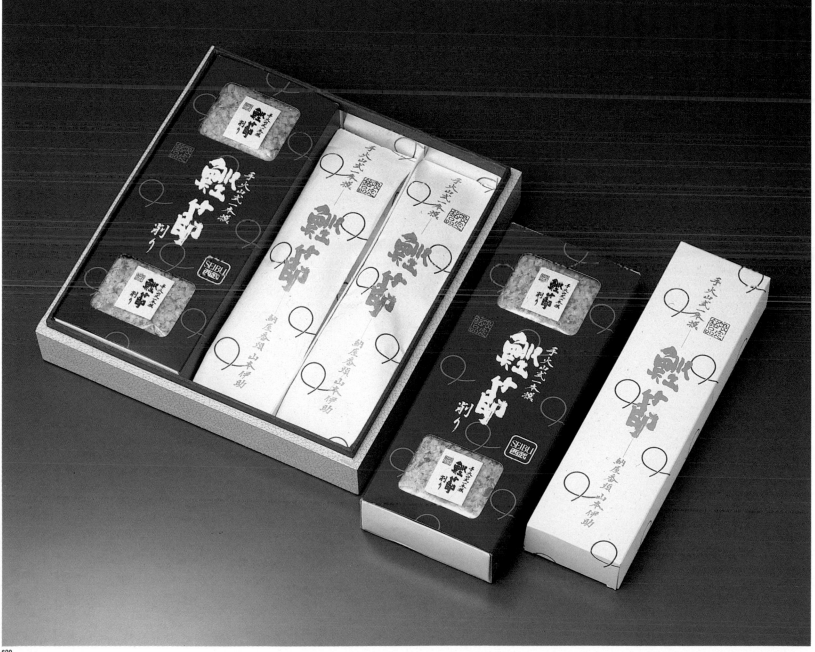

629

630

631

632

ARTIST / KÜNSTLER / ARTISTE:

630 Harry Willock
631 Victor Flatt/Bryce Atwell
632 Tobie Beele
633 Hans Reisinger
634 Peter Walton

DESIGNER / GESTALTER / MAQUETTISTE:

630, 631 Patricia Perchal
632 Elsabe Gelderblom
633 Joep Bergmans
634 Heinz Grunwald

ART DIRECTOR / DIRECTEUR ARTISTIQUE:

630, 631 Patricia Perchal
632 Robbie de Villiers
633 Joep Bergmans
634 Heinz Grunwald

AGENCY / AGENTUR / AGENCE – STUDIO:

630, 631 Michael Peters & Partners
632 Janice Ashby Design Studios
633 Ten Cate Bergmans Design
634 Grunwald Corporate Communication

630, 631 Packaging design for deep-frozen products by *Surgela*. Shown here: a 450 gram pack containing small peas and a minestrone pack (containing twelve selected vegetables). (ITA)
632 Design concept for fruit preserves by the *Koo* brand. The glass jars allow for an easy check of the contents. Shown here: peach halves, pear halves and fruit salad. (SAF)
633 Plastic beaker for *Mona* kefir, made according to a recipe from the Caucasus. (NLD)
634 Packaging design for the introduction of a new high-fibre cereal from the *Nabisco* foodstuffs company. A photographic illustration to show the ingredients of this muesli, made with whole-wheat bran, dried fruit and nuts. (AUS)

630, 631 Packungsgestaltung für Tiefkühlprodukte der Marke *Surgela*, hier 450-Gramm-Packungen mit feinen Erbsen und zwölf Gemüsesorten für Minestrone. (ITA)
632 Gestaltungskonzept für Früchtekonserven der Marke *Koo*. Die Glasverpackung erlaubt ungehindertes Prüfen des Inhalts – Pfirsich- und Birnenhälften sowie Fruchtsalat. (SAF)
633 Kunststoffbecher für *Mona*-Kefir, nach einem Rezept aus dem Kaukasus hergestellt. (NLD)
634 Packungsgestaltung für die Einführung einer neuen Müesli-Sorte der Marke *Nabisco*, die reich an Lebensmittelfasern sein soll. Die photographische Illustration verdeutlicht den Inhalt: Getreide mit Kleie, Früchten und Nüssen. (AUS)

630, 631 Emballages conçus pour des produits surgelés de la marque *Surgela*. Paquets de 450 grammes avec petits pois et douze sortes de légumes pour le minestrone. (ITA)
632 Programme de conditionnements pour les conserves de fruits de la marque *Koo*. Les bocaux de verre permettent de vérifier directement la qualité du contenu: moitiés de pêches et de poires, salade de fruits. (SAF)
633 Gobelet synthétique de kéfir *Mona*, fait d'après une recette caucasienne. (NLD)
634 Emballage conçu pour un nouveau muesli de *Nabisco*, riche en fibres végétales. Sur la photo, on peut en voir le contenu: céréales, son, fruits, noisettes. (AUS)

633

634

635

636

635–637 Trademark and label design for *Lawry's*, producer of gourmet foodstuffs. Shown here: classic salad sauces and the "special edition" range comprising sauces and also spices and herbs in jars with screw tops which are presented and sold in pairs complete with a small wooden box. (USA)
638 Packaging design for two sorts of French fries for the *Cordon Bleu* brand. The illustrations make for easy identification between the two variations in the cut of the potatoes. (GBR)
639 Design concept for carrier bags, folded cartons, beakers and paper bags for a fancy takeout food shop specializing in all-American foods. (USA)

635–637 Schutzmarke und Etikettgestaltung für *Lawry's*, Hersteller von Gourmet-Lebensmitteln. Hier die klassischen Salatsaucen und eine «Sonderausgabe» davon sowie Gewürzmischungen in Gläsern mit Schraubverschluss, die in kleinen Holzkisten verkauft werden. (USA)
638 Packungsgestaltung für zwei Sorten Pommes frites der Marke *Cordon Bleu*. Die Illustrationen zeigen deutlich, um welche Schnittart es sich bei dem Inhalt handelt. (GBR)
639 Gestaltungskonzeption für Tragtaschen, Faltkartons, Becher und Papiertüten eines Delikatess-Ladens, der sich auf amerikanische Esswaren spezialisiert hat. (USA)

638

637

ARTIST / KÜNSTLER / ARTISTE:

638 Bob Haberfield

DESIGNER / GESTALTER / MAQUETTISTE:

635–637 Art Goodman/Chuk Yee Cheng/Brenda Hayden
638 Glenn Tutssel/Carolyn Reed
639 Tom Geismar/Susan Schunick

ART DIRECTOR / DIRECTEUR ARTISTIQUE:

635–637 Art Goodman
638 Glenn Tutssel
639 Tom Geismar

AGENCY / AGENTUR / AGENCE – STUDIO:

635–637 Bass/Yager & Assoc.
638 Michael Peters & Partners
639 Chermayeff & Geismar Associates

635–637 Marque déposée et étiquettes conçues pour *Lawry's*, fabricant de produits pour gourmets. Ici: sauces à salades classiques ou spéciales; herbes arômatiques dans des bocaux à couvercle vissé, vendus dans des petites caisses en bois. (USA)
638 Emballages conçus pour deux sortes de pommes frites de la marque *Cordon Bleu*. Les illustrations montrent clairement la façon dont sont coupées les pommes de terre. (GBR)
639 Toute la gamme d'emballages conçus pour un magasin spécialisé dans les nourritures américaines: sacs portatifs, cartons pliants, gobelets et sachets. (USA)

639

640

ARTIST / KÜNSTLER / ARTISTE:

641 Bob Haberfield
643 Dennis Tani

DESIGNER / GESTALTER:

640 Zengo Yoshida
641 Glenn Tutssel/
Carolyn Reed
642 Ken Cato/George Arvanitis
643 Dennis Tani
644 Les Mason

ART DIRECTOR:

640 Ken Parkhurst
641 Glenn Tutssel
642 Ken Cato
643 Dennis Tani
644 Les Mason/
Russell Springham

AGENCY / AGENTUR / AGENCE:

640 Bright & Associates
641 Michael Peters & Partners
642 Ken Cato Design Co Pty Ltd
643 Dennis Tani Design, Inc.
644 Russell Springham/
Les Mason Design

641

Packaging
Packungen
Emballages

640 Packaging developed for *El Molino's* new line of homogenized salad dressings for sale in health-food stores and grocery chains. The packaging, for maximum display and shelf impact, highlights the health-food aspect—no oil or preservatives, low calories etc. (USA)
641 Packaging design for a series of deep-frozen vegetables of the *Cordon Bleu* brand. (GBR)
642 Bottle livery for *Arthur Brunt's* brandy syrup dessert sauce for ice-cream or pudding. (AUS)
643 Carrying-carton design and bottle styling for a cooling drink (wine with mineral water, sugar, citric acid etc.). Here "Plum Crazy"—one of four flavours. The lower half of the carton in plum colour, the upper half in grey-blue, the puffins in natural colours. (USA)
644 Bottle and label styling for an Australian vintage port wine. (AUS)

640 Gestaltungskonzeption für die Einführung einer neuen Linie von Salatsaucen der Marke *El Molino's* in Reformhäusern und Lebensmittelketten. Das Hauptgewicht liegt auf dem gesundheitlichen Aspekt (wenige Kalorien, keine Konservierungsmittel) und der visuellen Wirkung des Inhalts. (USA)
641 Packungsgestaltung für eine Reihe von Tiefkühlgemüsen der Marke *Cordon Bleu*. (GBR)
642 Flaschenausstattung für einen Weinbrand–Sirup der Marke *Arthur Brunt's*, der als Sauce für Nachspeisen wie Eis und Pudding empfohlen wird. (AUS)
643 Gestaltung des Tragkartons und Flaschenausstattung für ein Mischgetränk mit Wein mit dem Namen «Arktischer Erfrischer», hier «Pflaume», eine der vier Geschmacksrichtungen. Untere Hälfte des Kartons und des Etiketts in Pflaumenblau, obere Hälfte in hellem Graublau. (USA)
644 Flaschenausstattung für einen australischen Portwein. (AUS)

640 Conception d'une nouvelle ligne de sauces à salades de la marque *El Molino's*, mises en vente dans les magasins diététiques et chaînes d'alimentation. L'accent est mis sur la santé (moins de calories, sans conservateurs) et l'effet visuel du contenu. (USA)
641 Emballages conçus pour une gamme de légumes surgelés de la marque *Cordon Bleu*. (GBR)
642 Etude de bouteille pour un sirop de Brandy de chez *Arthur Brunt's* recommandé pour accompagner la glace ou le pudding. (AUS)
643 Carton de transport et étude de bouteille pour une boisson au vin appelée «Rafraîchisseur polaire»; ici, «Prune», l'un des quatre parfums. Couleur prune en bas du carton et de l'étiquette, gris bleu dans la partie supérieure. (USA)
644 Etude de bouteille pour un porto australien. (AUS)

642

643

644

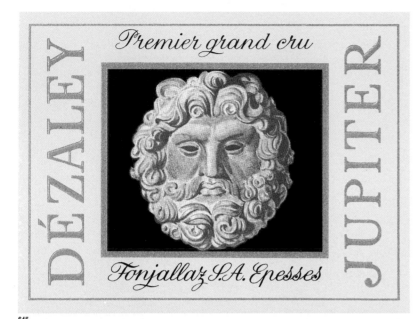

DÉZALEY JUPITER
Premier grand cru
Fonjallaz S.A. Epesses

645

645 Design of the label for a Swiss white wine. Light brown Jupiter head on deep purple ground, display type gold-toned, reading text black, on white ground. (SWI)
646 Carton for a wine cooler with the contents clearly illustrated. (SAF)
647 Design of the carton packaging and bottle livery for a Japanese drink. The colours are olive green, purple and a gold tone. (JPN)
648 Carton packaging for a Japanese spirits bottle. Silvery grey with picture-writing in white, black and red; the name and the circle in turquoise. (JPN)
649 Bottle livery for a kiwifruit cocktail produced in South Africa. (SAF)
650 Bottle and label styling for *Fosters Country Cooler*, a light-alcoholic drink. (SAF)

645 Etikettengestaltung für einen Schweizer Weisswein. Hellbrauner Jupiterkopf auf violettem Grund, Beschriftung goldfarben und schwarz auf weissem Grund. (SWI)
646 Kartonverpackung für einen Weinflaschenkühler, mit klarer Darstellung des Inhalts. (SAF)
647 Gestaltung der Kartonverpackung und Flaschenausstattung für ein japanisches Getränk. Die Grundfarben sind Olivgrün, Violett und ein matter Goldton. (JPN)
648 Kartonverpackung für einen japanischen Schnaps. Silbriges Grau, Beschriftung in Weiss, Schwarz, Rot und Türkis. (JPN)
649 Flaschenausstattung für einen Kiwi-Cocktail, der für den südafrikanischen Markt bestimmt ist. (SAF)
650 Etikettgestaltung für *Fosters Country Cooler*, ein alkoholisches Getränk. (SAF)

645 Etiquette conçue pour un vin blanc suisse. Tête de Jupiter brun clair sur fond violet, inscription or et noir sur fond blanc. (SWI)
646 Emballage de carton pour un seau á vin avec image du contenu. (SAF)
647 Conception d'un emballage de carton et étude de bouteille pour une boisson japonaise. Couleurs prédominantes: vert olive, violet et or mat. (JPN)
648 Emballage de carton pour un eau-de-vie japonais. Gris argenté, inscription en blanc, noir, rouge et turquoise. (JPN)
649 Etude de bouteille pour un cocktail de kiwis destiné au marché sud-africain. (SAF)
650 Etiquette conçue pour *Fosters Country Cooler*, une boisson alcoolisée. (SAF)

646

647

648

ARTIST / KÜNSTLER / ARTISTE:

645 I. de Grandi
646 Gary Silberman
648 Shozo Kakutani
649 Drexler Kyzer
650 Anthony Lane

DESIGNER / GESTALTER / MAQUETTISTE:

645 I. de Grandi
646 Helene Swart
647 Kenji Maezawa
648 Shozo Kakutani
649 Robbie de Villiers/Anthony Lane
650 Anthony Lane

ART DIRECTOR / DIRECTEUR ARTISTIQUE:

645 Michel Logoz
646 Helene Swart
647 Kenji Maezawa
648 Shozo Kakutani
649, 650 Robbie de Villiers

AGENCY / AGENTUR / AGENCE – STUDIO:

645 Roth & Sauter SA
646, 649, 650 Janice Ashby Design Studios

649

650

651

652

ARTIST / KÜNSTLER / ARTISTE:

652, 653 Dale K. Johnston
655, 656 Shigeru Akizuki

DESIGNER / GESTALTER:

651 John Nowland/
     Kelly Burton
652, 653 Dale K. Johnston
654 Harry Elbers
655, 656 Shigeru Akizuki

ART DIRECTOR:

654 Harry Elbers
655, 656 Shigeru Akizuki

AGENCY / AGENTUR / AGENCE:

651 John Nowland
     Graphic Design
652, 653 Design Center
654 H. & E. Elbers

654

655

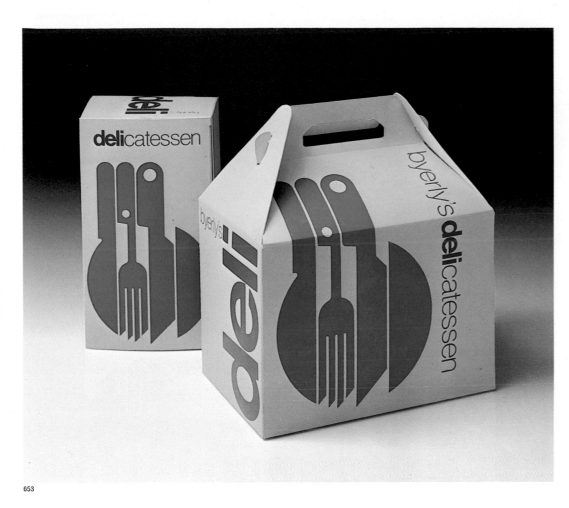

651 This bottle bears an invitation (by way of the label) to an inspection of the brewery and a celebration to mark the most successful year (1984) since its foundation in 1862. (AUS)
652, 653 Carton design for *Byerly's*, a food chain-store. The design in Fig. 652 shows packaging for wines and spirits, and allows for a special display effect; Fig. 653 shows two variations of cartons for foodstuffs. (USA)
654 Bottle livery for *Napoleon* brandy imported and bottled in the Netherlands. (NLD)
655, 656 Example from a series of wooden packagings for diverse products promoted by the Japanese Wood Package Committee. Here, a partly opened wooden case with hinges, for three different sorts of wine, and the presentation of the contents with the case fully opened. (JPN)

651 Als Einladung zur Besichtigung einer Bierbrauerei und Feier des erfolgreichsten Geschäftsjahres (1984) seit der Gründung im Jahre 1862 gestaltetes Etikett. (AUS)
652, 653 Kartongestaltung für *Byerly's*, eine Lebensmittelkette. Das Design der in Abb. 652 gezeigten Verpackung für alkoholische Getränke ermöglicht einen speziellen Ausstellungseffekt; Abb. 653 zeigt zwei Kartonvarianten für Esswaren. (USA)
654 Flaschenausstattung für *Napoleon*-Cognac, der für den niederländischen Markt bestimmt ist. (NLD)
655, 656 Beispiel aus einer Serie von Holzverpackungen für verschiedene Waren, die von einem japanischen Komitee für Holzverpackungen lanciert wurden. Hier ein halb geöffnetes Holzkistchen für Wein, mit Scharnieren ausgestattet, und Präsentation des Inhalts bei ganz geöffneter Verpackung. (JPN)

651 Etiquette conçue aussi comme invitation à la visite d'une brasserie et à la fête célébrant l'année-record 1984, la meilleure depuis la fondation en 1862. (AUS)
652, 653 Emballages de carton conçus pour *Byerly's*, une chaîne de magasins d'alimentation. Le décor graphique des emballages de boissons alcoolisées (fig. 652) permet de varier la présentation à l'étalage. La fig. 653 montre deux variations de cartons pour denrées alimentaires. (USA)
654 Etude de bouteille de cognac *Napoléon*, mis en bouteilles aux Pays-Bas et destiné au marché hollandais. (NLD)
655, 656 Un exemple choisi parmi une série de boîtes en bois à usages divers lancée par un comité japonais d'emballages en bois: petit coffret à charnières pour le vin, ouvert à demi, et présentation du contenu du coffret ouvert. (JPN)

653

656

657

ARTIST / KÜNSTLER / ARTISTE:

657 Susanna Vallebona
658 Shigeru Akizuki

DESIGNER / GESTALTER / MAQUETTISTE:

657 Anna Luraschi
658 Shigeru Akizuki

ART DIRECTOR / DIRECTEUR ARTISTIQUE:

657 Susanna Vallebona
658 Shigeru Akizuki

AGENCY / AGENTUR / AGENCE – STUDIO:

657 Esseblu

657 Bottle styling for three cordials—peppermint, raspberry with citrus fruit, and orange—on the *Lazza* label. The naturalistic illustrations enable an easy identification. (ITA)
658 Wooden boxes in two sizes, with hinged flap tops, in natural colour. The bottles are wrapped in black paper, bearing gold-edged labels; the printing on both boxes is in black with red. (JPN)

657 Flaschenausstattung für drei Sirup-Sorten der Marke *Lazza*. Die naturalistischen Illustrationen sorgen für eindeutige Identifizierung, unterstützt von der Farbe des Getränks. (ITA)
658 Holzkistchen in zwei Grössen, mit Klappdeckeln an Scharnieren. Flaschen mit schwarzem Papierwickler und goldumrandetem Etikett, die Kistchen naturfarben, schwarz und rot bedruckt. (JPN)

657 Etude de bouteille pour trois sortes de sirop de la marque *Lazza*. Les illustrations réalistes et la couleur de la boisson permettent de reconnaître immédiatement chaque sirop. (ITA)
658 Deux petites caisses en bois avec rabats à charnières. Bouteilles enveloppés de papier noir, étiquettes à bordure dorée; caisses de bois naturel, imprimées en rouge et noir. (JPN)

659

660

659 Packungsgestaltung für Magnetdisketten für Computerdaten von *Capital Data Systems*. (USA)
660 Verpackung für *Apple*-Computer-Disketten. Schwarze Kontur, grünes Blatt auf Weiss. (USA)
661 Packungsgestaltung für die Einführung von zwei Waschpulversorten von *Fine Fare*. (GBR)
662 Verpackung für ein neues Software-Produkt der *Xanaro Technologies*. Sie enthält zwei Fächer, wovon eines Platz für die fünf Programmdisketten sowie Zusatzdisketten bietet, das andere enthält die Dokumentation über das Programm. (CAN)
663 Geschenkverpackung in Form einer leuchtend gelben Stülpdeckelschachtel für verschiedene Sorten japanischen Konfekts, nochmals in kleine Schachteln verpackt, von *Zeniya*. (JPN)
664 Wellkartonschachtel mit Apfel-Kerze, die als Werbegeschenk von *Ciba-Geigy*, mit Hinweis auf das Pflanzenschutzmittel *Topaz C*, an südafrikanische Apfelbauern versandt wurde. (SWI)

659 Packaging design for boxes of ten disks in the *Platinum* series for *Capitol Data Systems*. (USA)
660 Packaging for *Apple* computer disks. Black contour, green leaf on white. (USA)
661 Range of packaging for the introduction of two kinds of washing powders by *Fine Fare*. (GBR)
662 Packaging for a new software product by *Xanaro Technologies*, containing two compartments, one for the five programme-disks with space for backup disks, the other for documentation. The box is made of high-impact polystyrene in flat black, printed in luminous green. (CAN)
663 Gift packaging in the form of a box with a glossy bright yellow lid, for various kinds of Japanese confectionery already packed in small boxes, by *Zeniya*. (JPN)
664 Corrugated cardboard box with an apple candle sent as a gift by *Ciba-Geigy* to the South African apple growers to promote the plant-care product *Topaz C*. (SWI)

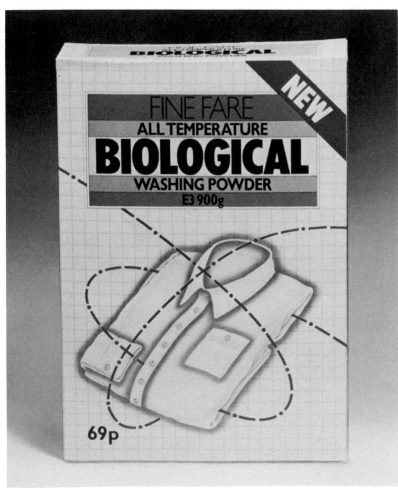

661

662

ARTIST / KÜNSTLER / ARTISTE:

660 John Casado
661 Bob Haberfield/Harry Willock
664 Paul Bergmeier

DESIGNER / GESTALTER / MAQUETTISTE:

659 Art Goodman/G. Dean Smith/Saul Bass
660 Clement Monk/Ellen Romano
661 Mark Wilkens/Gail Sharp
662 Paul Hodgson/Gary Ludwig
663 Yasuo Itou
664 Christian Lang/Marcel Berlinger

ART DIRECTOR / DIRECTEUR ARTISTIQUE:

659 Saul Bass
660 Tom Hughes
661 Gail Sharp
662 Paul Hodgson/Gary Ludwig
663 Yasuo Itou
664 Christian Lang/Marcel Berlinger

AGENCY / AGENTUR / AGENCE – STUDIO:

659 Bass/Yager & Assoc.
660 Apple Creative Service
661 Michael Peters & Partners
662 Spencer/Francey Inc.
663 Tac Co., Ltd.
664 Ciba-Geigy/Werbung

663

659 Emballages pour les disquettes d'ordinateurs *Platinum* series de *Capital Data Systems*. (USA)
660 Emballage pour les disquettes d'ordinateurs *Apple*. Contour noir, feuille verte sur fond blanc. (USA)
661 Emballages conçus pour deux nouvelles sortes de lessive en poudre de *Fine Fare*. (GBR)
662 Emballage pour un nouveau produit de logiciel de *Xanaro Technologies*. Il comprend deux compartiments, l'un pour les cinq disquettes de programme et celles supplémentaires, l'autre pour la documentation concernant le programme. (CAN)
663 Paquet-cadeau de *Zeniya*, jaune vif, à couvercle emboîté, contenant diverses sortes de friandises japonaises, elles-mêmes emballées dans de petites boîtes. (JPN)
664 Boîtes en carton ondulé renfermant des bougies en forme de pommes envoyées comme cadeau publicitaire à des agriculteurs sud-africains par *Ciba-Geigy*, afin de promouvoir *Topaz C*, produit pour le traitement des arbres fruitiers. (SWI)

664

665

666

667

668

ARTIST / KÜNSTLER / ARTISTE:

665 Kirsten Roberts
667 Denis Parkhurst
671, 672 David Stevenson

DESIGNER / GESTALTER / MAQUETTISTE:

665 Clive Gay
666 Ian Mullan
667 Peter Sargent
668, 669 Ken Cato
670 Heinz Grundwald
671, 672 James Nevins

665 Can design for a deodorant line for men. (SAF)
666 Design of the plastic containers for hair shampoo and conditioner which give extra body to the hair and "scientifically adjust to the hair type". (AUS)
667 Design concept for bottles and jars for a line of skin and hair products mainly sold in health-food stores. The packaging reflects the natural ingredients in the products and projects a high quality image. (USA)
668, 669 Packaging design for a hair-care line. The emphasis is on the natural extracts in the composition. The colours of the plastic bottles and lids support the botanical illustrations. Fig. 669: Shampoo and conditioner. (AUS)
670 Tube design for a medicated shampoo with a new formula for users who have scalp problems. (AUS)
671, 672 Tin with plastic lid and vacuum packaging for coffee by *Chase & Sanborn*. Easy identification of the sort is through the colours (see Fig. 672). (USA)

665 Dosenausstattung für eine Deodorant-Linie für Männer. Die beiden Sorten heissen «Kreuzfahrer-Stahl» und «Inka-Gold». (SAF)
666 Gestaltung der Plastikbehälter für Spezial-Shampoo und -Pflegemittel, das dem Haar Volumen verleihen soll. (AUS)
667 Ausstattungskonzept für Flaschen und Töpfe einer Haut- und Haarpflegeprodukt-Linie, die vor allem in Reformhäusern angeboten wird. Die botanischen Illustrationen und die Produktbezeichnungen unterstreichen den Naturprodukt- und Qualitätsanspruch. (USA)
668, 669 Packungsgestaltung für eine Haarpflege-Linie, mit Hauptgewicht auf den Ingredienzen, deren naturalistische Darstellung auf den Etiketten durch die Farbe der Plastikflaschen und Deckel unterstützt wird. Abb. 669: Shampoo und Pflegemittel. (AUS)
670 Tubenausstattung für ein medizinisches Shampoo gegen Kopfhautprobleme. (AUS)
671, 672 Dose mit Plastikdeckel und Vakuumpackungen für Kaffee von *Chase & Sanborn*. Leichte Sortenidentifizierung durch die Farbgebung (s. Abb. 672). (USA)

669

670

ART DIRECTOR / DIRECTEUR ARTISTIQUE:

665 Clive Gay
666 Ian Mullan
667 Ken Parkhurst
668, 669 Ken Cato
670 Heinz Grunwald
671, 672 Nicolas Sidjakov/Jerry Berman

AGENCY / AGENTUR / AGENCE – STUDIO:

665 Pentagraph
666 Mullan Pettigrew Design
667 Bright & Associates
668, 669 Ken Cato Design Company Pty Ltd
670 Grunwald Corporate Communication
671, 762 Sidjakov Berman & Gomez

665 Etude d'atomiseurs pour une ligne de déodorant pour hommes. Deux sortes. «Acier croiseur» et «Or Inca». (SAF)
666 Flacons de plastique conçus pour un shampooing spécial et un produit qui donne du gonflant aux cheveux. (AUS)
667 Gamme de produits pour la peau et les soins capillaires vendus surtout dans des magasins de diététique. Les dessins botaniques et les noms des produits soulignent le caractère naturel et la qualité de la marque. (USA)
668, 669 Conditionnements d'une ligne de soins capillaires. Les dessins réalistes des étiquettes et les couleurs des flacons de plastique et des bouchons mettent en valeur les composants. Fig. 669: shampooing et traitement. (AUS)
670 Etude de tubes pour un shampooing médicinal contre les problèmes de cuir chevelu. (AUS)
671, 672 Boîte ronde avec couvercle de plastique et emballages sous vide des divers cafés *Chase & Sanborn*. (USA)

Packaging / Packungen / Emballages

671

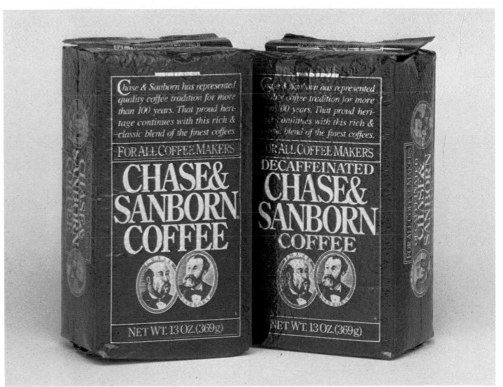

672

673

673 Packaging design for *Le Royal* cosmetic by the Japanese producer *Albion*. A connecting element is the special shape of the lids. (JPN)
674 Presentation case with powder compact and lipstick of the brand *Yume Urushi*, designed for Albion Cosmetics of Tokyo. (JPN)
675 Sleek metal box containing a Japanese speciality. (JPN)
676 Packaging for a line in dental hygiene, designed for Tesco Foodstores. (GBR)
677 Design concept for the men's line from *Cacharel*, here for toilet-water, soap, deodorant, after-shave and balsam. The flask on the right is in a real leather case. (FRA)

673 Packungsgestaltung für *Le Royal* Kosmetikprodukte des japanischen Herstellers *Albion*. Ein verbindendes Element ist die spezielle Deckelform. (JPN)
674 Geschenkschachtel mit Puderdose und Lippenstift der Marke *Yume Urushi*, für Albion Cosmetics in Tokio konzipiert. (JPN)
675 Blechdose als Verpackung für eine japanische Spezialität. (JPN)
676 Verpackungslinie für dentalhygienische Produkte: Mundwasser und Zahnbürsten. (GBR)
677 Verpackungsreihe für die Herrenlinie von *Cacharel*, hier für Toilettenwasser, Seife, Deodorant, Rasierwasser und Balsam. «Flachmann» in Hülle aus echtem Leder. (FRA)

673 Conditionnements conçus pour les cosmétiques *Le Royal* du fabricant japonais *Albion*. La forme du couvercle constitue un élément commun à ces produits. (JPN)
674 Emballage-cadeau, poudrier et bâton de rouge à lèvres de la marque *Yume Urushi*, conçus pour Albion Cosmetics, Tōkyō. (JPN)
675 Boîte en fer-blanc contenant une spécialité japonaise. (JPN)
676 Conditionnements conçus pour des produits d'hygiène dentaire: solutions pour bains de bouche et brosses à dents. (GBR)
677 Gamme de conditionnements de la ligne pour hommes de *Cacharel*: eau de toilette, savon, déodorant, lotion après-rasage et baume; à droite, flacon recouvert de cuir. (FRA)

674

675

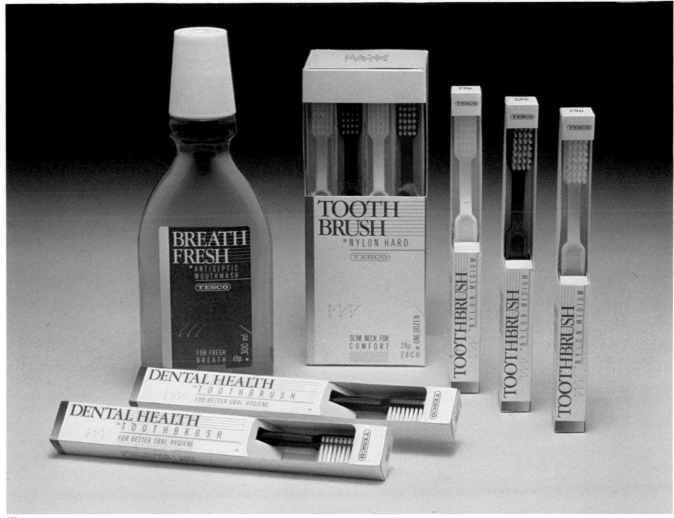

676

ARTIST/KÜNSTLER/ARTISTE:

673 Yoshiharu Yasumura
674 Hitomi Minoda
677 Annegret Beier

DESIGNER/GESTALTER:

673 Norio Noda/
    Saori Kurashige
674 Takako Nagai/
    Saori Kurashige
675 Hiroyuki Ban
676 Mark Wilkens/Gail Sharpe
677 Annegret Beier

ART DIRECTOR:

673 Naomi Hosoya/
    Shozo Nishigori
674 Naomi Hosoya
675 Nobuyuki Ban
677 Annegret Beier

AGENCY/AGENTUR/AGENCE:

673, 674 Albion Cosmetics
    Design Room
675 Ban Package Design Center
676 Michael Peters & Partners
677 Annegret Beier

677

678

679

ARTIST / KÜNSTLER / ARTISTE:

678 Patrick M. Redmond
679 Luis Acevedo
680 Kazumasa Nagai
681 Tim Girvin
682 Takenobu Igarashi

DESIGNER / GESTALTER / MAQUETTISTE:

678 Patrick M. Redmond
679 Woody Pirtle
682 Takenobu Igarashi

680

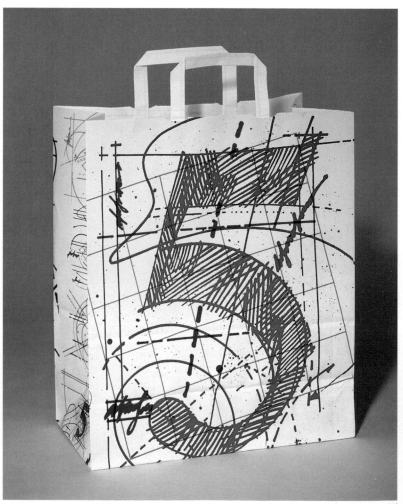

681

ART DIRECTOR / DIRECTEUR ARTISTIQUE:

678 David Brown / Patrick M. Redmond
679 Woody Pirtle
680, 681 David Au
682 Takenobu Igarashi

AGENCY / AGENTUR / AGENCE – STUDIO:

678 Patrick Redmond Design
679 Pirtle Design
680, 681 Bloomingdale's
682 Takenobu Igarashi Design

678 Summer shopping-bag with sailing information, for *Dayton's* store. (USA)
679 Paper carrier for the fashion department of Dallas's shopping complex *Galleria*. (USA)
680 For the Japan Weeks at *Bloomingdale's* —a specially designed carrier. (USA)
681 "Five" on one side of this carrier bag for *Bloomingdale's* and "eight" on the other to make "85" (the year). (USA)
682 White dots in rows on black ground offer a sleek, tense and compact effect for the design of a paper carrier for the Museum of Modern Arts' shop in New York. The same design was also used for a poster and for notepads. (USA)

678 Sommer-Einkaufstasche mit Segelinformationen, für das Kaufhaus *Dayton's*. (USA)
679 Papiertragtaschen für den Modesektor des Ladenkomplexes *Galleria* in Dallas. (USA)
680 Für die Japan-Wochen im Kaufhaus *Bloomingdale's* konzipierte Tasche. (USA)
681 «Fünf» als Teil der Jahreszahl auf einer Tragtasche für *Bloomingdale's*; auf der Rückseite ist die «Acht» abgebildet. (USA)
682 Weisse Punkte auf schwarzem Grund, in Linien angeordnet, bewirken eine spannungsreiche, dichte Atmosphäre auf der für den Museums-Kiosk des Museums of Modern Art in New York konzipierten Papiertasche. Das gleiche Design wurde auch für einen Poster und für Notizblöcke verwendet. (USA)

678 Sac d'été orné d'illustrations explicatives sur les bateaux à voile pour les grands magasins *Dayton's*. (USA)
679 Sac de papier pour les articles de mode des magasins *Galleria* à Dallas. (USA)
680 Pour les semaines japonaises des grands magasins *Bloomingdale's*. (USA)
681 «Cinq» commme chiffre de l'année sur un sac de *Bloomingdale's*; le «huit» se trouve de l'autre côté. (USA)
682 Des points blancs alignés sur un fond noir créent une atmosphère de tension sur ce sac de papier conçu pour le kiosque du Musée d'Art Moderne de New York. La même composition graphique a été employée pour une affiche et des blocs-notes. (USA)

The Museum of Modern Art

682

Paper / Papier: Papierfabrik Biberist—Biber art paper, super white, glaced,
130 gm² and Biber Offset SK3, pure white, machine-finished, 140 gm² /
Biber-Kunstdruck ultra weiss, glaciert, 130 gm²
und Biber-Offset SK3, hochweiss, maschinenglatt, 140 gm²

Printed by / gedruckt von: Offset + Buchdruck AG,
Staffelstrasse 12, CH-8021 Zürich

Typesetting / Lichtsatz: Sauerländer AG, Aarau
(Univers, MONOTYPE-Lasercomp)

Binding / Einband: Buchbinderei Schumacher AG, Bern / Schmitten

Glossy lamination / Glanzfoliierung: Durolit AG, Pfäffikon SZ